ROUTLEDGE LIBRARY EDITIONS: WW2

Volume 24

POLAND, SOE AND THE ALLIES

POLAND, SOE AND THE ALLIES

JOZEF GARLINSKI

LONDON AND NEW YORK

First published in 1969 by George Allen & Unwin Ltd

This edition first published in 2022
by Routledge
2 Park Square, Milton Park, Abingdon, Oxon OX14 4RN

and by Routledge
605 Third Avenue, New York, NY 10158

Routledge is an imprint of the Taylor & Francis Group, an informa business

© 1969 Jozef Garlinski

All rights reserved. No part of this book may be reprinted or reproduced or utilised in any form or by any electronic, mechanical, or other means, now known or hereafter invented, including photocopying and recording, or in any information storage or retrieval system, without permission in writing from the publishers.

Trademark notice: Product or corporate names may be trademarks or registered trademarks, and are used only for identification and explanation without intent to infringe.

British Library Cataloguing in Publication Data
A catalogue record for this book is available from the British Library

ISBN: 978-1-03-201217-9 (Set)
ISBN: 978-1-00-319367-8 (Set) (ebk)
ISBN: 978-1-03-203978-7 (Volume 24) (hbk)
ISBN: 978-1-03-203981-7 (Volume 24) (pbk)
ISBN: 978-1-00-319006-6 (Volume 24) (ebk)

DOI: 10.4324/9781003190066

Publisher's Note
The publisher has gone to great lengths to ensure the quality of this reprint but points out that some imperfections in the original copies may be apparent.

Disclaimer
The publisher has made every effort to trace copyright holders and would welcome correspondence from those they have been unable to trace.

POLAND, SOE and the ALLIES

by

JOZEF GARLINSKI

TRANSLATED FROM THE ORIGINAL POLISH
BY PAUL STEVENSON

LONDON
George Allen and Unwin Ltd
RUSKIN HOUSE. MUSEUM STREET

FIRST PUBLISHED IN 1969

This book is copyright under the Berne Convention. Apart from any fair dealing for the purpose of private study, research, criticism or review, as permitted under the Copyright Act 1956, no portion may be reproduced by any process without written permission. Enquiry should be made to the publisher.

© *Jozef Garlinski, 1969*

SBN 04 355006 1

PRINTED IN GREAT BRITAIN
BY GRYF PRINTERS (H.C.) LTD
171, BATTERSEA CHURCH ROAD, LONDON, S.W. 11.

CONTENTS

	Page
List of illustrations and maps	7
Foreword by Major-General Sir Colin Gubbins, K.C.M.G., D.S.O., M.C.	9
Abbreviations	13
Introduction	15
PART I: IN THE DARK	17 - 53

First Poles on British soil in 1940. British preparations for subversion in Europe; building up of SOE; its Polish section. Organization of underground forces in occupied Poland. New Polish Government in France. Defeat in the West. Further building up of the Polish underground. Reconstruction of Armed Forces in Britain; liaison with the home country by the Polish General Staff (Sixth Bureau). Development of aviation since World War I. SOE applies for aircraft. First drop on Polish territory. First plan, prepared in Warsaw, for a general rising.

PART II: BY THE LIGHT OF THE MOON	55 - 100

Polish training courses in Britain. 138 Squadron and first Polish crews for night flights. Two first routes to Poland. General Sikorski in America. Independent Polish Flight in 138 Squadron. Polish holding station, action stations, alarm and take-off. Secret radio liaison with Poland; use of the BBC. Flight and drops of six Polish parachutists. Secret dropping zones in Poland; reception stations and the organization for distribution of supplies. Problem of equipping Polish forces in the West; dependence on Britain. American aid, Lend-Lease. Description of containers and supplies sent.

PART III: NIGHT AND VENGEANCE   101 - 165

Diversionary operations in the East of Poland; the "Fan" organization. Successes and failures. Parachutist *Ponury* carries out armed raid on the prison at Pinsk. Attempted raid on another prison and betrayal by Russian communists. Difficulties with Soviet Russia. Proposal to bomb Auschwitz. Tragic days for Poland in summer 1943: arrest of General Rowecki and death of General Sikorski. Problems of manpower, aircraft and supplies. *Ponury* as a partisan leader. Two conceptions of how to fight the German occupants. Polish partisans in the north-east near Wilno. Soviet partisans and their hostility towards Poles. Further building up of flights to Poland; transfer of bases from Britain to Italy. Difficulties with the Western Allies; exclusion of Poland from allied operational plans. Teheran conference. Home Army intelligence provides information on the German "new weapons"; discovery of V2 testing ground. Securing of V2 rocket intact. First attempt at a night landing in Poland. Bringing to London of the V2 plans and parts of the rocket. Losses among parachutists dropped in Poland.

PART IV: INTO THE ABYSS   167 - 233

General Okulicki lands in Poland and joins Home Army H.Q. Change of plans and decision to launch a rising in Warsaw. Differences of opinions among Poles regarding operations in Poland. July 1944: "We are ready to fight for Warsaw." Technical difficulties of sending the Parachute Brigade to Poland. Could the Polish Air Force have helped Warsaw? Outbreak of rising. Polish efforts to secure aid in the West. First supply flights to Warsaw and first losses; Air Marshal Slessor's views. Russia's attitude towards rising. Mikolajczyk in Moscow; attempt to get Stalin to help Warsaw. Churchill and Roosevelt try to prevail on Stalin to allow landings on Soviet airfields. Russian "No". Preparations for flight by U.S. Air Force and further representations to Stalin. Belated Soviet agreement. Supply flight of American Flying Fortresses. Further flights from Italy. Capitulation of Warsaw. Summing-up of results and losses. Table of all flights and drops over Warsaw. General Okulicki as new commander of the Home Army. Reconstruction of its H.Q. Renewal of flights to Poland. British Military Mission. The last drop into Poland. Soviet winter offensive. Yalta conference. Home Army disbanded. Arrest of sixteen leaders of the Polish underground by the Bolsheviks. San Francisco conference. Polish political leaders in the Lubianka prison. Show trial in Moscow. General Okulicki's defence and his last words.

APPENDICES

Statistics of drops during the four operational seasons	235
Sources	239
Index	244

ILLUSTRATIONS AND MAPS

	Page
Poland in October 1939	16
Routes to Poland from England	66

Wladyslaw Sikorski
Kazimierz Sosnkowski
Stefan Rowecki
Tadeusz *Bor* Komorowski
Colin Gubbins
John Slessor
H. B. Perkins
Henry McLeod Threlfall
Leopold Okulicki
Kazimierz Iranek Osmecki } Following page 104
Jozef Hartman
Maciej Kalenkiewicz
Tadeusz Klimowski
Adolf Pilch
Ponury
Zygmunt Milewicz
A Halifax
Polish airmen from 1586 Flight

Routes to Poland from Italy 144

Photographs of K. Sosnkowski, S. Rowecki, T. *Bor* Komorowski, L. Okulicki, M. Kalenkiewicz and *Ponury* from the Polish Underground Movement (1939—45) Study Trust; photograph of W. Sikorski from the Polish Institute and Sikorski Museum; the rest from private sources.

FOREWORD
by
Major-General Sir Colin Gubbins, K.C.M.G., D.S.O., M.C.

The history of the unceasing armed struggle of the Polish nation against the German occupation forces following her defeat in September 1939 by the overwhelming might of the Reich, whilst her Allies stood helpless to come to her succour, is almost unknown in our own country and in the world at large. Alone the culmination of this bitter and remorseless warfare in the heroic Warsaw Rising of 1st August, 1944, has received any general recognition.

Now at last after prolonged and intense research from all available records and sources the story of this unrelenting underground war has been pieced together in all its epic and tragic aspects: the author himself as a Home Army officer was deeply involved in many of these happenings and thus writes from first-hand experience of the growth and development of the Home Army in Poland and its military operations against the occupying power.

This book explains in clear and objective terms the ineradicable dilemmas that continuously faced the Polish people and their Government: historically, in their situation between two massive and hostile neighbours which, with Austria, had until 1918 parcelled out and dominated their land for well over 100 years: immediately, at the war's beginning, in the renewed division of their whole country between the two dictator powers in cynical and expedient agreement: in mid stage and following Hitler's invasion of Russia, at first an uneasy alliance with Stalin, abrogated unilaterally by him following the disclosure of the Katyn massacres: and finally in the occupation and domination of the whole of Poland by Soviet Russia, still an indispensable ally of the West for the defeat of Germany and bearing the main weight of the land war in Europe.

In the circumstances it was inevitable and inescapable that there should be divided opinions and councils in all Polish circles, political, civil and military, both in London and in Warsaw, as to the policies and actions to be pursued at any given time throughout those desperate years. But until the death of Sikorski, Prime Minister and Commander in Chief, in a flying accident in Gibraltar in early July 1943, his firm and statesmanlike direction of affairs and handling of the complicated political and military problems facing his country's survival gave a remarkable unity of purpose and of effort. His death was a tragedy for Poland and a bitter blow for our country. He had more than once discussed with me the various possibilities that could surround the war's ending and of his hope and determination, if the physical circumstances permitted and other factors necessitated, to lead at least his Parachute Brigade back to Warsaw and re-establish his government there in face of everything. As is explained in this book, the final course of the war precluded any such gesture by either of Sikorski's successors.

S.O.E's role, under the charter of its constitution, was to aid and encourage all resistance to the enemy in the occupied territories. At its formation in July 1940 Poland had already the nucleus of a secret army, and collaboration between us and the Polish General Staff in London commenced immediately, with the immediate specific objective of establishing contact by air and parachute with the homeland so that arms, instructors, couriers, money etc could be delivered, and wireless communications built up. The physical difficulties were stupendous — the enormous distances involved at the very limit of endurance of aircraft then available, the frenetic and boundless activity of the German security services, the long passage over enemy-held territory with its fighter squadrons and "Flak". One is lost in admiration of the courage and skill of the pioneers of these flights, both Polish and R.A.F. and of the parachutists they carried. But the scale of these operations throughout the war remained always miniscule compared to the crying needs of the Home Army with its units scattered over a vast area: the adverse factors were too strong.

The bitterest cup remained still to be drunk. As the triumphant Red Armies swept through Poland again in 1944 following the massive defeats of Hitler's forces the local Home Army leaders made contact with them on Polish soil to co-ordinate operations. After seemingly friendly negotiations these leaders and their men were then swiftly liquidated on the spot or arrested and deported to Russia, eventually to suffer the same fate. And these were the Polish men and women who for years had fought the German enemy, had attacked and sabotaged his communications and transport serving the German armies in the East. Perfidy had reached its climax: we are left stunned by this appalling betrayal. I had suggested to Sosnkowski, the new Commander in Chief, that as the Russian troops entered Poland the Home Army units should avoid contact and withdraw as I feared their fate, but this was a Polish matter to be decided by their Government alone: Polish soil was Polish soil and not to be symbolically surrendered.

This book is sad but inspiring reading. Poland was our faithful ally from the beginning of the war to its very end: we won and in the event Poland lost, to be dominated again by a hostile and treacherous foe. Whatever may have been the divided counsels in her ranks as to policy, what was never in doubt was the courage and endurance and determination of the Polish people, whether fighting openly with the Allied forces in the West or secretly in the underground in their homeland, to continue the bitter struggle against Germany, faithful to their word to the bitter end, come what may. The author has done a great service to his countrymen in this meticulous and dispassionate account of a heroic epoch in their history: his book will not of course be permitted circulation in the Poland of today: let us hope for a Poland of tomorrow, free again.

ABBREVIATIONS AND CODE NAMES

AK	*Armia Krajowa* (Home Army)
"Bastion"	a dropping zone capable of receiving drops from several planes on a single night
BCRA	Bureau Central de Renseignements et d'Action.
"Bridge"	a two-way operation with a plane landing in Poland and returning to its base in allied territory
CD	executive director of SOE
"Duck"	a three-figure signal broadcast by the Polish Radio in Britain: see "Iodoform"
EU/P	sub-section of the Polish section of SOE dealing with the Polish minority in Northern France
F	SOE independent French section
"Fan"	a diversionary organization of the Home Army in the eastern territories
FANY	First Aid Nursing Yeomanry
Gestapo	*Geheime Staatspolizei*
GS/R	General Staff (Research)
"Intonation"	second period of drops into Poland
"Iodoform"	a system of secret signals sent by the Polish Radio in Britain through the BBC in connection with dropping and landing operations
"Jedrusie"	("Andrew Boys") a diversionary and partisan unit
"Kedyw"	*Komenda Dywersji* (Diversion and Sabotage Command of the Home Army)
KRIPO	*Kriminalpolizei*
MAAF	Mediterranean Allied Air Force
MD	mining and diversionary equipment sent to Poland in containers
MI R	Military Intelligence, Research
NKVD	*Narodny Komissariat Vnutrennich Dyel* (Peoples' Commissariat of Internal Affairs: used for Soviet secret police)

NOW	*Narodowa Organizacja Wojskowa* (National Military Organization)
NSZ	*Narodowe Sily Zbrojne* (National Armed Forces)
ORPO	*Ordnungspolizei*
OSS	Office of Strategic Services
OW	fighting equipment sent to Poland in containers
"Pond"	a secret landing ground for "Bridge" operations
"Retaliation"	fourth period of drops into Poland
RF	SOE section working directly with de Gaulle's BCRA
"Riposte"	third period of drops to Poland
RSHA	*Reichssicherheitshauptamt*
SAAF	South African Air Force
SD	*Sicherheitsdienst*
SIPO	*Sicherheitspolizei*
SOE	Special Operations Executive
SS	*Schutzstaffel*
SZP	*Sluzba Zwyciestwu Polski* (in the Service of Poland's Victory)
"Tempest"	an intensified diversionary operation consisting in local mobilization of larger units of the Home Army to attack retreating German units
"Tercet"	the second and third quarters of the moon
ZO	*Zwiazek Odwetu* (Reprisal Organization)
ZWZ	*Zwiazek Walki Zbrojnej* (Union for Armed Struggle)

INTRODUCTION

This book, which first appeared in Polish in 1968 under the title "Politicians and Soldiers", was originally written for the Polish reader. After the last war, from which Poland, in spite of her effort and her alliance with the West, did not emerge victorious, a number of simplifications and slogans were bandied around which distorted the historical truth. My object was to refute superficial judgments and present the events of those years in the light in which they ought to be generally known. I also wished to dig out the facts about certain matters and operations which for many years were secret and unavailable to both the historian and the reader. I wanted to give the Polish reader a true picture, unaffected by emotional judgments.

While the book was being written and as I found its scope expanding, I came to the conclusion that it should also interest the British reader. During the last war the Polish Government and General Staff were in London from 1940 onwards: it was from Britain that the planes took off to carry help to occupied Poland, it was here that the most important political and military decisions were taken. My country was very closely bound to Britain during the last war. British readers, especially of the younger generation, should also know why Poland to-day, in spite of an age-long tradition of freedom, is a communist country within the Soviet bloc. I wish, too, to remind people of the position Great Britain held during the war, of the important part she played and how unfortunately much of this moral capital was lost during the following years.

The book is almost an exact translation of the Polish version with some small omissions. In the main text a number of less important Polish names have been left out, and from the indices I have omitted a large table giving details of all the parachute flights to Poland. This table gave the code-name of each flight, the nationality of the crew, the type of aircraft, the navigator's name, the airfield from which it took off, the date of the flight, the location of the dropping zone, the names and code-names of the parachutists and details of the reception arrangements. It was considered that too many Polish names might confuse the British reader. Anyone interested in these details will find them in the Polish version.

J. G.

London, May 1969.

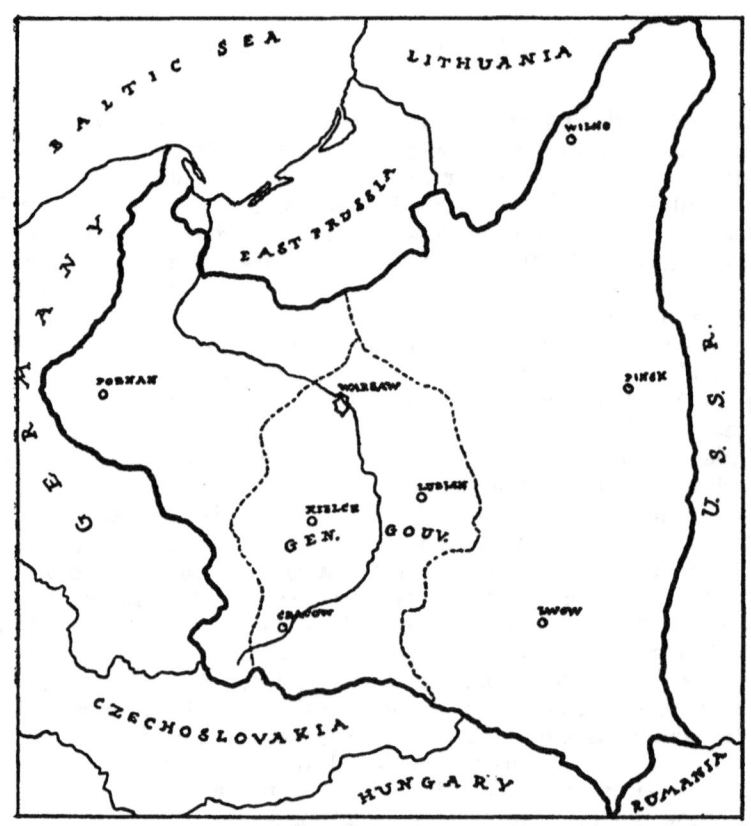

POLAND IN OCTOBER 1939

To the West, German occupied territory, to the East, Russian occupied territory, in the centre the General Gouvernement, created by the Germans and under their occupation.

IN THE DARK

I

The dirty green canvas flap was plucked aside violently and several strangely dressed young men rushed out of the tent. One was draped in the shreds of a sweater and in stained military breeches, another had a small sheepskin jacket thrown over his shoulders, although it was near the end of June and the sun was burning fiercely, a third wore sandals on his sockless feet.

It was obvious that they were in a state of extreme annoyance. They shouted, gesticulated violently and threw angry glances at the tent. They moved off a few hundred paces, climbed to the top of a small mound and sat down on the parched grass.

For several minutes they were unable to calm down. They were so unsettled by the quarrel, into which they had let themselves be drawn in the tent that they could scarcely remember when they had left that rowdy gathering or how they had found themselves on the hillock. They looked at the tents spread out below them and, still beside themselves, clenched their firsts in exasperation.

'What fools they are, what bloody fools' growled one of the young men, thumping his fist against the hardened earth.

Morale amongst the Polish rank and file was poor, which was not surprising. First the September defeat and then the collapse of France had hit everyone like a thunderclap. This was enough to break the spirit of many, but the young officers could not see why everyone in authority should be blamed for the misfortunes. They refused to listen as the soldiers began by complaining and proceeded, egged on by one another, to abuse and condemn everything and everyone, above all their commanders who, in their simple view, were capable of nothing and responsible for everything.

The small group of young officers, all friends, had tried to refute these sweeping generalisations and had only several minutes previously entered into an argument in which they had simply been outshouted. Discipline was none too good in those days, few people attached much importance to officers' rank, moreover hardly anyone was wearing correct uniform or could be distinguished by insignia from his oddly dressed comrades. Several days previously they had all escaped from a France in a state of collapse and had reached the south coast of England, whence they had travelled to Scotland and were now quartered in a temporary camp at Douglas near Biggar. They had not yet received their uniforms or been formed into a proper military unit, and they were still dazed by the crushing defeat of the Western allies.

The friends gradually calmed down. Waves of anger recurred every now and then, but with less force each time. Their anger was fading, to be followed by thoughts.

Soldiers, of course, were always the same. To-day they might be an unruly and demoralised bunch, but in a few weeks' time, once they were dressed in decent uniforms and could be trained afresh, the rabble would turn into a fine military unit. But the worst of it was that no-one knew whether there would be enough time for the uniforms to be delivered, for re-organization and for a return to military duties. These men had all encountered the Germans before, either during the September campaign in Poland or later in Norway or France, and each time they had found themselves up against such tremendous opposition that they could not imagine forces capable of stopping it. In Poland, after the collapse of the front and the disintegration of the great combat units, they had put their faith in the Western Allies, but after having actually come into contact with them, they had lost this uncritical faith and had had to exert great self-control so as not to flounder in the depths of pessimism. France frightened them by her slovenliness, lack of preparation and defeatism, the Norwegian campaign had flared up like a comet and promtly died down, leaving behind it a sense of frustrated intentions, while here in the British Isles they had encountered an atmosphere which they simply could not understand. In the port young, smiling girls had filled them up with tea, on the harbour wall they had seen civilians walking up and down with staves and pikes. Here and there they had seen wooden dummy field-guns; cheery men had clapped them on the shoulder and made signs indicative of complete self-confidence. They had had to look hard to find anywhere an armed soldier in proper uniform. They knew nothing as yet of Britain or the British, so they refrained from hasty conclusions, but everything they saw on landing and on the following day filled them with anxiety. They fought against it, tried to find arguments, had long conversations amongst themselves, told each other that Britain was, after all, the greatest power in the world; they sought logical reasons no longer for optimism, but for the slightest glimmer of hope. All to no avail.

'How can anyone now manage to stop Hitler and his victorious divisions? What forces are there to do it with? Today he is at the Channel, tomorrow he may already have landed!'

The friends' exasperation had by now completely died down. They got to their feet and looked towards the tents, feeling a newborn sense of solidarity and affection for the castaways whom they had just left in anger. How were the poor fellows to blame, thrown up like this on a foreign shore — how could they help failing to understand what had happened? After all, no one else could understand it either.

Would there still be a chance to supply the men with uniforms, to organize them and turn them into proper soldiers for the third time?

II

The long, sunny days were still for the most part untroubled by enemy attack; but towards dusk people in the streets began to walk faster, the buses too put on speed and the Underground stations and platforms began to fill with people carrying rugs and pillows. Without unnecessary fuss or irritation, and with a quiet sense of humour, the crowds bedded down amid the tiled walls and prepared in those cramped conditions to enjoy a few hours of rest. Only the police and air raid wardens still moved about the streets. The latter, in civilian dress with tin hats and gas-masks slung over their shoulders, patrolled the deserted thoroughfares and listened anxiously to the sounds of night. It was July, and the thin buzzing of insects might have been heard here and there; but no-one paid attention to them, for any moment might bring the threatening sound of vastly more powerful wings. Hundreds of Dorniers and Heinkels flew over London almost every night. Hitler's forces were just across the Channel, and his birds of prey swarmed over the British capital to clear the skies of resistance and blaze a path for the coming invasion.

On one such night in 1940, in the small hours, an important meeting was held in the Prime Minister's office in the Admiralty's underground stronghold. Those present were Anthony Eden, the Secretary of State for War; Hugh Dalton, the Minister of Economic Warfare; and Churchill, who had just taken over the Premiership and with it responsibility for the whole conduct of the war which had begun so disastrously. True, he had broad shoulders for the task, and had sought the supreme responsibility of his own accord. The Tories' new-found leader was sixty-five years old, but his strength and vigour might have been envied by many a young man. Full of optimism and the spirit of adventure, possessed of boundless energy and constantly brimming with fresh ideas, he worked ferociously day and night and knew how to extract the utmost effort out of those around him. He was endowed by nature with that extremely rare gift which is the dream of political leaders and commanders of great armies, as it is that of sportsmen training for great events: he could at any moment shut off his mind from the most baffling problems, forget the most shattering defeats and refresh his nerves and muscles by falling into a deep sleep, which in a few hours restored his mental brilliance and physical energy. So, while others wrestled with fatigue and struggled painfully to concentrate in the small night hours, Churchill, rested and full of dynamic vigour, with a cigar in his pursed lips and with his brow lowered like a charging bull, conducted the knottiest arguments and dazzled his entourage with ideas bordering on genius and seeming impracticability.

Of the two ministers present, Eden as Secretary of State for War was clearly involved with the subject in hand. A Conservative and close party associate of the new Premier, he was under the spell of the latter's personality and usually fell in with his arguments, so that Churchill could expect support from this quarter for even his most unexpected plans. The presence of Hugh Dalton, a socialist who had entered the government as a result of the wartime coalition, might have seemed more surprising. He had more than once crossed swords with Churchill, yet the latter had picked on him to carry out the government's most secret plan, believing as he did that the minister's abilities would overcome all difficulties and ensure success. No question could arise of any disunity or opposition based on party disagreements. This indeed is the great strength of British democracy and the four nations which inhabit the British Isles. In peace-time the parties struggle for leadership, and outsiders are often struck by the ferocity with which the opposition attacks the government's policies. Party strife often takes on violent forms, and it is hard to imagine that people thus divided can ever work together. But if war comes, the clamour of internal politics is suddenly stilled. A coalition government is formed under the leader of the party holding a parliamentary majority; the struggle is no longer for power at home, but for survival and victory in yet another of Britain's wars. The government enjoys unquestioned authority, the whole country is behind it, and this steady, tenacious and unshakable solidarity constitutes an invisible force which has many times broken the strength of more powerful and better prepared adversaries.

The subject of the present meeting was one close to Churchill's heart. From Britain's entry into the war on September 3, 1939 up to the present time, the Western powers had no success to their credit. The Royal standard flew over Buckingham Palace and Britain still dominated the seas, but on land, where she and her allies had come face to face with the enemy, the record was one of defeat almost without parallel in Britain's long history. Churchill could not forget the men evacuated from Dunkirk whom he had seen on the beaches of southern England. Haunted by Hitler's thin face with its absurd moustache and the strand of hair falling across the brow, he felt angrily that disaster might befall if he did not soon succeed in inflicting at least one blow on the hated enemy.

This was what the meeting had been called to discuss. Since the end of May 1940 plans had been afoot for the creation of a secret organization to carry the war into German-occupied territory. After Austria, Czechoslovakia, Poland, Denmark, Norway, Holland and Belgium, it was now France's turn. The Nazis, it is true, made differences between the occupied countries and did not treat them all with like severity, but they were hated everywhere and the more active elements in the population had at once gone over to underground resistance. It was necessary to make contact with these groups and use their readiness to fight by providing them with means and indicating the most vital targets. If the right people could be found and trained and if effective methods could be devised in the new circumstances, a serious blow might be dealt at Germany from within her European fortress. Precedents for this type of fighting were not lacking. Although it was centuries since the British had had to resort to underground methods in their own country, they had had much to do with such movements in the course of battling to maintain their empire. One had only to remember the Sinn Fein organization which for years harried British troops in Ireland. If Britain, which was still free and at war, extended a hand to the conquered but unsubdued peoples of Europe, German troops and authorities could be effectively attacked by unseen enemies. Trained experts in this type of warfare, along with supplies, could be sent from Britain. Sabotage, propaganda, attack on the lives of key officials, the disruption of work and industry and a general stirring-up of the occupied countries — such were the purposes for which it was proposed to set up a far-reaching secret organization. With plans so out of the ordinary, a completely independent instrument was necessary to ensure success. Although the objects of the proposed organization were primarily military, it was not to be placed under the War Office or staffed by ordinary officers. Naturally, this aspect aroused much opposition, and two months elapsed before the objections of the Admiralty, Air Ministry and Imperial General Staff were overcome, as they were thanks to Churchill's energy and enthusiasm. It was now July 16th: the broad plan was at last agreed, and the meeting was designed to give it practical shape.

After once more outlining his conception to the two ministers, Churchill proceeded to the executive aspect. If the others had any objections they would have found it difficult to put them forward. When Churchill's imagination was caught by a theme, discussion tended to turn into a monologue, and one to which it was worth paying the closest attention.

The secret plan had been carried to the point where it was known what the new organization would be called and who would be at the head of it. The title of "Special Operations Executive" (SOE) was appropriate to the aims described above, and the man designated to head the new body was sitting in front of the Prime Minister's desk.

Pausing for a moment in his address, Churchill looked closely at Dalton, who nodded in silence. Churchill did the same and resumed:

'You will have Vansittart to help you at the start, and you will need a big staff of officers and senior officials. They must be sought out and seconded from all over Whitehall, however much their superiors object. I will back you up in this. They must be chosen with care — we want fairly young men, with plenty of character and initiative. There must be as little red-tape as possible. The work will be highly secret, but of course it cannot be completely isolated from what the government and armed forces are doing. You must keep in touch with the Foreign Office and the Chiefs of Staff. The secret operations must fit into the general military picture, and you must keep the Services informed of your plans in general terms. In turn, SOE will be kept informed of our broad strategic planning.'

Churchill paused again and reached for a fresh cigar. Dalton took the opportunity to speak: he agreed with the plan, but was not quite certain of its exact aim. It was one thing to carry out sabotage close behind the front, and another to do so in the heart of the enemy's territory. At the present time, the Nazis held undisputed sway over the greater part of Europe. Any attempt to attack them from within might provoke reprisals against the population of the occupied countries.

The Prime Minister leaned forward with an impatient gesture.

'We cannot do anything without the help of the local population. We are talking about countries which have already started to conduct underground warfare. The war is on, and we cannot win it without victims.'

'So we are to go to work everywhere and with all available means?'

'Exactly. You are to set Europe ablaze!'[1]) said Churchill almost in a shout, thumping his desk. At that moment, the ceiling quivered and the heavy rumbling of a distant explosion was heard. Churchill smiled as he put a match to his cigar.

On July 22nd the War Cabinet approved the memorandum prepared for it. The record of the brief discussion merely states that the existence of SOE must be kept completely secret and that it was therefore not advisable for it to be debated in the House of Commons.

III

In 1939 the British were not prepared for war. Only the Navy, which had been kept up to strength and mobilized in good time, ruled the seas and protected the communications of Britain's far-flung empire.

Past strategy had been based on the principle that the Navy would also provide for the security of the British Isles, since only by defeating it could an enemy cross the Channel. Such had been the state of affairs for centuries. In the first world war the Germans made a breach in this principle by means of zeppelins, which dropped a few bombs on London and its environs. This largely symbolic attack was at the same time a warning that a new threat had come into existence — that of the air arm. Between the wars, aviation technique advanced at such a rate that the crude efforts of 1916-8 took on, in retrospect, a frightening character. It was no longer sufficient to control the seas: Britain must also control her air space if she was to be safe from enemy attack.

The practical British had grasped this fact at an early stage. In mid-1938, after Hitler's seizure of Austria, they began to organize the first flight training establishments in Canada, well away from threatened Europe. After the fall of France in June 1940, when the troops who had been miraculously rescued from Dunkirk lay on the beaches of southern England, not a moment was wasted in idle lamentation. The British people, tough despite their comfortable existence, devoted a

---

[1]) The actual phrase used by Churchill.

supreme effort to strengthening their Air Force. Day by day, factories working in three shifts turned out dozens of new aircraft, the bulk of which were fighters, and schools continued to be created for the training of war pilots.[2]) They might not be sure how to salute or which side their belts buckled on, but they must at all costs be able to fly. The pick of the nation's youth went through these crash courses. They were soon joined by large numbers of their Polish allies, for the Polish Air Force had been given priority in the evacuation from France, most of its pilots had seen actual fighting and their morale was better than might have been expected.

However, Britain's unpreparedness for war was not so great as it might seem from the outside. The practical islanders, while reluctant to sacrifice their comfort to timely rearmament, had foreseen the approach of war and had sought fields of activity in which they might achieve some results without setting in motion a whole large military machine. Looking back, they found many useful examples in their own history. It had not always been possible to act in the open, and soldiers in uniform had not always been the most effective argument. In the course of building up an empire they had often had recourse to secret action, subterfuge and the technique of weakening an enemy from within. The first world war, it is true, had gone down in history as a war of positions, of interminable trench warfare claiming millions of casualties, but even it had shown examples of the success of less orthodox methods — notably the legendary exploits of Lawrence of Arabia, whose guerilla warfare against the Turks in the Near East still stirs the imagination of artists and historians. Then there was the Boer war, in which British troops had been defied by an army of settlers ten times smaller but practising guerrilla tactics, and the Irish war of liberation in 1919-21, a further proof that war could be waged by other than textbook methods.

All these matters were of interest to those responsible for the nation's defence from 1938 onwards. A special section of the General Staff known as GS/R [3]) under Colonel Holland began to investigate the European scene. In spring 1939 Colonel Gubbins, later head of SOE, working with Holland, paid a number of secret visits to the Baltic States, Poland and the Danubian countries, examining the terrain with an eye to suitable areas for diversionary action. This was a good instance

---

[2]) At least six months of hard work were needed to train a completely raw young man to fly a modern machine. Great Britain at that time was more in need of aircraft than of trained pilots. Therefore, in spite of growing necessity, the period of basic training was never shortened.

[3]) General Staff (Research).

of far-sighted planning. At the same period GS/R was rechristened MI R[4] and undertook its first practical operations under Gubbins' direction: the latter had had personal experience of unorthodox methods of warfare in Ireland and had also served in Russia in 1919. In the summer before Hitler's attack on Poland secret sabotage courses were organized and were attended by young civilians who knew foreign languages well, had experience of such arts as mountaineering and potholing, or possessed wide commercial contacts abroad. Before the outbreak of war, before mobilization, when no one knew what turn events would take or how the Germans would overrun Europe, preparations were already in hand for underground warfare in territories that might fall under their control. In this field, Britain was better prepared for war than any other country.

War began for Poland on September 1, 1939 and for Britain and France two days later; but Hitler's first strokes were of earlier date. He had annexed Austria in March 1938 and Czechoslovakia a year later, and although there was no armed opposition, from then on these countries knew the hardships of occupation. We have no exact information about acts of sabotage on their territory during this period, but there must have been some, for there are always active spirits who refuse to submit to foreign rule. We may assume, however, that these acts were comparatively ineffectual, since people were still negotiating with Hitler instead of calling a halt to his aggression, and any saboteurs had only their own resources to rely on.

Matters took on a different complexion when, after the campaign of September 1939, the Germans occupied Western Poland, leaving the Eastern half of the country to their Soviet allies. From the very first day of the occupation the Polish underground movement began to operate, with sabotage as its chief aim. At this time, Russia was aiding Hitler with large raw material deliveries to enhance his war potential and his chances of defeating the West. Hundreds of trains were attacked by Polish saboteurs, often with major success in spite of primitive methods and the use of home-made explosives — for there was as yet no question of help from outside Poland.

An interesting detail may be quoted here concerning the first months of the war and early attempts at organizing sabotage. A Jewish writer of Polish origin named Dawid Wdowinski, who escaped by a miracle from the insurrection of the Warsaw ghetto in 1943, published in 1963 a book entitled *And We Are*

[4]) Military Intelligence, Research.

Not Saved,⁵) in which he mentions that Colonel R. Meinertzhagen, formerly Chief Political Officer in Palestine and Military Adviser to the Middle East Department of the Colonial Office, had several conversations with V. Jabotinsky, the noted Zionist leader who was one of the founders of the state of Israel. In the Colonel's *Middle East Diary*, published in 1959, we read:

"In December 1939, he [Jabotinsky] paid me a second visit, when he unfolded a plan for sabotaging German oil barges on the Danube. Could I get him suitable bombs? He explained that he had many reliable agents in the Balkans and that all he wanted was the explosive... After many formalities and consultations, including a visit to Woolwich where the handling of these weapons was demonstrated, 200 sticky-bombs, nasty green jelly, were placed on the ship and off they went. I shall never forget Jabotinsky's delight and enthusiasm when a demonstration was followed by the complete shattering of a thick steel plate; he threw his arms round me and kissed me; an unusual way of thanking a full colonel in uniform and before a large staff of experts. The venture was a success and many barges were destroyed."

When SOE was set up in July 1940, it took over the experience of MI R and set about energetically evolving plans. Dalton, the Minister of Economic Warfare and a member of the War Cabinet, was the political head of the new institution, but the all-important task of practical organization at this period fell on its civilian head, Sir Frank Nelson, whose functions were designated by the initials CD. Nelson had spent many years in commercial life in India, where he served in the army; he was later a Conservative M.P. and in the first year of the war was Consul at Berne. This background is characteristic of the British approach in such matters. As already mentioned, SOE was to be an unorthodox fighting service and was therefore removed from the control of the military and placed under a civilian head, despite strong military opposition. When Nelson retired owing to ill health in May 1942 he was succeeded by Sir Charles Hambro, another civilian and a professional banker. Brigadier Gubbins was seconded to SOE at Dalton's request in November 1940, and became its head three years later, in September 1943.⁶)

The first concern of the new organization was to recruit suitable staff. Churchill, as we saw, emphasized this at its

---

⁵) Published by the Philosophical Library, Inc., New York, 1963.
⁶) Sir Charles Hambro resigned because of differences of opinion with Lord Selborne, Dalton's successor from February 1942.

inception and promised help over secondments. By 1944 SOE had a huge staff numbering nearly 10,000 men and 3,200 women, a high proportion of whom (one in four of the men and one in eight of the women) were officers or agents. But at the outset, in summer 1940, recruiting was very slow. The abilities demanded by the job were so special that every applicant was treated rather like a candidate for membership of an exclusive club. Careful attention was paid to mental and physical qualities and education, and the applicant's past was scrutinized.

Once the preliminary staffing difficulties were overcome, further steps could be taken. Sections were created corresponding to the respective occupied countries, the first being the French section (code letter F), since France was the most important of the occupied countries and the nearest to Britain.[7] The Polish section got under way shortly afterwards, in the late summer of 1940. It was headed at first by B. Sweet Escott and later by Captain H. B. Perkins,[8]) who was directly subordinate to Captain P. A. Wilkinson: the latter also supervised a number of south-east European sections at SOE headquarters in London.[9]) The task of finding suitable personnel for the respective countries devolved on the sections themselves, since only they were competent to judge of a candidate's linguistic ability, knowledge of the country and its customs, local contacts and psychological suitability for operations in the specific area concerned.

It should be made clear that the Polish section differed from all the others in one fundamental respect. This we may see by comparing it with the French section, which was the biggest and most dynamic. The secret agents who were sent to France remained under SOE's instructions: their radio

[7]) SOE had the following sections: Albanian, Belgian, Czechoslovak, Danish, Dutch, French, German, Greek, Iberian peninsula, Italian, Norwegian, Polish and Yugoslav. Sabotage and the organization of secret armies, assisted from London, was carried out also in other fields and there is evidence that SOE dropped its agents into Austria and Hungary (in a report from Italy in 1944 of the VIth Bureau of the Polish General Staff there is mention of an operational holding school for drops into Hungary). In similar fashion work was carried out in the Far East (Malay, Burma and Borneo).

[8]) Captain (later Colonel) H. B. Perkins lived in Poland before the war, where he owned a small textile factory in Bielsko. Thanks to this he spoke Polish quite well and knew Polish likes and dislikes, their good and bad habits.

[9]) A little later, when in November 1940 Brigadier Gubbins went to SOE, Captain Wilkinson became his closest assistant. In the Autumn of 1942 he lost contact with the Polish section, as he was transferred to another post at the H.Q. of SOE. In the Summer of 1943 he went to Cairo to take up other duties, still for SOE. On December 3, 1943, on a secret mission, he landed in Yugoslavia.

links were with London, they sent in reports to London and returned there after completing their mission. (Incidentally, within the Polish section there was a subsection entitled EU/P which maintained liaison between SOE and the Polish Government in London in respect of the mining and industrial area around Lille and St Etienne in northern France, with its colony of about half a million Poles.[10]) To complete the picture it should also be mentioned that a section of SOE known as RF, independent of F section, worked directly with de Gaulle's BCRA. Besides the Poles and the Free French, there were in London in 1940-1 the legal and recognized governments of Belgium, Greece, Holland, Norway and later Czechoslovakia. But the Polish Government was the only one of these which enjoyed a special status as shown, *inter alia*, in its relations with SOE. The latter's Polish section co-operated closely with the Sixth Bureau of the Polish General Staff in London, but this was the limit of its authority in Polish affairs. All the agents, couriers and parachutists who travelled by air or otherwise from Britain to Poland came, as soon as they touched Polish soil, under the control of the Polish authorities in the homeland, to whom they reported. With one exception, they were invariably of Polish nationality.[11]) (The despatch of the British Military Mission to Poland on December 26, 1944, was, as I have described elsewhere, a special operation outside the normal sphere of SOE's Polish work).[12])

Every applicant who was selected and trained for operations in Poland took the same oath as was administered to the men of the AK (*Armia Krajowa* — the Home Army, underground

[10]) EU/P came into being in December 1940 as a result of an unofficial agreement between the Polish Government and SOE. The head of this sub-section from July 1941 to September 1944 was Ronald Hazell, a former English shipping agent on the Baltic Sea, who spoke Polish and German fluently. Up to D-day this sub-section sent 28 agents to France. Seven of them were lost. This short note concerns SOE solely and is not the full story of EU/P.

[11]) Two Hungarians, István Fehér and Iván Szabó, joined the Polish training courses. Later, on the night of March 13-14, 1943, one of the Polish parties included a Hungarian, probably one of the two above mentioned. The Home Army Headquarters were informed of this and instructed to send him on to Hungary. Having landed safely, he was sent to the Hungarian border escorted by two Polish policemen, who handcuffed him and pretended to have him under arrest. (Germans made some pre-war Polish policemen to co-operate for the maintainance of public order). In the archives of the Sixth Bureau in a report on jumps to Poland during 1942/43, ref. No. 1530/SP of April 5, 1943, there is a record of the arrival of a Hungarian (no name given) with one of the Polish parties.

[12]) The adventures of the British Military Mission to Poland have been fully described in a book (in Polish) by the present author entitled *Between London and Warsaw*, in the chapter *Operation Freston*.

forces who took their orders from the Polish Government in London), and as soon as he reached Poland he became, for as long as he remained there, a soldier of that Army. Political couriers took a somewhat different oath and, as soon as they arrived in Poland, became subject to the authority of the underground *Delegatura* (a political body headed by a Delegate appointed by London).

To sum up, SOE's influence in Polish affairs was confined to its contact with the Sixth Bureau in London. This was pointed out by the British historian H. T. Willetts in a paper presented to an Oxford conference in 1962 on Britain and European resistance:

"Its duties [those of the Polish section of SOE] were to assist the Polish Sixth Bureau in maintaining and developing communications with Poland, in training operatives, in obtaining supplies, and in arranging the delivery of supplies and personnel. Much of this work consisted in liaison between the Poles and interested British authorities."

The same historian further points out that of all the nationalities in London, the Poles were the only ones who retained the right to their own cipher for radio liaison with Poland, even when stringent censorship was imposed just before the invasion of the Continent.[13]) The code names which the parachutists chose for themselves and used while in Poland were known only to the Polish authorities, and the British had no access to them.

It may be presumed that British Intelligence had its own agents in Poland and communicated with them by means of couriers and other representatives; but it is certain that no agent was dropped there by SOE without the knowledge of the Polish authorities in London.[14])

In summer 1940 it was a matter of urgency to give form to the organization thus briefly outlined. Hitler's armies were poised on the Channel for their attack on Britain. The fortunes of the great air battle hung in the balance. There was hope of winning it, but even this would only mean preventing or at least delaying the German invasion of Britain. The war

---

[13]) The secret was kept so well that General de Gaulle himself heard of the landings from Churchill only when the ships were already at sea. A fierce quarrel took place between the two leaders as a result. The Polish Government also did not know the expected date of the landings, nor, of course, did the underground in Poland.

[14]) Any such person would almost certainly have fallen into German hands or to a Polish bullet, as an agent provocateur. In any case there was no need to send non-Polish SOE agents to Poland, for the only obstacle in the way of more widespread sabotage was lack of equipment and not of men.

had only begun; Poland had been overthrown and the Western alliance shattered. In order to contemplate a final victory whose shape could not yet be foreseen, it was necessary to undertake a counter-stroke which, at that stage of the war, could only take the form of sabotage and diversion.

As France was the nearest enemy-occupied territory, it was there that the first saboteurs were sent — via Portugal or Spain and across the Pyrenees, or by small boats or submarines which landed them on the French coast. The possibility of sending them in by parachute had been considered from the outbreak of war, but was not yet feasible.

The story of the last war is rich in paradoxes and surprises. France was close to Britain, its northern shores were even within the range of heavy-calibre guns. Poland was about a thousand miles away, and the aircraft of that time took between six and eight hours to reach its frontiers. Nevertheless, it was in Poland that the first parachute drop took place.

IV

Late in the evening of September 26, 1939, a Polish aircraft [15]) landed in beleaguered Warsaw. Its passenger, Major Edmund Galinat, made his way at once to General Julius Rommel, who was in command of the city's defence, and handed to him an order from Marshal Smigly-Rydz [16]) for the setting up of a military underground organization.

The order had been anticipated twenty-four hours earlier by General Michal Karaszewicz-Tokarzewski, who, as soon as he learned of the decision to surrender the capital, declared himself willing to take charge of underground activities. General Rommel, who had decided to surrender with his troops to the Germans, after some reflection signed an order on September 27th transferring his authority to General Tokarzewski, together with funds amounting to 500,000 zlote and a further 160,000 zlote in foreign currency. This order was co-signed by Stefan Starzynski as government commissar for the defence of Warsaw.

In this way, before the regular fighting was over and before the capital surrendered, an underground military organization known as SZP (*Sluzba Zwyciestwu Polski* — In the Service of Poland's Victory) came into existence and began operations. One of Tokarzewski's closest associates at

---

[15]) This aircraft was flown to Warsaw almost by a miracle, having been snatched away while under guard at an airfield in Rumania.

[16]) Polish C-in-C during the campaign of September 1939.

this time was Lieutenant-Colonel Leopold Okulicki, of whom we shall hear more.

A few days before or after the formation of SZP, various other independent underground bodies came into being throughout the country. The Nazi and Soviet conquerors, in accordance with the secret protocol for the partition of Poland annexed to their agreement of August 23, 1939, were administering the defeated country as if it were part of their own territory, but the Poles had no intention of acquiescing in this state of affairs. The enemies' strength might have seemed sufficient to cow all opposition, but this was not the case. In a very short time, Poland was honeycombed with resistance organizations representing the most various aims and shades of opinion. Those of a military type alone numbered over a hundred, but sooner or later almost all of these merged with the Home Army. In addition there were political and cultural organizations and groups of scouts and young people. On October 10th, when the ink was scarcely dry on the instrument of Warsaw's surrender, the first number appeared of the underground weekly *Polska Zyje* (Poland Lives). The occupying powers intensified their acts of repression, but these had the reverse of the desired effect. Every new report of the shooting of hostages, of arrests, expulsion and pillage, swelled the number of those who joined the underground movement. Acts of sabotage broke out spontaneously in a variety of distant places, before any orders could be given by a central authority. The invaders' press derided the "ephemeral" Polish state and denigrated its past, predicting a swift end to the war; but the Poles, fortified by their contempt of the enemy, ignored this venomous propaganda and put their trust in the West. Wireless bulletins, repeated from mouth to mouth, spoke of French and British preparations, the great armies poised behind the Maginot line and the exploits of the British Navy in distant seas.

The wireless also began to speak of the activities on French soil of the new Polish political and military authorities, and the name of General Sikorski was mentioned more and more frequently.

Before 1939, Poles had known little of Great Britain. Some aristocrats might follow British fashions, well-to-do people often travelled there, and the man in the street knew of Britain as the greatest world power, with the biggest fleet and a vast colonial empire; but he knew nothing more about it, and British politics and culture meant little to him.

France was a different matter. For centuries she had been linked with Poland by close cultural and political ties. The Napoleonic era had strengthened these ties a hundredfold, and during the Partitions Polish patriots had taken refuge in

France and carried on political activity there, while French literature had a profound effect on the intelligentsia. The first world war had still further enhanced France's prestige in Polish eyes. The mighty battles were remembered, Verdun stood out as a symbol of heroic resistance, and France was regarded as the chief agent of Germany's defeat. Today, when Hitler had unleashed a second European war which was bound to turn into a world struggle, the Poles, despite their country's overthrow, looked hopefully westwards. The Maginot line was invincible, so it was no wonder that Hitler had come to a halt. At the right time, the Allies would strike, and then the war would be over sooner than anyone expected.

Then came the fateful month of June 1940.

The catastrophe of September 1939 had been a profound shock to the Polish nation and it would be idle to belittle its gravity; but it is arguable that the collapse of the Western front came as an even greater blow. Those who understood military affairs must have realized that Poland could not hope to stand up to Germany, even without taking into account the treacherous Soviet attack; but the same knowledge of military affairs taught them that the Western allies were a force of a different order. And now in a few short weeks those allies had been routed, the British army had been driven back across the Channel and the French scattered to the four winds. When Hitler made his entry into Paris the Polish people, for the first time since the beginning of the war, began to doubt of its successful outcome. The timid began to steer clear of underground activity; the desperate committed suicide. It was many years since Poland had passed through such a dark night of affliction.

And then, when no one in Poland expected it, Winston Churchill's voice rang out — a strong voice full of energy, determination and faith in victory:

"We shall fight on the beaches, we shall fight on the landing grounds, we shall fight in the fields and in the streets, we shall fight in the hills; we shall never surrender!"

Only those who were living at that time in Poland, partitioned anew and groaning under foreign occupation — struck down and submerged by a wave of slander and vicious propaganda, yet determined not to surrender — only they could appreciate the full effect of the British premier's words. France was no more — at one stroke, the place she had occupied in the hearts of all Poles was taken by fighting Britain.

V

In the latter part of September 1939, the supreme authority of the Polish Republic resided for a few days in the person of Juliusz Lukasiewicz, the Ambassador in Paris. Fighting had not yet completely ceased in Poland, but the Government had already been interned in Rumania, together with the President, Ignacy Moscicki, and the Commander in Chief, Marshal Smigly-Rydz. The Rumanians impeded communications with the outside world, chaos was developing on every hand, while the pace of events grew ever faster and the need for decisions more urgent. All Polish eyes were turned to France, and every soldier and politician who managed to escape from Poland strove to make his way there. Thus the ambassador suddenly found himself not only in the position of a representative but in possession of powers and responsibilities which are normally held by others. Their exercise was made easier for him by the fact that he was popular with the French authorities. The latter threw open their frontiers to the Poles and allowed them to carry on political and military activities, but they also intervened in these from the very first moment. Before the month was out, the Poles driven from their country were discovering how bitter is the bread of exile.

Many factors pointed to General Sikorski as the man of the moment. He was an opponent of the political group which had governed pre-war Poland and was responsible for the débâcle; many Poles looked up to him, he was a senior officer of outstanding ability and enjoyed the trust and support of the French government. He was well aware of this and made for France with the utmost speed, arriving in Paris on September 24th. The pressure of events demanded immediate action, and on September 28th Lukasiewicz, after consulting those political leaders who were on the scene, appointed Sikorski commander of the Polish army in France. The French at once expressed their satisfaction and approval. Two days later, Moscicki's successor as President, Wladyslaw Raczkiewicz, without delay offered Sikorski the role of premier in the new Polish Government. Sikorski accepted both appointments, and within a few days had drawn into his own hands the chief political and military posts.

While events were taking this course in France, the military underground in Poland under General Tokarzewski had entered into co-operation with the political Advisory Council comprising representatives of the Peasant's Party (Maciej Rataj), the Nationalists (Nowodworski, a lawyer) and the Socialists (Kazimierz Puzak).

Sikorski followed closely what was going on in Poland:

he knew that important events were afoot there, but he had his own opinions and did not necessarily agree with all that was happening. In general he was opposed to initiatives taken without his authority, and he was not likely therefore to approve the actions of Tokarzewski, who was moreover a former supporter of Pilsudski. Although Tokarzewski placed his organization wholly under Sikorski's orders, the latter was not content with this and resolved to secure that all decisions affecting Poland were taken in Paris and not on the spot. General Sosnkowski had just arrived in Paris, and Sikorski decided to confide two important functions to him. The two did not belong to the same political camp (Sosnkowski had formerly been very close to the late Marshal Pilsudski), but this did not deter Sikorski, who rightly calculated that Sosnkowski's personality would neutralize much opposition to himself and that the centre of decision-making would remain firmly in Paris. By a decree issued on 13 November, Sosnkowski became chairman of a committee of ministers responsible for home affairs and also commander-in-chief of a new undergrounnd organization, the ZWZ (*Zwiazek Walki Zbrojnej* — Union for Armed Struggle).

The decision to confer both these functions on one person was sound in itself, but the decree created an artificial situation by providing that the ZWZ should supersede the SZP as the official Polish military underground. The decision meant that highly delicate and complicated activities in Poland were to be directed from Paris at a time when radio liaison was still in its infancy and communications had to be carried on by means of a slow courier service. To make matters even more complicated, the decree divided Poland into six areas [17]) whose commanders were to be separately responsible to Sosnkowski. In January 1940 this was modified so that there were only two commands for the German and Soviet zones of occupation, with headquarters at Warsaw and Lwow respectively; but both these remained severally responsible to Paris. Colonel Stefan Rowecki (known as *Rakon*, *Grabica* and later *Grot*), previously chief of staff of the SZP, was appointed commander in Warsaw, and Tokarzewski himself (*Torwid*) was appointed to Lwow with orders to proceed there immediately.

This was an unhappy decision, for before the war Tokarzewski had been the local corps commander at Lwow: everyone knew him there, and he was liable to be picked up at once by the Soviet secret police. Tokarzewski set out for Lwow but never got there, for on the night of March 6/7, 1940 he was

[17]) Warsaw, Bialystok, Lwow, Cracow, Poznan, Torun.

captured by a Soviet patrol at Jaroslaw, on the border between the German and Soviet zones of occupation.

Sosnkowski set to work energetically: he picked a staff and worked out a directive for ZWZ which was duly despatched to Poland by courier. But he realized that the system of command could not function on these lines for long, and despite Sikorski's opposition he was thinking of going to Poland and taking over effective command on the spot, when suddenly the collapse came. The German Panzer divisions surged forward, France was knocked out of the war and the Polish authorities were hastily evacuated to Britain, chiefly by way of France's southern and western ports. The last telegram of instructions from France was sent on June 18th: by force of circumstances it largely cancelled the existing artificial arrangement. Rowecki, now a general, was appointed deputy commander of ZWZ for the whole of Poland, with wide powers of action in the event of his losing touch with the government.

Two days later, Sikorski and his aide-de-camp stepped on board the bomber aircraft sent by the British premier, which carried them through the night to the embattled islands.

VI

It was the middle of February 1940. The streets of Paris were covered with slush and melting snow; spring might arrive any day, but winter maintained its grip and the sudden thaw only made the cold more penetrating.

Captain Maciej Kalenkiewicz, wearing the Polish four-cornered cap and a uniform made in France, stepped rapidly along the Seine embankment towards the Pont Alexandre III. He looked at his watch, slackened his pace and came to a halt beside the parapet. A slim, erect man of greater than average height, he would have been picked out as an officer even in plain clothes. He was barely 34 years old, though spectacles made him look older. He had had his share of active service, for after fighting in September in the 110th reserve regiment of lancers,[18]) he had served in Major Henryk Dobrzanski's [19])

---

[18]) The captain was a sapper, but just before the war was detailed for training to the 10th Lancers.

[19]) Major Henryk Dobrzanski *(Hubal)*, a world-wide known Polish rider in the thirties, did not cease fighting at the end of the September campaign and at the head of a small mounted detachment, in full uniform, carried out skirmishes against the Germans is South-West Poland. He was killed at the beginning of May, 1940. Soon after, the rest of his unit dispersed.

cavalry group till the end of November. In December he decided to join the Polish army in France, and made his way there via Hungary and Italy. His lively, inventive mind, and his studies as an engineer stood him in good stead. After the German *Blitzkrieg* and the collapse of Poland, everything had to be started from the ground up, and on the foreign though friendly soil of France there was much need for improvisation.

Today, he had made an appointment to meet his close friend Captain Jan Gorski for a strictly private conversation on a subject that interested them both greatly. The young officers, though again clad in uniform and serving with the regular forces, and though they had barely arrived in France, longed to return to their own country and dreamt of once more fighting there. To this end Kalenkiewicz had thought of a plan, which he was eager to discuss with his friend, for returning to Poland by air, landing either in a secret spot or by means of a parachute.

In the First World War, when aviation was in its infancy, landings had been effected but parachute drops were as yet unheard of. Between the wars experiments had taken place, with Russia in the lead: in the thirties the Red Army had not only demonstrated mass jumping by parachutists, but had made some experiments in landing larger military units with light equipment. Observers from Western armies had even been invited to one such display. In 1940 the Russians took their experiments a stage further during the occupation of Bessarabia, which they seized from Rumania. Light tanks, complete with their crews, were suspended by chains from transport aircraft; when these were airborne the chains were lengthened, and the planes, flying as low and as slowly as possible, deposited the tanks on the ground. The tanks' engines were started while they were still in the air, so that they sped forward the moment they reached the ground: this softened the impact and enabled them to go into action at once. The automatic uncoupling of the chains presented no great difficulty.[20])

However, these were all peace-time experiments. The first wartime parachute drops were used by the Germans to land saboteurs in Poland during the September campaign. Later they dropped parachutists in close formation in Norway, during their murderous attack on Rotterdam and on the Dutch and Belgian canals.

In prewar Poland too, parachute training had taken place, but it was in an elementary stage and no parachute units had

[20]) Information was given to the author by a Soviet officer in the German concentration camp of Neuengamme. Apparently this experiment resulted in heavy losses and was not repeated.

been formed. The modernization of the Polish army was a slow process, calling as it did for larger material resources than Poland possessed during her period of reconstruction after the wars of 1914-20 and more than a century of enslavement. What is more, modernization called for a change in the time-honoured attitudes of the individuals and groups who were then in charge of the country's politics and army; and to achieve such changes in the course of a few years is often harder than to raise money.

Kalenkiewicz and Gorski were both young men with up-to-date ideas: they were not burdened with service red tape, and their minds were fixed firmly on the subject in view. Their imagination was stirred by visions of the future and by the latest methods of combat, particularly everything to do with flying and the rapid transport of airborne troops. Moreover, although they had come to the West in order to put on uniform and fight their country's enemies openly, they felt ill at ease in the émigré world. They were irked by squabbles of a personal nature and could not understand the older generation's passion for paying off prewar political scores at this tragic period of the nation's history. They were also exasperated by the French, who treated the Poles with ill-concealed contempt while themselves revealing at every turn their lack of warlike spirit and technical preparedness. The young Polish officers, in their confidential talks, did not hide their fears for the immediate future and more than once lamented that they had been in such a hurry to leave their country. Their longing to return to it grew more intense every day. Meanwhile, they devoted their minds to the problem of rapid and effective liaison between Poland and the West. Wireless was adequate for information and intelligence purposes, but some other means was necessary for the transfer of personnel and supplies, and the obvious means was aviation.

Kalenkiewicz, who hoped to be attached to General Sosnkowski's staff, was in a better position to use influence and took on himself the task of knocking at various doors and trying to persuade important people. Tough and brilliant in argument, he was capable of painting a picture that would rouse the imagination, and in addition his personal charm sometimes prevailed even when argument had no effect on hidebound minds. In his favour too was the fact the need for rapid and continuous liaison with the home country was generally appreciated. Many were anxious to secure it on their own account: for instance, political groups sought to run their own couriers because they realized that the more influence they had at home, the greater their chance of power in the hour of victory.

Nevertheless, the young friends found it hard to gain

people's attention and convince them, and it was some time before they could claim any success. Hopeful ideas were not enough: they must also produce technical arguments. They drew up a series of memoranda examining various possibilities, and used these as ammunition for further attempts at persuasion.

The military authorities were slow to believe in the practicality of the friends' schemes, but they finally agreed to ask the French for a bomber. Nothing came of this, however: the French had few bombers and were expecting a German attack at any moment. Besides, aviation experts declared that there could be no question of flying over Germany and back by day, while night flying was impossible for technical reasons. A daytime flight avoiding Germany would involve too great a distance. Kalenkiewicz, undaunted, put forward an alternative plan for sending a small aircraft which would land at dawn and would not be intended to return, but would instead be destroyed or buried. The French having rejected this, a third plan was suggested, viz. to send a seaplane which would land on one of the bigger lakes. The French were still considering this when the German attack broke, putting an end to any further thought of operations from France.

The Western front collapsed so suddenly that even able men who were used to unpleasant surprises lost their heads. The ironic smiles disappeared from French officers' faces as the great army which was to beat off the Nazi attack dissolved and broke. Kalenkiewicz went south with Sosnkowski's staff and boarded a British ship which brought the party to England.

VII

Anyone who has lived for a time in London and takes an interest in the city knows that the huge metropolis, an agglomeration of many districts and small towns, is in a state of slow but unceasing evolution. As the years pass, quarters that were once fashionable become down-at-heel and their place is taken by others which, quite recently, were not regarded with much favour. From reading the Forsyte Saga we know, for instance, that Bayswater and Victoria, which are now rather shabby, were once regarded as fashionable districts. Bayswater is full of hotels of all sizes and some of its inhabitants are still rich, but few new houses are built there and it is not likely to regain its former status. Victoria is in somewhat better case thanks to the proximity of Buckingham Palace and the station which links Britain with the Continent, and accordingly parts of it are once more taking on a smart appearance with large new buildings containing offices and shops.

This was the area in which the General Staff of the Polish supreme command found a home after the defeat of France. After a brief stay in Bulstrode St., Marylebone, the staff moved to the Rubens Hotel in Buckingham Palace Road, whose name soon became a household word to the Polish community.

One of Sikorski's first acts after his arrival in Britain, was to send, on June 30th, a despatch to Warsaw via Budapest annulling the Paris arrangements for the control of the ZWZ and establishing its supreme command in Poland itself under Rowecki. This sensible decision also involved changes in London. Sosnkowski's staff, which had arrived from France, was no longer necessary now that responsibility for carrying on the war in Polish territory had been almost wholly transferred to the underground movement on the spot. However, there was still a need for liaison: the supreme authorities of the Polish state, now on allied soil, were responsible for the nation's policy and overall military effort, and the underground expected aid from them. The ZWZ had little difficulty in expanding its ranks, but was in dire need of arms and other supplies with which to carry on the struggle. After brief consideration in London it was decided to add a Bureau for liaison with Poland to the General Staff.

The Polish political and military authorities have been criticized for losing their hedas after the fall of France and so adding to the confusion, but this was not altogether so. The General Staff, which had dispersed into small groups in France, began to reach London at the end of June and was working in a more or less normal fashion in July. The liaison Bureau, headed by Colonel Josef Smolenski, was first organized in the middle of July: it consisted at that time of a single, general section with the duty of maintaining liaison with the Polish underground.

The first instrument of such liaison was the radio transmitter known as "Martha", which was brought over from France in an incomplete state by an NCO named Brekiewicz and restored to activity in London.[21]) By August it was possible to communicate with Poland via stations at Bucharest and Budapest: this was an important achievement, but did not meet all the needs of the high command. It was vital to find some quick means of sending men and supplies into Poland.

In a short time the Liaison Bureau was transformed into the Sixth (or Special) Bureau and began to expand its organization. A technical section, designated S, was set up

---

[21]) Details in the present author's book *Between London and Warsaw* (in Polish).

under Captain Jazwinski to work out plans for the transfer of men and supplies. A briefing section under Lieutenant Oranowski was responsible for instructing those who volunteered for parachute drops into Poland. Later, S Section was divided into an Operations group under Lt. Jan Podoski and a Supply group to which Lt. Oranowski was transferred. From the outset, the role of the Bureau as a whole was not merely that of a post-office: besides being an instrument of action for the Chief of Staff, it was the London mouthpiece of the home country's needs and in particular those of the ZWZ commander. In addition, its duties soon included liaison and co-operation with the Polish section of SOE.

While the Sixth Bureau was thus developing its organization and examining technical possibilities, it was compelled by the pressure of events to take practical action. At this stage of the war, the alliance with Poland was still of importance to Britain. France had collapsed, and Soviet Russia was Hitler's ally. The United States were neutral, the smaller European countries had either fallen into the Nazis' hands or were of no account, and something must be done at all costs to shake Hitler's power. Poland had not surrendered, she was still in the war, and her territory was traversed by countless Soviet trainloads of aid to Nazi Germany.[2]) Polish saboteurs had attacked and destroyed several of these, but they needed equipment and explosives to carry on the good work. It was vital to help these allies of Britain's as speedily as possible.

The Polish section of SOE came into existence at about the same time as the Sixth Bureau and was obliged, like it, to function while its organization was still developing. Its head, Captain Perkins, made contact with the Polish authorities at once and offered to place the whole of his resources at their disposal. He himself did not yet know how the technical difficulties would be overcome, he was still at the stage of feeling his way, but he understood clearly that it was urgent to establish liaison with Poland and that this could only be done by air. The officers of the Sixth Bureau were of the same opinion.

VIII

When Lindbergh in 1927 flew across the Atlantic — a distance of over 3,000 miles — in a single-engined monoplane

[2]) By a pact of February 10, 1940, Russia undertook to supply the Germans with 1,000,000 tons of fodder, 900,000 tons of crude oil, 100,000 tons of cotton, 500,000 tons of phosphates, 100,000 tons of chromium ore, 500,000 tons of iron ore, 300,000 tons of pig-iron, 2,400 kilograms of platinum and large quantities of other goods. The greater part of these supplies were delivered.

and was greeted in Paris by excited crowds, he behaved calmly and like a man who had done nothing out of the ordinary; yet his exploit was in fact an extraordinary one for that time. These were the days when the great development of avliation was just beginning: altitude and non-stop records were being set up, round-the-world flights were achieved and the speed of aircraft increased daily. But these were, so to speak, sporting records: the aircraft involved were light machines and were generally manned by a single pilot. Although they gave promise of great things to come, the application of these achievements to military, passenger and transport aviation was slow in developing.

When the second world war broke out, the fastest aircraft in the world was the German Messerschmitt 109 fighter, which could be adapted to attain a speed of 364 miles an hour. Military aircraft of ordinary types were slower. In the Battle of Britain, the Messerschmitts found worthy rivals in the Hurricanes and Spitfires, of which the latter proved to be the faster and more efficient. These were first-class machines and would no doubt have been favoured by the SOE planners had it not been that their use was confined to protecting bombers and to air battles. Their range was not much above 600 miles and they could carry scarcely anything besides the pilot and their own armament.

The types of bombers then available to the British authorities included the Whitley, Lysander, Albemarle, Halifax, Stirling, Liberator, Fortress and Dakota, the last three of which belonged to the U.S. air force. Bombers were of course slower than fighters, but they had a greater range and carrying capacity. It was a question of deciding which of them would be most suitable for clandestine and sabotage purposes.

The air battle was still raging over the British Isles and it was not the best time to seek to interest the air force authorities in other matters; but SOE could not wait, and neither could the Poles. Discussions were started, and the struggle for aircraft began. Not surprisingly, matters moved very slowly. On one side of the conference table were the representatives of the RAF with its experience and traditions dating from the first world war and with a rank second only to that of the Navy among the imperial fighting forces; on the other, a group of completely unknown people, some of them even civilians, representing a newly-fledged secret organization of which no-one knew anything and which had no past and no achievements to boast of. Senior officers listened, indulgent but unmoved, to the long arguments of those who sought to persuade them to hand over valuable crews and still more valuable aircraft for experiments whose purpose was obscure. The planes were to be adapted and manned by civilians in strange disguises for flights over German-occupied territory; not only by civilians, but sometimes even by women as well.

As long as it was a question of short, easy flights to France, Belgium and Holland, such as any old crate might undertake, the discussions progressed after a fashion; but when Poland was mentioned, the RAF officers' faces hardened. The distance from London to Warsaw was practically 1,000 miles, and this seemed quite out of the question.

During these difficult discussions, it more than once occurred to the SOE representatives that if their organization possessed its own squadron or flight of aircraft, they would not need to spend so much time in fruitless argument. But at that early stage such a solution was not to be thought of, and so they battled on.[23])

The first round of argument would probably have ended in victory for the RAF, or at best a draw, had SOE not possessed a strong ally in Churchill, whose mighty shadow loomed over the conference table and did much to turn the scale in favour of the organizers of sabotage. The latter's personal calibre was also not without its effect. In accordance with the principle adopted at the outset they had been recruited with great care and were men of high intelligence, initiative and independence. Thanks to these factors the RAF authorities finally gave in and agreed to trial operations, though without much faith in their success.

At the initial stage it was difficult to envisage using American aircraft, if only because the US was not yet in the war. Among the RAF bombers the choice fell on the twin-engined Whitley, a slow, cumbrous machine with a range of about 870 miles. It had never been used for parachute jumps; clearly it could not fly to Poland and return without landing, but the experts believed that it could be adapted for the purpose in view. Extra fuel tanks were fitted, an opening was made in the floor of the aircraft and fastenings were provided for parachute lines. The tanks and extra weight lowered the plane's carrying capacity, but it was thought that it could still carry several passengers with their equipment besides its crew and could fly about 1,550 miles in 12 hours. Experiments began accordingly.

At that early stage, when SOE was in the course of being set up and was seeking aid from the RAF, the Polish military authorities, though much interested, were unable to join in the discussions. The General Staff was not yet fully organized,

---

[23]) This idea was reverted to during various phases of the development of SOE, but was never realized, even in the peak year of 1944. Formal and technical considerations stood in the way.

the Sixth Bureau was in its infancy, and Polish pilots were engaged in the Battle of Britain partly as members of RAF flights and squadrons. The first Polish bomber flight (the "Mazovian", No. 300) was formed on July 1, 1940, but it was hard to imagine that it could in the foreseeable future be placed at the disposal of the Polish authorities for the exclusive purpose of carrying out flights to Poland. This was as yet nothing more than a hope, and one that was in fact never fully realized.

While efforts were being devoted to obtaining and adapting aircraft, attention was also given to the problem of training parachutists. This too was a matter of trial and error, for no experiments had as yet been carried out in the West as regards nocturnal sabotage by means of parachute drops.

The first and perhaps the hardest task was to find suitable recruits. What was wanted were young male or female volunteers who must be in perfect physical condition, intelligent, with plenty of initiative and self-reliance but at the same time disciplined and capable of standing up to arduous training. They must be able to take risks consciously but without bravado, good at keeping secrets, courageous, tough and at times even brutal. These were formidable requirements, and few were able to satisfy them. Volunteers were forthcoming, but at least half of them had to be rejected as unsuitable.

Fortunately there was a great deal of excellent material among the Polish troops then in Britain. These included many officers and NCO's who had proved themselves in September 1939 and in France, and many young people who had grown up in independent Poland, who thought along modern lines and were inspired by high ideals.

Since the whole enterprise was kept in the darkest secrecy, recruiting had to be carried on in like manner; but how were volunteers to be had when the existence of a recruiting list could not be divulged? The method adopted was to inform unit commanders secretly of the general plan and invite them to select suitable candidates. Each man was to have the task explained to him in a private and confidential talk, and then be free to decide for himself. After the first few dozen were recruited in this way, no further difficulty was encountered. Those who were chosen might recommend their friends, and in any case the plan gradually became known in spite of all security measures.

Among the first volunteers were the two friends, Maciej Kalenkiewicz and Jan Gorski. They were still fascinated by the problem of parachute troops and sabotage operations, and were still active in studying theoretical aspects and drawing up memoranda on the methods of effecting landings in Poland. They were certainly forerunners of the idea of creating a parachute brigade, which was later taken up by others.[24]) They felt as restless in Britain as in France, and it is not surprising that for both practical and idealistic reasons they were among the first to volunteer for night expeditions.

Hundreds of other volunteers followed close behind them, and the next stage was to put applicants through a variety of tests. Courses were organized by SOE, but both the Poles and British were impatient for actual operations. They needed the experience of carrying out a first jump in enemy-occupied territory, of seeing how the aircrews performed their tasks on a lonely night-time flight, how the parachutists would react, whether their reception on the ground would go off according to plan, and how the equipment, material and instructions would pass muster, planned as they had had to be without knowledge of actual conditions. SOE might carry out tests in France, Belgium or Holland, but what was the value of the experience gained with flights lasting only an hour or so, when there was no difficulty in waiting for good weather or other favourable circumstances? What was needed was to go further afield, to a territory so remote that it could hardly be reached by the aircraft of that time (which had to make the return journey also) — one which, moreover, was of especial importance in itself and was honeycombed with German occupation and police forces. It should be a territory, too, which was suited to sabotage activities because inhabited by a nation full of fighting spirit, unreconciled to defeat and enemy occupation.

After many discussions between SOE and the Sixth Bureau, after trials of aircraft and consideration of all difficulties, dangers and objections, the answer to these requirements emerged with increasing clarity in a single word: Poland.

IX

Next to Hitler, Heinrich Himmler was the most powerful man in Nazi Germany. A slightly-built, bespectacled figure, he might have been taken for a clerk or a small shopkeeper; but the demonic energy that lurked within his undistinguished frame gave a different cast to his career. For him as for many, the unlooked-for success of the Nazi movement opened up extraordinary possibilities. In 1929 when barely 29 years

---

[24]) The Polish Independent Parachute Brigade was formed in Scotland from the 4th Rifle Brigade. It began to be organized during the first months of 1941.

of age, he was appointed by Hitler *Reichsführer* of the SS, a band consisting at he time of only 250 men. By 1933, when Hitler attained power, the figure had grown to 50,000. Himmler's strength of will, ice-cold temperament and total lack of scruple enabled him to break down one obstacle after another in the pursuit of his goal, namely absolute power second only to that of the *Führer* himself.

Apart from a ruthlessness bordering on sadism, Himmler was distinguished by his ingenuity. His head was constantly full of new plans which, if he so decided, took shape in the form of orders and action. It was his idea to raise the birth-rate by setting up establishments in which young unmarried German girls received SS-men in order to bear their children, which were then brought up in state nurseries. In Poland, it was also his idea to depopulate the Zamosc area in order to make room for an SS state. Thousands of adults were slaughtered on this occasion; their children, if they had fair hair and blue eyes, were sent to Germany to be denationalized. This was indeed only a fragment of a much wider plan. Himmler was obsessed with a mania for deportation and re-settling and thought nothing of transferring millions of people over distances of several hundred miles, unless of course the nationality in question was earmarked for extermination.

The combination of boundless energy with a complete lack of moral sense added up to murder on a gigantic scale. There was something uncanny about this man, who would talk quietly about rose-growing and be preoccupied for hours with the fate of a single blossom, and then in the same placid tone give orders for the gassing or burning to death of hundreds of thousands of innocent and defenceless people. Such was the head of the SS, who in a few years gained control of the various branches of the police system, being first Vice-Minister and then, in 1943, Minister of Internal Affairs. He was the creator of the Reich Security Headquarters (*Reichssicherheitshauptamt* — RSHA) and took over personal command of this body after its first head, Reinhard Heydrich,[25]) was killed in 1942.

[25]) Reinhard Heydrich (who was 38 at the time of his assasination) was appointed by Hitler at the beginning of 1942 to be Protector of Bohemia and Moravia and took up this position while remaining head of the RSHA. On May 27, 1942 two parachutists from the Czechoslovak Brigade, the NCO's Jan Kubis and Jozef Gabcik, made an attempt on his life in the suburbs of Prague, by throwing a grenade at his car. Heydrich was badly wounded in the spine and in spite of an operation died on June 4, 1942. Hitler ordered reprisals; as a result thousands of hostages were arrested — some of them killed and the village of Lidice, not far from Prague, razed to the ground. All the men were murdered and the women sent to concentration camps. The children were sent to Germany to be denationalized.

In general, the inhabitants of the occupied countries lumped together the various German security authorities under the title Gestapo; but in fact matters were more complicated. To begin with, in all occupied territories the German army was present and the military intelligence body known as *Abwehr* carried on its functions under the overall control of Admiral Canaris.[26]) It had a counter-espionage department with thousands of civilian agents who kept an eye on all foreign intelligence agencies and potential enemies of the German armed forces, including the local resistance movement. The Abwehr was vigilant enough, but could not be compared in this respect with the police forces under Himmler, which fell into two main groups. These were the ordinary civil police (*Ordnungspolizei* — ORPO), which functioned only in German territory and was of little importance to the occupied countries, and the security police (*Sicherheitspolizei* — SIPO). The latter operated in all territories where there was a German occupation administration, and was therefore best known to the peoples of Europe; but it too was subdivided. The *Kriminalpolizei* (KRIPO) was responsible for the pursuit of ordinary criminals, and any member of a resistance movement who was arrested thought himself lucky if he fell into its hands, since he stood a chance of being freed if he could raise a sufficiently high ransom. But as a rule political offenders were dealt with by the other branch of SIPO, the notorious and much-execrated Gestapo (*Geheime Staatspolizei* — Secret State Police). Incidentally, the Nazis did not invent this body but took it over from the Weimar Republic, though of course they greatly increased its size and efficiency.

SS, *Abwehr*, ORPO, SIPO, KRIPO, Gestapo — it might be thought that these were enough. However, there was still another body: the Party's security system known as the *Sicherheitsdienst* (SD). This large force was closely allied with the Gestapo and shares with it responsibility for the death of millions. Nor is even this quite the end. We must remember the railway police and the special detachments guarding roads, bridges, river traffic, forests and factories;

---

[26]) Admiral Canaris, of Greek descent, was one of the most controversial German figures during the last war. From the very beginning he was regarded in certain circles as being opposed to it. Some even say that he secretly sabotaged the German war effort and was in touch with the Allies. Himmler fought him in every possible way and tried to deprive him of power and importance by undermining and liquidating the *Abwehr*. In this he was succesful and the *Abwehr* finally ceased to exist on June 1, 1944, when the remnants of its staff were absorbed by the *Sicherheitsdienst* (SD). After the attempt on Hitler's life Canaris himself, who was already in prison, was accused of being in the plot. He was executed in April 1945 in the concentration camp of Flossenburg. On Hitler's personal orders he was hanged twice over.

not to mention, as far as Poland was concerned, the Ukrainian Gestapo and the Byelorussian and Lithuanian police. It would take a modest-sized book to enumerate all the various forms of the German security service, to distinguish their respective capacities and describe their innumerable badges and uniforms.

All these uniformed and secret police and countless security agencies — all these cold, ruthless, unscrupulous wielders of authority, the depraved and sadistic guardians of law and order, spent their days and nights tracking people who were for the most part unarmed and defenceless, breaking into their houses by night, dragging their wives and children into the street and cramming the victims into nameless graves, camps and prisons.

All this was well known to the three young Polish officers who, on the night of February 15-16, 1941, sat huddled together in an aircraft which carried them over occupied Europe. During their training they had purposely been given a thorough account of all aspects of the German terror system. One or other of them, during lectures and exercises, may have felt his heart beat faster and wondered if he could dare to face the risk. There was time to reflect and withdraw; but such understandable moments of weakness passed, and as they now sat in the plane, the grim facts they had been told about seemed to sink away far behind them into the night. The knowledge that in a few hours they would again be on Polish soil, surrounded by their brothers of the underground army, filled their minds to the exclusion of all other thoughts.

Thanks to the strict security governing clandestine operations, the three young officers did not know the whole picture and it did not enter heads that they were making history — that they were pioneers of a type of expedition that was new not only as regards Poland but as regards the whole SOE effort in occupied Europe.[27]) Night flights had been made over France, Belgium and Holland, but only for the purpose of dropping equipment and explosives.

In accordance with the views held about landing possibilities, a moonlit night had been chosen. Some clouds were gathering, but there was still sufficient visibility. The aircraft was a slow Whitley whose radius of action was barely sufficient to reach the Polish frontier and return, so there was no question of a choice of route. The pilot was making for

---

[27]) The first flight was to have taken place in December 1940, but at the last moment, when the parachutists were already at the airfield and getting into their overalls the flight was called off. It had been decided that the range of the aircraft (a Whitley) was not sufficient. This flight was organized by Wing-Com. Knowles of the Air Ministry, in agreement with SOE and the Sixth Bureau.

Düsseldorf and Berlin. Raids on Germany were infrequent at that time and it was hoped that a single machine could get through unobserved. The crew were all British, for the Poles were still in process of forming a special-duties flight following Sikorski's intervention with the British authorities.

At the beginning of the flight the parachutists had disposed themselves on the floor of the aircraft, but they soon began to move about, for the flight was high and the interior of the plane became chilly. This fact, small as it was, had an effect on their state of mind; they began to feel less strained, and their minds were distracted from the adventure before them. After a while tension gave way to a human sense of grievance against those who had sent them on this risky expedition without due regard for their comfort *en route*. Examining their surroundings further, they were surprised to find that there was no opening in the floor of the plane to jump through and they were expected to use the doors in its side. Another grievance — why had they been trained to jump through a trapdoor?

The aircraft droned on, and the three young men continued to be assailed by a medley of feelings. Their imagination painted fantastic pictures of what awaited them on the ground; their eyes took in the sights about them, and they recalled yet again General Sosnkowski's parting words:

"You are flying to Poland as our advance guard. Your task is to prove that we are able maintain liaison with the home country."

The pilot's voice came over the intercom: 'We are getting near Berlin.'

After a moment's attention, they were again lost in memories, thoughts and imaginations. Then came the pilot's voice again: 'We are over Poland.' The crucial moment was at hand. Alert, watchful and concentrated, they nevertheless could not restrain their excitement. They collected their equipment, buttoned up their overalls and once again checked the fastening of their parachutes. Each of them kept repeating subconsciously the name "Janek" [28]) — the password that had been drilled into them.

'Get ready,' came the order.

The side-door was opened, and the cold rays of an enormous moon streamed into the aircraft. The dispatcher touched the first man on the shoulder:

'Go!'

[28]) The counter sign was "Adam".

After him equipment, then another jump. The second. The third.

Each in turn heard the roar of the engines and a rushing sound in his ears as he sped dizzily downwards and saw the earth swaying beneath him. The forests threw their dark shadow; the fields lay white with snow under the cold moon.

The three men, two of whom were officers and one a political courier,[29]) had in fact been dropped sooner than planned, for the pilot had not been able to find the dropping zone; he had not enough reserve of fuel to circle in search of it, and his orders were that the drop must be carried out at all costs. As a result, the men landed in German territory, close to the pre-war Polish frontier in the neighbourhood of Bielsko. This part of Poland had been annexed to Germany after September 1939, and it was some way from the border of the *General-Gouvernement* which ranked as a separate, German-occupied territory. The party lost all their equipment, but the officers, travelling by different routes, managed to reach the meeting-place. One of them, Lieutenant Zabielski, injured his legs seriously when landing.

This first landing from the air in occupied Polish territory had a tremendous effect on the population's morale and the development of the resistance movement. The infuriated German authorities stuck up all over the country little red posters calling on the people to help in the search for three exceptionally dangerous bandits. The effectiveness of the grapevine was such that from the moment these posters appeared, the whole of German-occupied Poland knew that the men in question were members of the underground army who had come in some mysterious fashion from the West. As the days passed more such men arrived, bringing ever more effective means of combat. Polish hearts beat faster and hopes rose higher — the Western allies were at last making their presence felt.

The episode of the posters was one of the most signal defeats suffered by German propaganda: the Nazis had shown yet again their complete lack of understanding of the minds of the occupied peoples.

X

General Stefan Rowecki, who was barely 45 years of age, was a man of great energy with a fresh mind unencumbered

---

[29]) They were: Ft. Lieutenant Stanislaw Krzymowski *(Kostka)*, Lieutenant Jozef Zabielski *(Zbik)* and a political courier Czeslaw Raczkowski *(Wlodek)*.

with grudges and political animosities. From the outset, his line of action was simple and forthright.

An unexpected series of events had turned him in a few months from a little-known colonel into the most important figure in underground Poland, with all-absorbing tasks and a large territory under his command. Knowing himself to be the nation's leader, aware of the possibilities and moral strength inherent in his position, he was also conscious of the limitations of clandestine action. He well knew that even the biggest and best organized underground movement could not win a war against Hitler's armoured divisions, not to mention the fact that Russia was on Germany's side. The underground could and must harry the enemy in every possible way, but the blows which would decide the fate of the war must be struck from outside. Only then, when the German war machine had begun to falter, could the underground venture on open acts of war with any hope of success.

Before he became Tokarzewski's chief of staff, Rowecki had intended to escape via Hungary to join the new Polish army in France. Instead, he remained in the home country and was soon bound to it by the most special ties, but he did not cease to look westward. He was convinced that final victory could only come as a result of joint, concerted, open action by the underground and the Western forces.

The Polish forces were in France for too short a time to achieve much, but they did establish liaison between Paris and Warsaw and create the beginnings of an organization. While Kalenkiewicz and Gorski were still in Paris planning flights to Poland and improved military liaison, Rowecki was thinking along the same lines. The underground needed money and arms in order to expand its forces, and these could only come from the West.

After the fall of France and the move of the Polish Government to London, the underground leaders in Warsaw began to work out their first plans for a general rising. The moment might seem a strange one, since if ever the prospects of victory and expelling the Nazis looked hopeless it was in that autumn of 1940. Nevertheless, the high command of the ZWZ grappled with the difficult task, in which Rowecki took a major part. From the psychological point of view their decision was justified. The catastrophe in the West had come as a deathblow to the hopes that had begun to stir again after the previous September. At all costs these hopes must be revived. As far as the general public was concerned, the optimistic communiqués of the clandestine press helped to do so; but the staff of the underground army, which put little faith in the communiqués, found comfort in devising plans for a rising.

Naturally these were kept highly secret, but their existence was known to a select few and did much to keep up their spirits. It was therefore no bad thing for the high command to ponder over the last stages of the war and how best to expel the hated invader. For this, of course, it needed information about the secret plans of the Western allies and a true appreciation of their strength.

This is not to say, however, that the only purpose of preparing plans for a rising was a psychological one. Certainly Rowecki wanted to distract his companions' minds from gloomy thoughts, and no doubt he himself felt the need of such distraction; but he also saw the practical necessity of considering what Poland's political and military situation might be towards the end of the war, and what courses of action would then be the most effective. These problems were still far off in the future, but that was all the more reason for thinking about them now. The underground Polish state was still in course of formation, and for the second time Polish armed forces were being reconstituted in the West. By planning for the long term, it might be possible to avoid improvisation at the critical moment and ensure unity of leadership and action, thus sparing the country fresh defeats and disappointments.

The first plan for a rising, contained in Report No 54, was an elaborate document in four parts, with eight annexes. It consisted of an analysis of the political and military situation that might be expected to prevail during the last phase of the war, followed by recommendations for action. In the political field various contingencies were envisaged, since Poland at the time had two enemies who between them occupied the whole of her territory. Despite the optimism which inspired the plan as a whole, this section consisted of a sober examination of possibilities and contains some interesting predictions of what might occur. It emphasized that insurrectionary action could only begin when German power began to crack.

On the other hand, there were some surprising evaluations of the aid to be expected from the West and the part that would be played in it by Polish troops. At this time, in autumn 1940, the Polish units that had been shattered in France were only beginning to re-form in Britain, and we had literally no forces except a few air squadrons and ships. Nevertheless, Rowecki's plan provided for massive participation by air forces, which were to bomb major objectives in at least four cities, as well as parachute landings in various places and the putting ashore of large motorized units which would occupy the coast around Danzig and Gdynia. The annexes comprised long lists of equipment which would have to be delivered in good time to the Polish underground if it were to play an effective part.

This plan, with its exaggeration of current possibilities and disregard of the fact that the Polish armed forces in the West were completely dependent upon the British, shows that the officers concerned had no idea of the actual possibilities or of conditions in Britain, and had not even an approximate notion of the size of forces and the sort of action on which it would be reasonable to rely. This point deserves closer examination. What was the reason for their optimism, and how could experienced officers err so wildly in their forecasts? Was there no way of explaining to them with brutal frankness the situation of our armed forces in a foreign, though allied country?

To answer this we must consider the picture from two points of view. Firstly, the situation in Poland. The country had been invaded and conquered, divided into two occupation zones, honeycombed with troops and police, subjected to lying propaganda and to a régime of unexampled terror — yet the morale of the population was surprisingly good, especially in the German-occupied zone where the ZWZ headquarters were situated. Hitler's police system strove with the utmost cruelty to put down all manifestations of independence, but its methods were so primitive and brutal that they achieved, contrary to expectation no doubt, the result of uniting all Poles. Any member of the underground in trouble could rely on help from any member of the population. He was offered a place in which to live and install clandestine equipment, while friends hid him from German eyes and warned him of any danger. A soldier pursued by the police could enter any premises and knock at the door of anyone's flat, in the certainty of finding a helping hand. A saboteur could rely on the secrecy of railway workers at all levels. Throughout the country, the inhabitants of remote villages and settlements watched out for the arrival of a soldier from the woods in order to give him food and shelter and send their sons to fight by his side.

Knowing this, and with the sense of strength that such an atmosphere imparts, the underground leaders tended unconsciously to look at the future more optimistically than was justified by the facts. It is not surprising that they should have felt more optimistic still about the prospects of the armed forces in the West, which were being organized in the free world with all its power, riches and inexhaustible resources.

Let us now consider the position in the West. As long as France held out, there was no question of any message that reached Poland containing a pessimistic or even restrained account of the military situation. Sikorski was an old friend and protégé of the French, who had lived for years in Paris and was a sentimental, more or less uncritical francophile.

The French authorities might make difficulties for the Poles, refuse them supplies, interfere in their political and military affairs and even express contempt for the allied nation which had stood up to Germany for so short a time; but Sikorski was impervious to all this, he had no eyes for France's own weakness, and he believed absolutely in the solidity of the Western front and in final victory. When France went down like a house of cards before the German attack, he refused to the very last minute to believe what was happening. What can his thoughts and expectations have been when, late on the evening of June 20th, he stepped on board the bomber Churchill had sent to fetch him? He knew no English and next to nothing about Britain and the British; all he knew was that they were going on fighting and that he must ally himself with them for better or worse. Before him lay the prospect of once again painfully building up his country's shattered forces, concluding a new military agreement with his British ally and struggling in the nightmare of politics to form as strong a government as circumstances might permit. How could he afford to be pessimistic? How, in those black days after the disaster, could he send to Poland messages of warning, hesitation and doubtful augury? Would any premier and commander in chief of his country's forces have done so?

Whatever criticism may be made of its contents, Report No. 54 is a remarkable document, drawn up with care and having the great merit of showing clearly the plans, calculations and hopes that the Polish underground entertained in connection with the West and the armed forces there. Rowecki signed it on February 5, 1941. Its transmission to the West by way of Switzerland, together with enciphering and deciphering, took so long that it was not on Sikorski's desk until June 25th. But by this time a fresh epoch had dawned in Europe, for on the 22nd Germany had attacked Soviet Russia.

BY THE LIGHT OF THE MOON

I

Even the best athlete would feel tired after a six-mile run, so it was not surprising that the young men were less cheerful and lively than usual. Without the customary shouts and joking, they silently took off their shirts and, towel in hand, went into the shower-room, where they began to recover their lost energy. Streams of hot water restored the elasticity of their muscles; their hearts began to beat more calmly and steadily, their panting breath subsided. Already refreshed, they returned to the changing-room and donned their shirts and uniforms.

The group, which numbered a few dozen, included a tall, well-built man with greying hair, who had also taken part in the run and had not yet got his breath back. He was clearly a man of some importance, for the young officers treated him with respect; clearly too he was popular, for friendly glances were cast in his direction.

This was Major Josef Hartman, who was in charge of the course for carefully selected volunteers who had applied to be sent on missions to Poland. Although 44 years old, he made it a point of honour to undergo the same training as the applicants. This demanded first-class physical fitness in preparation for the nocturnal landing in enemy-occupied territory. Not only did Major Hartman seek to emulate his pupils and set them a good example, but he secretly cherished the ambition of making a parachute landing himself. He knew that his superior officers would not look kindly on this, but he hoped that in the end he would somehow get round their objections.

As often happens in life, things were decided by a coincidence. Before the war Hartman had been aide-de-camp to Marshal Pilsudski in his retreat at Sulejowek and, after 1934, to President Moscicki. He was well-known in Poland, where his trim, virile figure was familiar to many; this, no doubt, was rather pleasant than otherwise at the time, but was now unexpectedly a source of chagrin. He longed to return to his country and was training as thoroughly as he could to be a parachutist, but he knew that his appearance was a security risk. If he moved about in Poland the Germans would probably soon be on his trial, and many others might be arrested in consequence.

These were not empty fears. The German police had been prepared for war no less thoroughly than the armed forces, and had on their files photographs of all Poles of any distinction in political or military life. They were not likely to overlook a man whose duties had led him to be much photographed and whose face had appeared throughout the country on magazine covers and in film newsreels.

Torn by these doubts, he nevertheless threw himself heart and soul into his responsibilities as head of the training course. These had both a pleasant and a disagreeable side. The requirements were extremely stiff and the rules of selection were rigorously applied, so that any volunteer who was not wholly suitable was rejected without mercy. It was heart-rending to have to send back to his unit a young man who, with tears in his eyes, mutely begged you to reconsider the decision; but it was impossible to relent. Messages from the underground made quite clear what was required, and they could not be disregarded, nor could the risk be taken of sending on an exceptionally difficult mission anyone who might not make the grade. Among other things, Warsaw's wishes were reflected in the fact that those sent out were mainly officers; there was no discrimination at the London end, but the underground made clear its need for trained men who could assume command functions. Exceptions to this were radio operators and saboteurs with special skills.

At the outset, the process of selection involved many hard decisions and much soul-searching; but later, as the course got into its stride, the commander had good reason to congratulate himself. A volunteer army is always better than any other; but no formation or crack detachment, no body of volunteers however highly trained, could compare with the glorious band of young men who offered themselves and were accepted for service in Poland. Undeterred by difficulties or obstacles, they executed every task with the utmost zeal and discipline and with a precision worthy of all praise. These incomparable soldiers had only one object in view: to come to grips with the enemy. But their attitude was not one of mere simple-minded hostility. None of them belonged to the swashbuckling type which is content to possess a weapon and to kill. Every man felt himself charged with responsibility, a unit in a world-wide struggle which was to bring his country freedom, after which it would be for him and the rest of his generation to guide its fortunes aright. After each exercise, even the most strenuous, the young men would start discussing problems of all kinds — political, scientific, economic, military and administrative. Many of them were well informed and had a university education; all were intelligent above the average and each one felt himself indebted to his country, which had given him freedom, schooling and the chance of a better future. Naturally there were occasional difficulties and clashes of temperament, quarrels and animosities, but these were of small account and soon gave way to the commander's tactful handling. A more suitable man than the latter would have been hard to find. Hartman had no son of his own, and treated the lads like members of his own family: he loved them, and they loved him, so that a unique bond was formed between the commander and his pupils.

A few of the volunteers had had some experience of parachute jumping before the war; but it was in different conditions and with different equipment, so that in effect everyone started from scratch. However, parachuting was not the beginning of the course. Spending a few hours in an aircraft and jumping at the end of the trip was a way of getting oneself speedily into Poland, but that was not the essential purpose for which they were trained. The underground army required specialists, above all in sabotage, intelligence and communications, and every man underwent extensive training in these fields. Staff officers with some background of military experience were wanted too, but they also could benefit from acquiring special skills.

Training usually began with a course in marksmanship, together with topography, the first principles of handling mines, and elaborate training in physical fitness. This course, lasting four weeks, was the first major hurdle and deprived many of their hopes of a quick return to Poland.

The second basic course was in clandestine activity and various forms of sabotage. This lasted 5-8 weeks and familiarized the applicant with tasks very like those he would have to perform when he reached Poland.

After these two courses the men were allowed to specialize, at their own choice, in such subjects as sabotage, communications, intelligence, propaganda, or the use of armoured vehicles and methods of fighting them. The first three of these required the longest period of training, usually six months or even more. Those who had passed out of a senior military college were allowed to train for higher command posts. The object was that each applicant should qualify in at least two specialities. In the early stages, all candidates were also put through a course in 'living off the land': they had to remain under canvas and sustain themselves only with what they could catch in the form of wild life or glean in the way of berries etc. Later this course was discontinued.

After all these hoops had been gone through, the successful candidates who, not belonging to the Parachute Brigade, had not yet done any jumping, were sent to train in Scotland at a place they christened "Monkey Wood." After various forms of gymnastics and acrobatics, trapeze work and jumping from towers, they graduated to Ringway, a large parachute training establishment near Manchester. Here each of them made two jumps from a balloon and at least two from an aircraft, and one at night.

The final stage of the long process of "natural selection" was the briefing course. This took about a month. Candidates were instructed about everyday life in occupied Poland, including police regulations and the various German security forces; they were acquainted with the routine of the dropping zones, told what to do if they landed in the wrong place, shown how to pack and unpack their equipment and how to use the apparatus which would assist them to find their destination. Finally they were dropped by night and drilled in the procedure whereby parachutists were received by those on the ground and made their way to contact addresses.

All this time they had to keep in first-class physical and mental condition. They might, in theory at least, be called on any day to make a real jump and fend for themselves in occupied territory, and therefore they must be prepared at all times to practise deception and camouflage, to take swift, automatic action and guard themselves agains surprise. Each man repeated over and over again the details of his personal cover story, identifying as closely as he could with his new, fictitious personality, while his superiors kept setting him the most fantastic and varied tasks. He might be ordered to take part in a brawl, an attack or an ambush. Local police and civil defence authorities were warned that they might be subjected to sudden acts of violence which would not necessarily be due to criminals or enemy action. If any candidate allowed himself to be caught or, when arrested, did not tell a sufficiently convincing story to get himself out of trouble — if he showed any hesitation, weakness or indecision, then even at this last stage of all he might be dismissed in a few brief words and returned to his unit.

These nocturnal alarms and excursions were an excellent means of final training, but they were risky too. The police and Home Guard could not tell who was attacking them, and defended themselves for all they were worth. Usually the chasing, uproar and exchange of shots ended with a drink in some local pub and there was much laughter over the absurd situations that arose, but on other occasions heads were broken and serious fighting took place in which people were maimed; in two cases the casualties were fatal.

At the end of the briefing course, all those who were to be parachuted took an oath in the customary form, and were now ready to be dropped in Poland and begin service there. Each man was trained to his finger-tips, in perfect physical condition, alert as a wild beast, with all his instincts sharpened — like an Olympic boxer, impatient to enter the ring for his long-awaited final contest.

At the beginning of 1941, when the first Polish candidates were enrolled for the introductory course, SOE already had a good deal of experience behind it. Investigation of sabotage techniques had begun before the war, and for some months past a few agents landed by sea had been operating in France and Belgium. Their experience of the real thing was now supplemented by the results of the first drop in Poland. SOE Headquarters were much interested, demanded the fullest details and analysed every aspect of the flight — the equipment carried, the success of the jump, the reception on the ground etc. Naturally the details were of interest to all sections of SOE, and on this account, as well as for reasons of economy, the secret training courses were in general run on a joint basis for all the nationalities concerned. Each section had its own supervisor, generally an older man with experience of active service, whose task was to smooth out difficulties and misunderstandings and to act as interpreter. However, an exception to this principle was made for the Norwegians, who had a permanent base in Scotland, and for the Poles, who were allowed from the outset to organize their own courses in all subjects other than parachute jumping. The Poles, British and other nationalities always did their practice jumping at Ringway.

This exceptional treatment for the Poles was due to the fact that the Polish section of SOE was on a different basis from the other national sections and, as already mentioned, its role in Polish affairs was confined to liaison with the Sixth Bureau. This special status gave rise to many administrative difficulties, but it was an aid to secrecy [1] and the exact adaptation of training to the end in view. Nearly all the instructors were members of the Polish armed forces, and the lectures and training were usually carried on in Polish, which was an advantage for the first year or two. Apart from the occasional use of British instructors, the only exception to the Polish nature of the courses was that each

---

[1] Although every possible security measure was observed, the German Intelligence Service got to know of even the best camouflaged training centres. One parachutist, arrested in Warsaw and taken to Gestapo H.Q., was shown a photograph of one of the centres in Great Britain where part of his training had taken place.

individual station was placed under a British administrative commandant. These officers took no part in the training but were concerned with commissariat duties and the provision of technical equipment. They were also formally responsible for discipline, and for this purpose had authority over the Polish course supervisors. In theory this arrangement might have led to friction and misunderstanding, but in practice it never did, as the British officers, who were senior in both age and rank, showed the utmost tact and friendliness and did all they could to help the work along.

The stations occupied by the Poles were not always at their exclusive disposal. Other nationalities might be quartered there for a longer or shorter period, but the Polish group was always treated as a separate unit, with its own commander and generally its own instructors.

The first Polish attempts to train parachutists began in the autumn of 1940, when Colonel S. Sosabowski, later commander of the Parachute Brigade, sent a dozen or so officers and cadets to an SOE course in mining and marksmanship at Inverlochy Castle near Fort William in Scotland. This castle, the home of Lord Abingdon, was close to Ben Nevis, the highest peak in the British Isles. The station was under the command of Major Stacey and the mining instructor was Captain Strawinski of the Polish engineering corps, who was killed during exercises with explosives in Italy in 1944.

A month or two later, in January 1941, the Poles set up their first course, at SOE's secret station No. 38. For security reasons these stations were generally established in out-of-the-way areas, safe from prying eyes, or on large country estates. This one was at Lord Aldenham's home in the middle of a large park at Briggens, Hertfordshire. The surrounding country was beautiful, hilly and thickly wooded. Lord Aldenham was a well-built man of about fifty with important business interests that absorbed the whole of his attention. He gave the Poles a hearty welcome but made clear at the outset that he would not have time to see much of them; his wife, however, would do whatever she could. This promise proved to be of the greatest value. Lady Aldenham, who had four children from her first marriage, including three sons on active service, behaved like a mother to the fair-haired Polish boys who once again filled her house with the clamour of youthful voices. She looked after their comfort, gave them the best food that could be had, did her best to make their brief spells of recreation pleasant, drove them in and out of the local village, and carried in the boot of her car, hidden amongst piles of assorted objects, the explosives and other gear which it was necessary to keep from public view.

The station commandant was Lt.-Colonel Evans, a friendly,

obliging officer with grizzled hair, who threw himself heart and soul into the exercise. He performed his duties with great tact and, while never intruding, was always ready with advice and help. When he found that the young officers liked him and sought his company, he abandoned his British phlegm and joined in the course with youthful enthusiasm. He would change his clothes, put on a false beard and startle the lads by suddenly appearing in the midst of a sham battle.

The Polish commander of the course was Captain Franciszek Koprowski, who had been known before the war as a P.T. instructor at the Grudziadz cavalry school. The sabotage and mining courses were in the hands of Captain Jerzy Szymanski and Lieutenant Morawicz respectively. The greatest importance was of course attached to this training in clandestine warfare.

After a few groups of volunteers had passed through the course (they numbered about 20 at a time) and in the light of the experience gained, changes were made in the station personnel. The new commandant was a Scot, Major Angus Kennedy, who was as friendly and helpful as his predecessor. The Polish command was taken over by Major Hartman, who was in charge of all Polish training matters under the Sixth Bureau. He arrived at Briggens on July 7, 1941 and remained for the rest of the period. Thanks to mutual tact, relations between the two were harmonious and efficient: no disagreement over responsibilities marred the peace and good order of the lectures and exercises.

In course of time other courses were started, for which different locations were required. SOE possessed several in the vicinity and made some over to the Poles, including Nos. 17, 18 and 20 at Chalfont and Latimer. Later a station at Inchmery near Southampton was taken over from the French section. Here the organization was somewhat different from that at Briggens. The Polish group, whose commander was subordinate to the British commandant, led a fairly independent existence and constituted a separate unit, but trained frequently with groups from other countries. When the training system was at its full extent, the Poles possessed ten stations in all.

On May 1, 1942 the clandestine warfare course was moved further north, to Lady Dorothy Braybrooke's home at Audley End, Saffron Walden, not far from Cambridge. Here, at SOE station No. 43, under Col. Terry Roper-Caldbeck, Major Hartman set up his training headquarters. Here also two of the most important courses were located: that in clandestine warfare, under Major A. Mackus, and the briefing course, under Major A. Wejtko and afterwards Colonel Wieronski.

This set-up under Major Hartman lasted until special operations were discontinued at the end of December 1944. The Major was active till the end, inspecting courses at his own and other stations, joining in the instruction and helping and encouraging candidates. He knew all the young men well and was a devoted mentor to them, tactfully drawing out the less self-assured and calming the over-boisterous. He longed to see active service himself and in fact took part in two commando raids on the French coast, but his ambition to land in Poland was not realized. He knew that if he overcame the obstacles that stood in its way, he would be acting from selfish motives and not for the good of the cause to which he was devoted. Accordingly he stifled his warlike aspirations and worked steadily on, regardless of long hours and fatigue. Not even those closest to him would have guessed his inner conflict, or the sadness and resignation which lay behind his calm exterior and expression of absolute confidence.

But his pupils were flying over Poland — the lads he had trained and bore for ever afterwards in his heart.[2])

II

There is no doubt that before the "Battle of Britain" began Marshal Goering's staff possessed a fairly accurate plan of the positions of all the military and civil airfields in the British Isles. The life of a foreign agent in Britain was not and has never been easy, thanks to the solidarity of the population, the language difficulty and the great experience of the security forces, but the Germans had prepared for war very thoroughly, had indeed begun to think about it immediately after the signing of the treaty of Versailles and would not have neglected such an elementary matter.

[2]) The call for volunteers to work in Poland, addressed to the Polish Army, Air Force and Navy, both in Great Britain and from the end of 1943 the Middle East and Italy brought 2.413 applications. Among them were several women. 28 candidates applied to become political couriers. Altogether the following number underwent training in the activities indicated:

1) marksmanship — 282 (this number only refers to those who underwent advanced training)
2) underground warfare — 630
3) sabotage — 325
4) liaison — 75
5) intelligence — 50
6) propaganda — 64
7) armoured and anti-tank weapons — 161
8) staff officers and others of field rank — 91 (including 22 specialist airmen)
9) briefing — 606
10) parachute training — 703
11) political couriers — 28
12) qualified as fit to jump — 579 soldiers and couriers.

Nothing could be done about this fact, but as soon as military operations began, new airfields were established, and these had to be guarded, as far as might be possible, from unauthorised observers. True they were as a rule large, noisy and of necessity well-lit targets, but rigorous security measures lessened the chance of their being pin-pointed too soon. They could also be photographed from the air, but this involved daylight raids, which, after the Germans had lost the great battle in the air, became almost impossible for them.

Strict security was necessary to protect ordinary military airfields, but it could not compare with the measures required on those airfields which were used for special purposes. The bombing and destroying of any other airfield hampered air operations only to a certain extent, whereas the destroying of the appliances and planes which served the highly complicated night sabotage operations would have completely upset the whole of their planning.

For this reason, after SOE had come to an agreement with the Air Ministry as to co-operation, it ruled out all the existing airfields and began to look around for other possibilities. Having surveyed the Midlands and East coast, the experts decided on the racecourse at Newmarket. It was inspected and measured, the neighbourhood investigated and work began. This was wartime, so there were no lengthy breaks for tea or a cigarette and in a few weeks an airfield was built, suitable for heavy bombers and very strictly guarded. Whitleys began to assemble there and on August 20, 1940 they were formed into 1419 Flight under Wing-Commander E. M. Fielden, nicknamed "Mouse". The Flight was earmarked for work for SOE, but it remained throughout under the command of the RAF.

The first successful flight to Poland, combined with a drop of parachutists, who all luckily reached their destinations, brought SOE headquarters a lot of material, but above all it electrified the Polish General Staff in London. There, in the spring, they had discussed and worked out plans for using all the Polish Armed Forces in the West to help the mother-country. The successful flight gave life to these disucssions, transferring them from the plane of abstract argument to that of practical deliberation, although definite decisions were still a long way off.

Less than a month after London received word that the first parachutists had touched Polish soil, Sikorski approached the British authorities with an application for Polish aircrews to be attached to the unit which was carrying out these special flights. Polish airmen, he felt, had a better right than any others to fly over Poland. In September 1941 permission was given for three Polish bomber crews to be attached to 138 Squadron, which on August 25th had taken over duties from 1419 Flight and was stationed on the airfield at Newmarket. In accordance with the principle in force at that time they were volunteer crews, who had already carried out their full quota of operational flights and undergone extra training in low-level night flying and special methods of navigation. Poland was not covered by the system of radar signals, and therefore a night flight to that country required astronomical navigation and visual observation.

On October 25th three Polish aircrews reported to Wing-Commander Knowles of 138 Squadron. This was a magnificent squadron, and the history of the Polish crews, the drops to Poland and other countries and the secret night flights is irrevocably bound up with it. Its badge was symbolic: a sword cutting a knotted rope, and its motto "For Freedom" could not have been more expressive.

In December two further Polish crews joined the squadron and were immediately put on to night flights. It should be stressed that although all the Polish crews in the special squadron were supposed first and foremost to carry out flights to their own country, this principle was never fully observed. Every crew in 138 Squadron, whether Polish or British, could be ordered to fly to any accessible country within the sphere of interest of SOE. All the efforts of the Polish authorities to get this pratice changed came up against arguments which could not be gainsaid. Flights to Poland, on account of the distance, were only possible in autumn, winter and spring, when the longer nights allowed the aircraft to reach their objectives, make their drops and return to base under cover of darkness. What were the crews to do during the summer, when the nights were short and flights to Poland suspended, while other, nearer countries waited for supplies? So they flew also to Norway, France and even Austria [3]) and Czechoslovakia. In return British crews flew quite often to Poland, generally with equipment, but also with parachutists. The Royal Air Force at that time was too over-burdened by the incessant and ever-growing needs of the numerous fronts to be able to allow crews and aircraft to stand idle.[4])

When discussing these problems from the perspective of twenty-odd years later, one must remember that in the meantime there has been a colossal advance in aviation technique.

[3]) It was during a flight to Austria on April 20, 1942 that the first Polish crew from 138 Squadron was lost, flying in a Halifax commanded by Fl.-Lieutenant Antoni Voelnagel.

[4]) The liberal use of Polish crews destined and trained for flights to Poland, sometimes exceeded the bounds of reasonable planning. A crew, captained by Fl.-Lieutenant Idzikowski, was shot down near Malta carrying out transport duties. This loss was not easily made good.

What was at that time a dream and an unattainable ideal can to-day be experienced by anybody who wants to fly and has the money for the fare. One has only to provide oneself with passport and ticket, go out to the huge London Airport and board the most modern jet plane, in order to soar up to 30,000 feet and, in a pressurised, well-heated cabin, in great comfort, with a well-stocked bar and high-class cuisine, fly in a couple of hours to Rome, Vienna or Barcelona. On a trip to Paris, the drive to and from each airport takes longer than the actual time spent in the air. A flight across the Atlantic, which 40 years ago brought Lindbergh fame, is to-day a commonplace.

How different it was in 138 Squadron!

After the slow heavy Whitley had been abandoned, four-engined Halifaxes were brought into use. These were bombers, also slow, which offered the passenger no comfort, not even heating, not even a seat; they had a normal range of 1,500 miles and a load-carrying capacity of 4,180 lbs. The distance from London to Warsaw is almost 900 miles, so there could be no question of flying to Poland and back without landing; it must be remembered, too, that they did not fly by the shortest route, because the Germans, harassed by night bombing, had greatly strengthened their anti-aircraft defences and had hundreds of night fighters in readiness. By Route No. 1. which went across Denmark, it was a distance of 960 miles to the outskirts of Warsaw.

The Halifax was adapted, it was given an extra fuel tank and its range was increased to 2,100 miles, but at the expense of its maximum load, which fell to 2,420 lbs. The number of its crew could not be reduced below 7,[5]) nor could the aircraft be stripped of its armament, as it might be attacked during its long flight. Its speed was under 150 miles an hour, so that a flight to Central Poland and back took from 11 to 14 hours, depending on the weather. As the flights took place in winter, autumn and spring, there was always a danger of icing, and if there was an unfavourable wind the aircraft might well be unable to get back to base and have to land anywhere, sometimes even in the inhospitable waves of the North Sea.

While describing the aircraft, the navigational problems, the difficulties and discomforts of these night operations, it must be added that the technique of dropping at that time required

---

[5]) The crew of a Halifax, adapted for special flights, at the outset always consisted of nine men. The record of a flight to Poland in March 1942 gives the full crew of a Halifax No 9618. Later, to increase carrying capacity, the crew was reduced to seven men, one gunner and one mechanic being left out.

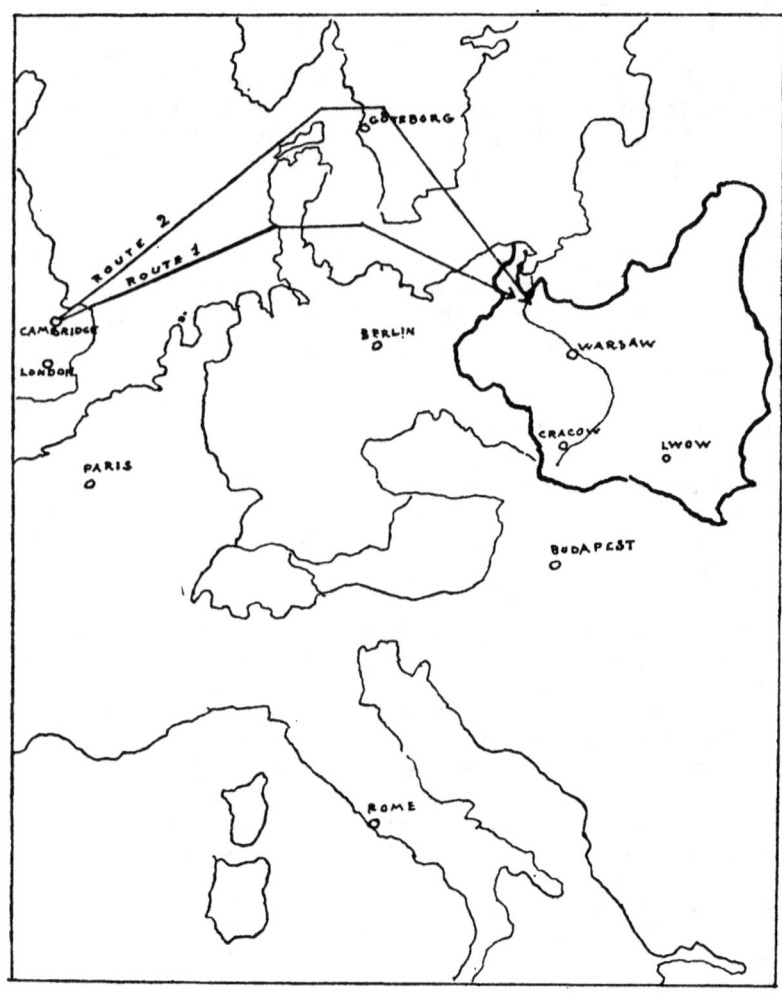

The first two routes used on flights from Britain to Poland

a full moon.⁶) Without it the navigator could not guide the aircraft to its destination or find the dropping zone, where faint lights signalled that it was ready to receive the drop. As long as the flights were based on Britain, they could be carried out during only six or seven months of the year. Taking into account the moon's phases, this meant at most about 40 operational nights over the whole 12 months, and the weather did not always permit of an operation. Nobody thought then of danger or discomfort, but only of the minimum conditions allowing a given operation to be considered as a military flight and not simply as suicide.

In November 1941 138 Squadron, together with the Polish crews, was moved for some months to the airfield at Stradishall.⁷) Wing-Commander Farley took over the command. This move may have been made for security reasons, or the racecourse at Newmarket may have turned out to be too well-known.

While the squadron resumed its night flights from its temporary base, squads of workmen began in great secrecy and haste to built a new airfield near the village of Tempsford, in Bedfordshire, north-west of London, on ground belonging to a farm called Gibraltar. Low-built living-quarters, workshops and hangars were erected, concrete was laid for the runways, water and electricity were laid on. The whole was surrounded by wire fences and secured by low gates and guards. The patient and expert eyes of foreign agents might have ferreted out the airfield, but it would have been by no means an easy task.⁸)

In February 1942 the first Lysanders and Hudsons landed at Tempsford and were formed into the special 161 Squadron, which was mainly intended for night landings on occupied territory, especially in France, Belgium and Holland. Its commander was E. M. ("Mouse") Fielden of the former 1419 Flight. A month later, on March 14th, 138 Squadron moved

⁶) This was the period of the second and third quarters of the moon. It was given the code name "Tercet". When this time approached, the alert was called both in the operational holding stations in Britain, where the parachutists were assembled, and on the dropping zones in Poland.

⁷) Stradishall did not have runways long enough for the heavy, specially adapted bombers flying to Poland. For this reason the flights to Poland took off from a near-by small airfield where there were no messes or other amenities.

⁸) The Germans knew of the existence of the special duties squadrons and furiously searched for their airfield. The secret was, however, very well kept, for it was only once in danger. One night in 1942 a solitary German bomber flew over the airfield and dropped flares along the main runway. The ack-ack kept silent, not wishing to betray the camouflaged objective too soon. The German circled for some time but apparently noticed nothing, for he flew away and dropped his bombs on a perfectly innocent nursery-garden, gleaming with greenhouse glass.

to Tempsford, where it remained until the last months of the war.

From this airfield, hidden among farm buildings, during three years almost night after night the steel birds took wing and flew over Europe to bring her help; from here the teams of parachutists went out to France, Belgium, Holland and Norway, to blow up bridges, destroy railway-lines and burn down factories working for Hitler. Here members of the Polish armed forces boarded Halifaxes and flew to the East, where, after their secret jump, they joined the underground army and fought on their native soil. It is hard to describe in a few words the enormous effort and self-sacrifice of these two squadrons; hard to reckon the thousands of night hours flown under the fire of quick-firing and machine guns, hard to imagine the agony of the return flights on the last drops of fuel with shot-up wings and dying engine, hard to picture the torment of the frozen men who had to land in the North Sea. If anyone was close, very close to those fighting in the underground forces, it was these boys from 138 and 161 Squadrons, from the airfield at Tempsford.[9])

Getting five Polish crews into the special squadron was a step forward, but Sikorski could not stop at that. He continued to press the British authorities for an independent Polish flight for liaison with Poland and at the same time looked around for better equipment on the technical side. Immediately after the first flight, which was made in a Whitley, he turned his eyes to the West, knowing that there had been great advances in aviation. In England work had begun on altering Halifaxes and adapting them for longer flights, but the Polish Staff, while keeping this fact in view, began to make enquiries of its own. In April 1941 the Polish Chief of Staff, General Klimecki, sent secret instructions to the Air Attaché in Washington to take up urgently the matter of American aircraft for flights to Poland. He had in mind two four-engined giants: the Consolidated M. 32 and the Boeing B. 17. The United States were still neutral, but it was an armed neutrality and favourable to Hitler's enemies. Britain had already received help from the States and it could be presumed that the Polish request would meet with a friendly reception. So it did, but after consideration of the technical aspects, efforts were directed to securing a number of four-engined Liberator bombers. General Klimecki's letter prepared the ground for Sikorski, who visited the United States that April and had several talks with President Roosevelt.

[9]) 138 Squadron, while it was based at Tempsford, carried out: 2,562 flights; dropped: 995 parachutists, 29,000 containers, 10,000 parcels; lost: 70 aircraft.

It turned out to be much easier to start talks and present the problem than to bring the matter to a happy conclusion. The first proposal for an independent Polish Flight for special operations was turned down by the British authorities and the latter were not pleased to find the Poles independently negotiating for aircraft with the Americans. Poland was within the British sphere of interests, and this was one of the grounds on which objection was raised. It was not only a question of prestige, however: Britain herself was very dependent on help from the Western hemisphere. She needed every plane, every ton of war material.

Thus there began prolonged negotiations on two fronts which lasted for nearly two years. The question of Liberators was settled first. General Sikorski, knowing that whatever he got, he would only receive through the British channel, went to the United States a second time and there, about the turn of the year 1942-43, he was promised that the Polish Air Force would get twelve of the greatly-desired bombers. This was not a gift. Everything that the United States gave went on to the Lend-Lease account. The thin end of the wedge of British intervention immediately became apparent. The Secretary of State for Air, Sir Archibald Sinclair, at the end of January 1943 promised Sikorski to allocate three Liberators, but only after they had been adapted for night operations.[10])

Before the Liberators were delivered and before Polish pilots went aboard them, a second matter was settled. The Air Ministry at last decided on the establishment of the independent Polish Flight within 138 Squadron (it was the Squadron's third flight). The establishment was six crews and one reserve, three Halifaxes, three Liberators and maintenance crews.[11]) The command of the Flight was given to an experienced airman who had already flown over Poland several times, Fl.-Lieutenant Stanislaw Krol. In July the Flight was given the number 301, thus preserving the memory of the bomber squadron of the same number, which had had to be disbanded to bring the new unit up to strength.

At last a way had been found out of the harmful impasse. It was high time, especially where aircraft were concerned, for flights to Poland by Route No. 1 over Denmark were becoming more and more dangerous every month. The Germans had brought into action a large number of anti-aircraft

---

[10]) This technical consideration was not a mere pretext. The Liberator, built as a daytime bomber, had no suppressor on the exhaust pipe, which emitted flames visible for a long way at night. It was several months before American and British technicians found a solution to this problem.

[11]) Only 81% of the strength of the maintenance crews was filled, for the Polish Air Force always suffered from lack of men.

guns and night fighters which were beginning to be a serious threat. While waiting for the Liberators to be adapted, flights were carried out as before, for the Halifaxes could not take any more roundabout way, and the losses were heavy. During two nights, September 14th and 16th 1943, out of 16 Halifaxes sent to Poland, 7 were shot down, including two Polish crews, and the rest so seriously damaged that they had to be sent for general repairs which lasted 8 weeks. Although the Squadron consisted of three flights, after these two terrible nights it had only two undamaged machines.

Luckily in October the long-awaited three Liberators arrived.[12]) They were manned by Polish crews and flights began over Route No. 2, via Southern Sweden — more than 120 miles longer than the first, but very much safer.

These three American aircraft, although much fewer than what was needed and hoped for, were all the same a token of better days. Immediately after the first flights, plans were begun to increase the number of secret flights, especially as the long winter nights were coming on. In Poland the underground began to reckon on a bigger supply of arms, when a new complication arose. The Allies conquered a large part of Italy and a project was formed to transfer the bases for the flights to Poland to the Apennine peninsula. This decreased the distance and so was an excellent idea, but it required time to carry out. Once again there was a break in the night operations to the fighting country that was crying out for help.

III

The winter evening was closing in, and it was growing dark in the huge baronial hall with its sombre oak panelling. The lights had not been turned on, and the blinds and black-out curtains were still undrawn. Through the large windows one could see patches of snow here and there on the lawn, and beyond it a dark cluster of trees with jagged tops.

Second Lieutenant Klimowski, a slim figure in spectacles, of medium height, looked down from the first-floor landing. Seeing the hall deserted, he came downstairs, walked briskly across it and half-opened a door leading into the grounds. Met by a gust of chilly air he pushed harder, flung open the

---

[12]) Fl.-Lieutenant Krol made a list of the advantages of the Liberators as compared to the Halifaxes. As well as the greater range (Liberators 2,210 miles — Halifaxes 2,100 miles) and load-carrying capacity, the Liberator was easier to jump from, it was not so sensitive to icing and to a crosswind on take-off and it had better engines. It only required a general overhaul after 700 flying hours, while the Halifax needed one after 250. Both planes, adapted for night drops, had a minimum crew of 7.

door and stepped out on to the gravel path which surrounded the lawn and disappeared beneath the trees. Somewhere out of doors he expected to find his comrades, for it was their habit to take a long walk before supper to get up an appetite and dispel boredom. As the damp, penetrating wind grew stronger he thrust his hands into his trouser pockets and ran at the double across the lawn towards the looming expanse of the ancient park.

For over a month a dozen or so of young men who had passed through the whole gamut of courses had been waiting at the holding station twenty-odd miles north-west of London, whence almost any evening they might be ordered to report at once to the airfield. The station was in an ancestral home whose owners had moved out, leaving it at SOE's disposal with all its portraits, heirlooms and suits of armour. It stood in a large park, which was excellent for walks and training as well as for cover purposes.[13])

The station's permanent staff consisted of the British commandant and a middle-aged lady in charge of a score of girls belonging to the First Aid Nursing Yeomanry (FANY). Their duty, which might seem easy but was in fact most delicate, was to supplement the purely domestic services of the place by keeping the young men company, beguiling the long hours and days of nervous waiting and creating a calm, friendly, home-like atmosphere. It is easy to imagine the sort of scabrous jokes to which such an arrangement might give rise, the knowing winks and smiles and the more or less improbable anecdotes. But in fact no such jokes were made, no-one ever told tales of nocturnal adventures and none of the young men who passed through the holding stations ever made the slightest allusion of this kind. On the contrary, whenever they spoke of the last, anxious days of waiting, the young officers' eyes would brighten and their voices take on a note of tenderness. These girls of good family, often well-to-do, were generally pretty and full of charm; their upbringing had accustomed them to discipline, but also to luxury, admiration and attentions of all kinds; yet in the hard days of war they threw themselves into the common effort and performed their duties admirably. They drove field ambulances, served in canteens and worked hard at the various SOE stations. One team of parachutists succeeded another: they might differ in nationality, language, habits and temperament, but the girls had the same pleasant smile for all of them — the same quiet understanding when a boy had

---

[13]) This was station No. 17 near Hartford, borrowed for a short time from the French. At the beginning of 1942 probably in January they moved to station No. 18 near Stevenage.

trouble expressing himself in English, the same friendly readiness to receive his confidences, keep up his spirits and comfort him in moments of impatience or despair.

Following the direction from which he could hear loud shouts of laughter, Klimowski soon found his comrades, who had divided into two teams and were having a snowfight, with girls supporting each side. On seeing him, one of the young men called out "Supper-time!"; the fight ceased, and they set about dusting the snow off their clothes. They were all in civilian dress, as the parachutists at holding stations did not wear uniform. They were, so to speak, already half-way to Poland, and only a night's flight lay between them and life with the underground.

After supper that evening they did not turn on the gramophone for a dance, as the leader of the group had arranged an important conference. The time was shortly before Christmas 1941; three separate parties were anxiously awaiting orders to take off, but the fateful evening had not yet arrived and no-one knew when to expect it. Several times already the first team had been driven to the airfield, but the flight had not taken place: the weather had changed at the last minute, either along the route or at the reception centre in Poland, and plans had to be called off, thus increasing the young men's ardour and impatience. Nor was this the worst. The weather might clear and a fresh flight might be ordered at any time during the full moon, but a secret message had just been received from Poland announcing that the reception station had been "blown". In those early days alternative stations had not yet been organized, and flights were possible only to a small area of the country. Again there was apparently nothing to be done but wait.

Waiting was the last thing the young men felt inclined for. It was over a year since they had volunteered for special duty; they had gone through every possible course and training school and been drilled in every detail of their cover story. Their final super-secret briefing and the period spent at the holding station had cut them off from ordinary life and concentrated their minds wholly on Polish conditions; they could not imagine returning to their units, nor could they bear waiting any longer. Only their superiors tactful handling and the girls' friendly charm made it possible for them to behave calmly, but tension was liable to break through at any moment. A general discussion provided some outlet for their ill-humour and enabled them to ventilate ideas for breaking the spell of inaction.

They had all grown so used to the idea that they would be flying before the end of the year that they refused to hear of further delays and spurned the most reasonable arguments. Nothing could be done about the bad weather, which was for the pilots to judge, but why should they be deterred by the lack of an organized reception station? One of the more impatient among them declared that he would feel safer jumping "into the blue", since the Germans were bound to have an eye on the reception committee and this would only bring trouble to the parachutists. This unorthodox view, which was contrary to all the rules of planning and security, commanded unexpectedly wide support. Many who would have laughed at it in normal times sought, in their eagerness for action, to find arguments in its favour.

Klimowski, who had his nerves under control, did not press his own views over-strongly. He well knew how risky a blind drop would be, involving almost certainly the loss of one's whole equipment; on the other hand, he was eager to fly and the party to which he belonged was first in the queue. Those in the majority would not let themselves be overruled, but it was another question whether they could convince the Sixth Bureau, which had the last word.

In a few days the latter's answer came. The flight was urgent and was to take place as soon as weather permitted, despite the lack of reception arrangements.[14])

That afternoon, as Klimowski was getting his equipment in order, Kalenkiewicz came up, took him by the arm and led him out of doors.

'Listen, old chap, I quite agree with you that it's wrong and unsafe to land without a reception station. What's the point of organizing everything in detail and giving the people at home all this trouble and risk, if we're going to revert to slapdash methods at the first sign of difficulty? I'm saying this because you know how long I've been working on this problem of the jumps and how much I've thought about it."

'Yes, I know, but they've decided we're to go.'

'They have, and I want you to do something for me.'

'What is it? You know we're not allowed to take anything extra with us.'

---

[14]) In the archives of the Sixth Bureau there has been preserved a report of Staff Captain Jazwinski, dated Dec. 28, 1941, i.e. the day after the parachutists took off — they jumped on the night of December 27/28. From this it appears that the heads of the Sixth Bureau were opposed to "blind" drops but gave way to pressure by the Air Ministry. It has proved very difficult to find any document indicating the point of view of the British authorities. In Brigadier Gubbins' opinion the difficult decision was taken by both sides jointly. Without doubt the Sixth Bureau could have resisted any pressure if it had been totally opposed to the flight. Usually it was the Poles who were willing to take any risk and fretted at delay, and the British who held them back and advised caution.

'Of course not. What I want you to do is to let me take your place.'

Klimowski stopped short and looked at his friend.

'How on earth can I do that?'

'You can if you want to. As I say, I agree with you about the landing; but I'm a courier for the C-in-C, and there's some important and urgent mail.'

'And you want to make a blind landing with it?'

'Well, what can I do? If the people at the top think it's all right...'

Klimowski thought for a moment. There was some justice in his friend's request; moreover he knew that Kalenkiewicz, though a sensible and somewhat older man, was as much under the spell of the calendar as he himself. For both of them, December 31st was a far better date than January 1st. Klimowski agreed.

The flight took place accordingly, on the night of December 27/28. The parachutists dropped in the immediate neighbourhood of a police station in the territory annexed by the Germans, and were caught in trees as they fell. In the ensuing fight two were killed. The others, including Kalenkiewicz, managed to get through to the *General-Gouvernement* with their despatches and money intact. Their equipment was of course a total loss.

The experiment proved once and for all that it was no use jumping without a reception committee. In future, teams would have to wait.

As the men at the holding stations were already fully trained, no special exercises took place there. There would be a short morning period of P.T., a walk or a run during the day, some pistol practice and coaching in one's cover story. The pistol practice took up most time and attention: each of the young men accumulated as many of these weapons as he could, by fair means or foul. It was a sort of competitive collector's mania. Those who had numerous pistols of different types spent their energies on the hunt for ammunition, which was hard to come by. A firing-range, bordered by sandbags, was improvised in the park, and whenever the weather was fine enough shots resounded there by the hour. Every weapon was fired off to test its accuracy and the best manner of handling it. After long trials each man would decide which of his pistols was the most efficient and reliable, and would then bestow the most loving care upon it, obtaining as many cartridges as he could and polishing it till the dark steel gleamed. At night the weapon reposed under its master's pillow, and by day it lay close to hand in his trouser pocket.

Klimowski had a Colt from which he never parted: it fitted

his hand perfectly and never missed its target. His other weapons and his civilian clothes were kept in a locker beside his bed. Each garment had been carefully checked for anything that might betray the wearer's origin.[15]) Every shirt and pair of socks, all toilet and personal articles had been specially brought from Poland or made to the Polish pattern. Everything a man carried in his pockets was rigorously checked not once but many times. Letters were specially manufactured; notebooks, pencils and photographs alike indicated that their possessor lived in Poland. His cover story was confirmed by identity papers forged in the Sixth Bureau with the aid of specimens brought from the home country. They had to be altered frequently in accordance with changing police regulations, which were reported in the utmost detail in telegrams from Warsaw.

Apart from clothing, each man's locker contained the equipment he would need for his nocturnal parachute jump.[16])

The gloomy January days dragged wearily on. The moon was nearly full again; at dusk the young men went outside and, instead of larking about or going for a walk, stood silently gazing at the sky. Major Perkins, who had joined the station a few days before, was among them. A tall, broad-shouldered man in the prime of life, usually fond of a laugh or a drink, this evening he was ill-humoured. What was the good of staring up like this every night? Here it was nearly full moon, and they were still waiting, waiting, waiting.

Suddenly the telephone rang in the hall. The major dashed to answer it and the lads ran after him. Yes, it was London, to say in coded language that the new reception station was organized and ready. No orders for departure had been given, but the young men rushed upstairs in a body and began sorting out their equipment.

Next day Major Jazwinski arrived with pre-departure instructions. The men had already been assigned to parties, each with its leader, and these were now ordered to assemble

---

[15]) Every parachutist received a civilian suit, a pair of shoes, a coat, headgear, a scarf, a woollen sweater, 2 shirts, 2 pairs of thick underpants, 3 pairs of thick socks, 3 handkerchieves, a pair of warm gloves, German razor-blades and several packets of German cigarettes. He was also given six months' pay in dollars. On his own account he was supposed to get himself a watch (if he had not got one of his own from Poland, he had to get hold of another, either Polish or German) and toilet accessories which did not bear any English marks.

[16]) This equipment consisted of white overalls, a helmet, elastic bandages, rubber inner soles, leather gloves, 2 automatic pistols with 50 rounds for each, a clasp-knife, a small shovel, an electric torch, a large compass, a penknife, a small bottle of spirits, an iron ration, first aid kit and a small amount of poison concealed in a button. The parachutists could refuse to take the poison.

and await their turn for final briefing. Separately, for security reasons, each man was given details of the dropping zone and was shown its location on a 1:100,000 map, a copy of which was given to each leader. The men were told the name of the nearest inhabited place and made to repeat the password and countersign several times. The lights to be displayed on the ground were chiefly of interest to the pilots, but the parachutists were informed of them also. Finally, in a whisper, each man was given the addresses and passwords of two contact points to which he was to report in Warsaw: a main one and an auxiliary one. The order now was to stand by.

Two days later, just after the midday meal, the telephone rang again. Major Perkins grabbed the receiver and, while still holding it, waved his other arm and shouted "This is it!"

Mastering his excitement with an effort, Klimowski made for his room. It was a cold day and the night promised to be even colder, so he put on an extra shirt and sweater — they would be needed in Poland anyway. Into a briefcase he thrust a change of linen, toilet gear and a few packets of German cigarettes. He threw on his coat and overcoat and reached for his white overalls, inside which fitted various items of small but by no means light equipment. Two Colts went into his pocket, and instead of a beret he donned a silver-grey rubber helmet. Finally he drew on a pair of long white silk gloves reaching above the elbow, and over them a pair of equally long brown gloves made of strong leather.

The six men of the first party, all similarly accoutred, came downstairs and stood in the vast hall. Major Perkins cast an eye over them and checked the exact time. He did not verify their names, for he already knew them well by sight.

It was a longish drive to the airfield in a closed vehicle, and it was dark when they got out and felt the tarmac of the runway beneath their feet. A good way off, they saw the huge winged shadow of an aircraft, quivering and with engines throbbing. It was a four-engined Halifax with a Polish crew, ready to take off and warming up before the long, dangerous flight.

They stepped into a low shed and were met by Colonel Smolenski [17]) and Major Jazwinski, who had come to give them final instructions. Gazing with feigned indifference about them in the dark, they saw other groups in a similar get-up to their own. Few of the men spoke, but from time to time they caught a foreign-sounding word or two. So more than one plane was taking off over Europe that night.

[17]) Colonel Smolenski was recalled from the Sixth Bureau in September 1941, but he continued in command for a few months until the new chief of the Bureau, Lt.-Colonel Rudnicki, learnt the ropes.

Major Jazwinski began to summon the members of the party one by one. Each of them had been minutely drilled in his duties and had had the rules of security drummed into him day after day, but that was still not enough. He was once more scrupulously searched: every pocket, every scrap of paper, every trifling object. One man turned out to have on his person a London bus ticket, another some English matches. After the search was over, the major reached into a sack and drew out a broad, heavy belt made of strong material, which fastened over the shoulders by means of webbing and contained money for the underground army: generally gold dollars and dollar bills, sometimes sovereigns or gold roubles, German marks or occupation zlote.[18]) Each man, as he received a belt, signed for its contents. He also received and signed for a tin container a few inches long, which fitted into the pocket and contained only paper money.[19])

The men slipped out of their overalls, threw off their coats and fastened the new, precious load about them. The weight was considerable, and they realized that from now on their movements would have to be slow and cautious.

[18]) The rate of exchange of hard currency during the war was much higher that that of paper money. At the beginning of 1943 the gold dollar fetched 480 zlote on the black market in Warsaw and the dollar bill only 120. Before the war it sometimes happened that the rate of exchange of gold dollars was slightly less than bills — they were heavier, and so transport costs were higher. Tsarist gold roubles were also sought after on the black market, although they were not officially recognized in any country. In Soviet Russia anyone found in possession of them went to prison. They were worth more than the black market value of the gold in them. Tricksters took advantage of this and during the occupation began to forge "real" gold roubles with the full percentage of high-carat gold. Among paper money only dollars had high value on the black market. Pounds hardly circulated at all. The fact that the Germans forged quantities of five-pound notes (in one of the concentration camps) had nothing to do with this, since during the occupation nobody knew about these forgeries. A special department of the Home Army H.Q. was responsible for changing the money received from Britain. It was impossible to avoid using the black market, which was very efficient. Every day, through special contacts, it was possible to check the rate of exchange of dollars and other currencies (there was always a difference of a few points between the buying and selling price).

It was not always the case that all the parachutists in a party were equipped with money-belts. The number of belts issued depended on the amount of cash ready for transport. The value of the gold dollars sewn into a belt was usually $3,600 but sometimes as low as $2,400. The amount of paper money, considerably lighter, was naturally greater. A party of six parachutists usually took altogether $15-18,000 in gold and 50-100,000 in bills.

[19]) These tins were made in the shape of a cone, so that it was easier to bury them. A flexible wire about 6 feet long was fastened to the base, with a nail at its other end. Therefore these tins were called "nails" or "wedges". If the tin had to be buried, this nail was driven into the nearest tree to mark the place.

Colonel Smolenski took the leader of the party aside and handed him a small black metal box containing secret despatches for the ZWZ[20]) commander. Inside it was a smaller box with microfilm and a tiny incendiary bomb. If the outer container were struck by someone trying to break it or cut it open, the impact on the smaller box would produce an explosion which would destroy the film. In the ordinary way the container was opened by means of two screws in its base.

Last came the parachutes themselves. They were brought from a special store where they had been kept at the proper temperature and free from damp. As the most important part of the equipment, they were of course treated with special care. The safety of human lives and the success of the whole nocturnal adventure depended on their friendly aid, on the rustle of obediently unfolding silk. The men bent over them eagerly and began to examine them from every side, turning them over and measuring them against their own clothing.

Major Perkins, whose duty was to bring the latest weather report, stepped briskly into the hut. Without a word, he grinned and gave the "thumbs up" sign.

The last farewells took place under the wing of the quivering monster, as Colonel Smolenski embraced each man heartily in turn. Tiny lights glowed at the wing-tips as the throb swelled into a roar.

IV

One of the first German police measures in Poland was to order the population to hand over their wireless sets. As usual, the penalty for disobedience was death. Measures of this sort are not popular with the Poles, especially when backed by threats, and many of them were simply ignored; but in this case it was not so easy. Wireless receivers are hard to hide: they need an aerial and batteries or electric current, and they make a noise. So some people destroyed their sets, while others piled up in local police stations.

But not all. When the order was issued in November 1939, the underground resistance was already well under way. The first shock of defeat had worn off, and few Poles were prepared tamely to acquiesce in German regulations.

However, while many clandestine sets were in operation, they were of use only to a select few. The general public had no means of listening in, getting to know announcers' voices or hearing new programmes, talks and music. It was

---

[20]) A few weeks later, on Feb. 14, 1942, by order of General Sikorski the name ZWZ was changed to "Home Army".

not until the Warsaw rising in 1944, when a large part of the city was in Polish hands, that the radio could be listened to freely. Those who were in the capital in those days and are still alive will remember the irritation with which soldiers and civilians alike greeted the incessant repetition by the BBC of the chant *Z dymem pozarow* ("Mid flames and smoke").[21] The city was indeed wrapped in the smoke of war, but in spite of fire, bombing and destruction it was fighting on: each house defended itself, no-one thought of surrender, and the doleful melody aroused ever-louder protests.

'Tell London to stop burying us,' cried the soldier on the barricade. 'Hell's bells, not that again,' exclaimed the factory foreman with his bristling moustache, as the familiar tune once more came round.

For once in a way, these worthy people were blaming their exiled countrymen unjustly. The dirge-like tune was not a reflection of London's morale but, on the contrary, a secret signal to units of the Home Army throughout Poland.

Wireless, like the air arm, performed a prodigious and many-sided role in the last war. Statesmen and commanders used it to inspire their countrymen, and generals to give orders in the field; mighty engines of propaganda churned out slogans and twisted facts this way and that in the endless battles of psychological warfare. Hundreds of millions of people were locked in an all-out effort, and a babel of voices on every wavelength sought to reach the ears of each one of them. It was no wonder therefore that wireless also became the chosen instrument of the most occult plans and secret services.

The Polish Radio, with BBC transmitters at its disposal, was involved at an early stage in the organization of parachute drops into Poland. The initiative came from the Sixth Bureau, which, worked out a plan and broached it with the British authorities. The idea was not new to them, for the BBC had been used for various secret activities since the beginning of the war. Agreement was soon reached with the Poles, who were given a fairly free hand on condition that everything done under the aegis of the BBC must be agreed to and supervised by the latter's own security organization, under a mysterious Miss J. Thompson.

Almost every programme of Polish Radio contained musical interludes, and attention was now devoted to these. Certain tunes were selected and earmarked "reserved", and the Polish

---

[21] This was a political lament written during the Partition period. The melody was broadcast in connection with the carrying out of operation "Tempest", a local mobilization of larger units of the Home Army whose task was to harass the retreating German troops.

underground was given the details in strictest secrecy. The tunes were then divided into groups and communicated to the various dropping zones. In due course a cipher message would be sent from London to Warsaw by radio to the effect that it was intended, during a specified period of time (generally a few days), to send men or supplies by plane to a particular dropping zone. The size of the party would be indicated, and as far as possible the number of packages or containers. The reception committee would stand by, but no-one yet knew for certain whether the drop would take place. Only if the appropriate tune was played at the end of the Polish Radio transmission at lunch-time would those on the ground know that the planes were to be expected that very evening, about midnight.

The musical signal was always broadcast immediately before closing down and was introduced by a special form of words. At 1.45 p.m. the announcer would say: "And now in conclusion we will play to you...", whereas other transmissions ended with "And now comes a short programme of Polish music."

The broadcasting of a given "reserved" tune served to inform either the underground as a whole or a particular area that planes would be taking off that night, but it was still not known at the Polish end which dropping zones they would be making for. As time went on and the number of flights grew, the zones also multiplied, so that on receipt of a given signal some dozens of them would be alerted. To avoid this a system was adopted whereby the announcer inserted groups of three figures — known to the Poles as "ducks" — into the broadcast which contained the signal. This, of course, had to be done so as not to attract attention, and the key figures were recited in a normal voice as part of a long series. Their message was thus conveyed only to the initiated listener, crouching by his set in the immediate neighbourhood of the dropping zone. Sometimes, before broadcasting the musical signal, the announcer would, as a warning, utter a code sentence, such as "The sun shines through the mist."

Naturally a great many songs and tunes were broadcast which had no special meaning. These were called "cover tunes" and were skilfully mingled with the others so as to put unauthorized listeners off the scent, especially the German monitoring service which strained every effort to break the musical cipher.

The radio code system as a whole bore the cover name "Iodoform" and was known in full to only one member of the Polish Radio staff — its single announcer, Lieutenant Czeslaw Halski, to whom the oath of a Home Army soldier had been administered by the Sixth Bureau. He alone, on receipt of an emergency telephone call, could change the gramophone record scheduled for close-down and substitute one that would inform his listeners that the flight was off. This happened often enough for reasons of weather or other unforeseen circumstances. Halski never went off duty during a broadcast containing a "reserved" tune. If he were to fall ill on some occasion when a signal announcing a flight had to be cancelled, his place would be taken by a fully-briefed Sixth Bureau officer.

Unfortunately it also happened quite often that although the signal tune was played and the mystic numbers given, the longed-for consignment did not reach the dropping zone. This might be because the flight had been called off at the very last moment or because the plane had had to turn back owing to a sudden change of weather or to icing, or had failed to find the reception area.

At times the system also had comic results. The programme-planners were ignorant of the musical cipher, and this led to misunderstandings which were remembered for many years. Whatever the circumstances, the lunch-time broadcast had to end with the signal tune and no other. On one occasion a long obituary of Cardinal Hinsley, who had been a good friend of the Poles, had to be rounded off with a jovial Polish folk-song beginning: "Poor old Matthew's dead and gone."

However, such incongruities were as a rule noticed only by close followers of the radio programmes in Britain or in some safe neutral country where a handful of Poles could listen in peace on the BBC wavelength without fearing that the police would suddenly knock on the door. Those who listened in Poland itself, knowing full well that they would be put to death or sent to Auschwitz if their hiding-place were discovered, paid hardly any attention to the programmes as a whole. All they were concerned with was political and military news: it was their responsibility, among other things, to pass on to the clandestine press the latest communiqués from the various fronts. These were at once printed in the form of radio bulletins: some appeared daily, and were circulated with a punctuality and speed that astonished the layman. They were distributed everywhere, cheering up those of faltering courage and keeping alive the timid flame of hope and optimism.

Nor were the oddities of the programme noticed by the armed men, with set faces, who lay in hiding near the secret dropping zones, for long days and nights that might turn into weeks and even months. Their sharpened hearing was sensitive to two sounds only: the distant hum of heavy engines and the strains of a single, longed-for tune. That tune, hackneyed and commonplace as it might be, was for them the most desired, the most intoxicating melody in the world.

V

The manager of the *Zachodni* (Western) Bank in Cracow immediately before the war was Zygmunt Milewicz, a man in his forty-fourth year and a lieutenant in the reserve. He was still physically fit, but the days had gone by when he could perform the sort of sporting feats that required elastic muscles and a young man's heart.

He was called up at the end of August, fought in the September campaign, escaped to Rumania and thence to France, where he again put on uniform. After the collapse of the Western front he was one of the many who made their way to Britain.

Then came the call for volunteers to undertake special duties in Poland. The authorities were looking for athletic young men, full of endurance, and Milewicz hesitated for a long time before putting in his name. He was afraid his commander would send for him, take one ironical glance, bawl him out and send him back to quarters. However, this did not happen. He was accepted for training, went through the full course and made seven practice jumps. Now, on a dark evening, he and five comrades, all in full parachute gear, with a beltful of money and two pistols each, had climbed aboard a great four-engined Halifax.

Shortly before seven o'clock the lumbering machine rose off the tarmac and began slowly to gain altitude. With a crew of nine besides the six parachutists, a heavy load of containers and specially-fitted extra fuel tanks, the aircraft vibrated with effort, all its engines roaring. Its underside was painted black. Painfully it rose to a height of 11,500 feet, where the rarefied air enabled it to fly faster and with greater safety, though even here it was liable to be attacked by night fighters over the further shore of the North Sea.

The parachutists arranged themselves as comfortably as they could on the floor of the aircraft. They showed no special excitement; they were in a sense veterans of such trips, since they had been called out several times during the weeks of waiting and had actually flown over Poland twice, but had had to turn back on each occasion. On the first, they were over the dropping zone and a few hundred yards from their native soil when a local fog closed in and made the operation impossible. The second time, their aircraft was hit by flak which damaged one of the engines. They had got safely back to base, but were so depressed that they could scarcely bear the period of waiting till their third flight. Now they lay quietly, nestled in sleeping-bags, their teeth chattering — the plane was unheated — and doing their best to think of nothing at all, lest some idle word or movement should spoil their chances for the third time. In unusual and complicated circumstances, the best of men become superstitious.

Milewicz, who was a good deal older than his comrades, had the most philosophical approach to surprises and disappointments. He found waiting tedious and somewhat irritating, but managed to keep calm and collected; like the others, he disliked being called out for flights that did not take place, but he reflected that this was war and there was probably no help for it. The two unsuccessful flights over Poland had made him lose his temper, but that was exceptional. Now, as he lay for the third time in an aircraft that was taking him and his comrades to an unknown destination, he felt assured that that night the jump would come off. There were no logical reasons for his confidence other than the still, clear weather and the large moon that gazed blandly at the lonely craft as it made its way across the sky.

The drone of the engines and the slight vibration of the hull as they forged smoothly along above the clouds made the men feel sleepy, as did the rarefied air with its lower oxygen content. They lay quiet as if asleep; one or two used their oxygen masks.

An hour or two passed without incident; then the noise of the engines diminished and they felt the hull tilt forward as the plane lost height. The parachutists sat up expectantly. The dispatcher appeared and explained that they were approaching Denmark and would be hedge-hopping over steeples and factory chimneys, to avoid the enemy's flak and radar. He turned out the lights and uncovered a porthole through which they could look down. The plane was banking, and Milewicz was startled to see its great shadow falling across the earth as clearly as if they were flying not under a pale moon but in broad daylight. Their altitude was somewhere between three and five hundred feet. It was ten in the evening, and they could clearly pick out the roads with cars speeding along them and the tiny figures of pedestrians. The windows of the villages and townships over which they flew were carefully blacked out, but the houses threw long shadows across the streets.

Suddenly they heard three explosions, one after the other, and saw flashes in the air to one side of their plane and above it — the enemy's A.A. guns were trying to shoot down the intruder. Clustering round the portholes, the parachutists admired the display as more and more shells burst around them. They were mostly at a safe distance, as the low-flying plane had stolen a match on the A.A. batteries and the guns were unable to take proper aim.

Once more they were over the sea, this time the Baltic. The Halifax vibrated more strongly and began to climb again.

The parachutists lay down as before, but by now they were aroused and excited. It would not be long before the plane turned southward in the vicinity of Danzig at the mouth of the Vistula, Poland's river.

Milewicz got up and looked out once more. The moon was still bright, but its rays fell on dense cloud beneath which no land could be seen. The dispatcher appeared again.

'We're turning now and we shall be flying below the clouds, along the Vistula.'

The flight would not be over for an hour or so, but the party became feverishly active — checking their parachutes and pistols, feeling their pockets, taking a pull from their flasks. *Mak* (Poppy), the leader of the group, announced the password of the reception area and made them all repeat it together with the countersign. Then he went over the jumping order. Milewicz and a companion were first, then two others and then the leader himself with the last member of the party.

The men began to fasten on the rip-cords of their parachutes, which were attached by special rings to staples inside the hull.[22]) This was the most vital part of their drill, and despite their excitement they took care to follow it precisely.

The flight became bumpy as the plane again lost altitude, One of the party looked out. They were flying just over a forest; the moon was bright and visibility good. The plane banked, once and again. The navigator announced that they were in the zone and looking for the exact spot. A few minutes later, a red warning light glowed and the dispatcher came in once more.

'Their lights are showing. Stand by to jump.'

He opened the trapdoor in the floor of the aircraft; an icy blast swept in. Silently he beckoned as if inviting someone to dance. Milewicz approached and sat on the floor with his legs dangling through the black hole. The rest of the group crouched behind him in the prescribed order.

The aircraft banked yet again. The dispatcher listened intently to the intercom, raising his right hand. As the signal came through, the red light changed to green and the dispatcher's arm swept down. His shout of "Go!" was drowned by the engines' roar and the noise of a body slipping into the void below. Milewicz's companion was already sitting in his place, and disappeared at the second cry of "Go!"

---

[22]) The parachutes used by every section of SOE operated automatically by pulling a tape, fastened at one end to the tip of the parachute and the other to hook inside the aircraft. The tape broke under the parachutist's weight and the parachute opened. The parachutists had no means of opening the parachutes themselves if the apparatus failed to work. Once only during the jumps to Poland the tape failed to break and the parachutist, Lt.-Colonel Krizar, was killed.

The green light vanished; the plane banked and returned to the dropping zone, and the light came on again. Some containers and a second pair of parachutists were dropped. Then the process was repeated with the last two men and the rest of the cargo.

The Halifax turned for the last time; its wing-tip lights flashed and it swept round in a wide circle before flying off noisily.

In the bright moonlight, six white canopies at different heights floated lazily over a clearing in the forest and dropped to earth one by one.

VI

The process of sending supplies to Poland by air went through several phases as the war ran its course and technical methods improved.

The first phase began on the night of February 15, 1941, when a heavy Whitley took off from a secret airfield in Britain and made its way to Poland by the shortest route across Germany, carrying three parachutists who thus inaugurated the period of night flights and the secret dropping of supplies and men. During this experimental stage, which lasted until the end of April 1942, political factors did not play a major role; although Russia was in the allied camp from June 1941. Poland was still a valued ally and efforts were made to help her as much as possible, subject only to technical limitations.

Another factor bearing on the effectiveness of night flights and drops was the nature of German policy in occupied Poland.

If Hitler had conformed to the rules of international law concerning occupied territories and had not attempted to create a *fait accompli* before the end of the war, conditions would have been uniform throughout the area of western and central Poland which was Germany's share of the booty under the Nazi-Soviet pact. Unfortunately he did not do so. On the one hand, Poland's western and northern provinces were annexed to the Reich, whose frontier came to within twenty miles or so of Warsaw on the city's north-western side. To the westward the new German boundary took in Lodz, and in the south-west it came just short of Czestochowa. The remainder of the Polish territory occupied by Germany, including Warsaw, was turned into the so-called *General-Gouvernement*, a separate administrative entity with its seat of government at Cracow.

In the territory annexed to the Reich large-scale deportations were carried out, which seriously affected the preponderance of the Polish element. Owing to terrorism and police efficiency, the underground movement in this area developed very slowly. Its activities were cramped and there was no possibility of organizing reception centres for drops.

In the *General-Gouvernement*, things were different in this respect. Although the Gestapo was active and terrorism raged on an unprecedented scale, the Polish character of the area remained unaffected. Warsaw seethed with clandestine activity and was the capital of a whole underground state; other cities, towns, and villages were not far behind.

While air drops were thus possible in the *General-Gouvernement*, this meant that planes from the West had to fly considerably further than if their objective had been, for instance, in the neighbourhood of Poznan, Bydgoszcz or Gdynia.

As long as flights were carried out from Britain by converted Halifax bombers with a maximum range of some 2,200 miles, the only feasible dropping area was the northern part of the *General-Gouvernement* near Warsaw, and the first reception stations were in fact organized near Lowicz and the Kampinos Forest, a short distance west of the capital.

For a dropping zone it was necessary to find an open space, if possible slightly concave, measuring something over 650 by 200 yards, as remote as possible from main roads and difficult of access by German motorized transport. It might be a large forest clearing or an open field, tilled or otherwise. It must be free from stumps or large stones, so as not to increase the risk of injury to the parachutists. From the pilot's point of view it should ideally be a few miles from a lake or reservoir, a river-bend or the confluence of two rivers. This made it much easier to navigate and to locate the small but vital piece of ground.[23])

---

[23]) In 1942 SOE, after two years of experiments, produced a kind of short-wave telephone, called an S-phone, by means of which an aircraft could communicate with a dropping zone within a radius of up to 50 miles. In practice this radius was limited to under 25 miles and then, under favourable conditions, a conversation could be carried on in the same way as over an ordinary telepohne. This facilitated bringing the aircraft to the dropping zone. The Sixth Bureau was given 30 of these devices and sent them to Poland. They turned out to be rather ineffective, and in Poland they were hardly ever used.

Some time later, in the middle of 1943, another apparatus was produced in the SOE workshops called Eureka. This was an ultra-short wave transmitter weighing about 100 pounds which could be picked up at a distance of 40 miles. In the aircraft was installed a short wave receiver called Rebecca. When both these instruments were properly used it was possible to guide the aircraft to its target with great accuracy, to within a few dozen yards. Unfortunately Poland received very few Eurekas and so their usefulness was minimal. It is worth noting here that although France received a lot of them, they did not turn out as effective as might have been expected. The reason was that the members of the underground movement who prepared and manned the dropping zones did not know how to operate the complicated apparatus.

The reception station consisted of two parts, and this made it necessary to have a small hill near by, where one group would be stationed with a radio set and a red guiding light. At the actual dropping zone, a second group of underground soldiers were responsible for displaying a set of lights in arrow-formation to indicate the direction of the wind, taking charge of the parachutists after they landed and collecting the containers and packages. As long as the reception committees were wholly clandestine and were not reinforced by partisan detachments, they consisted of from 10 to 15 soldiers.

The commander of this small band was in charge of the whole operation; while it lasted, the parachutists were also under his authority, and so was the commander of partisans when these became part of the set-up. A representative of Home Army headquarters in Warsaw was supposed to be present at every drop and had specific duties of his own, but whatever his rank and function he too was under the orders of the local commander. Similar regulations prevailed on flights: one of the crew was in command and all passengers were under his orders, though they might be political or military leaders of the highest rank.[24])

The importance of air drops for the Home Army was such that its commander organized the reception arrangements on a centralized basis. All those who landed were under orders to report to Warsaw, and all supplies were to be taken there in the first instance. There was one exception to the centralization principle: the reception committees always consisted of local people. This had to be so, because the achievement of drops depended on so many factors that one never knew

---

[24]) Under Polish regulations the captain of the crew and therefore of the whole aircraft, including the passengers, was always the navigator, whereas under British regulations it was the pilot. The Polish Air Force in Great Britain came under the authority of the RAF and was therefore subject to British regulations. Nevertheless it appears that on the secret flights to Poland the navigator was in command of the crew and the whole aircraft. In any case the flight briefings and other papers issued before the flight, and the reports on return, were signed by the navigator. They are to be found in the archives of the Sixth Bureau. The author made enquiries of several Polish pilots who flew over Poland and got various replies. Some said that the pilot captained the aircraft, some the navigator. The author also made enquiries of the British Ministry of Defence and was informed by its historical department that all national air forces which operated during the last war from Great Britain came under the authority of the RAF and obeyed British regulations. This would mean that the captain of the aircraft was the pilot, but it seems that on the secret flights to Poland this was not laid down clearly. In the lists of parties drawn up on the basis of the archives of the Sixth Bureau and other available material, the code-names of the flights are given and the names of the airmen responsible for the flight. Without exception they are the names of the navigators, whether Polish or British.

whether a given flight would come off or the parachutes actually appear in the sky. Sometimes the reception committees had to remain mobilized for months in expectation of a particular drop, and this was only possible if they belonged to local villages.

This state of affairs had a curious consequence in respect of the organization of the Polish underground. Until the middle of 1943 the reception committees consisted not of Home Army soldiers but of local members of political bodies, in particular the Peasants' Party and the Peasants' Freedom Organization. The Home Army authorities explained this on the ground that it lessened the risk of their own organization being detected, but it seems doubtful whether this was the real reason. The air drops were too important, complicated and expensive to justify the Home Army commander in subordinating all other aspects to that of security and leaving the whole business of reception in other hands than his own. The explanation should probably be sought on other lines.

Apart from the Warsaw rising (August-September 1944), all drops took place in rural areas, and in these the Peasants' Party predominated, with its military organ known as the Peasant Battalions. The Home Army carried on long negotiations with a view to merging the two military forces; however, the Peasant Battalions remained independent till the middle of 1943, and as long as they did so they had the main voice in the countryside, especially in the western outskirts of Warsaw. The local villagers who formed the reception committees were full of patriotism and self-sacrifice, but they either belonged to the Peasant Battalions or were under their influence, and anyone operating in their territory had to take account of this.[25] It was therefore prudent of the Home Army commander to leave reception arrangements in their hands. When the merger took place in 1943 this, in the face of it, curious set-up ceased, and the reception centres passed under the control of the Home Army.

[25] Underground work encouraged the formation of a multiplicity of organizations, and in occupied Poland a number of clandestine military groups were formed, some very small, which fairly soon joined the main body of the Home Army. The political parties also had their military opposite numbers, and the process of bringing these into the Home Army was long and difficult. Part of the NSZ (*Narodowe Siły Zbrojne* — National Armed Forces) remained independent to the last. This state of affairs, harmful to united action, was partly due to the failure to form a coalition government when war threatened. In 1939 the opposition parties made proposals to the ruling group for the establishment of a government representing all the leading political bodies. The ruling party rejected this proposal, not wishing to share power and responsibility. After the defeat in September the political parties started to form their own clandestine military units to fight the occupants, but also foreseeing that they might be useful in a fight for power when the war was over.

It should be emphasized that this co-operation with a political group did not lead to any loss of security or needless casualties, nor to such tragic situations as occurred in France and Holland, when the reception organization was penetrated by the Germans.[26]) Members of the reception stations were chosen with the utmost care, and were made to take a special oath before each drop.

Precise instructions governed every aspect of the dropping operations, and great importance was attached to their observance, lest the already hair-raising risks be needlessly increased. It was vital not to make mistakes which might help the Germans, and not to fall into their hands after achieving a successful landing.

When a drop had taken place and the parachutists had been met by the waiting soldiers, they were taken at once to the local hide-out, where they handed over to the representative of headquarters their money-belts and their own pay in dollars which had been handed to them before take-off. They were given a receipt for these sums, which were carefully checked. The rule about handing over their own money was dictated by security. A routine police check on a railway station or aboard a train might otherwise lead to their downfall, whereas the identity papers they had brought would probably see them through. After they reached Warsaw, the financial section of the underground would, within a few days, return their own money to them in dollars, either in a lump or in instalments as they wished.

Meanwhile the commander of the reception station had been handed a list of the dropped supplies by the leader of the group of parachutists. His men set about collecting the packages and containers and loading them on to carts on which they were taken some distance away to a secret store. Thence, like the money, they were transferred to Warsaw, where they were kept in central depositories. The distribution of these priceless consignments of military equipment was one of the most jealously guarded functions of Home Army headquarters. However, one would have to be very ignorant of the ways of underground fighters to suppose that all the supplies collected at the dropping zones invariably reached Warsaw safely. Arms are as precious to a soldier as food or water, and ammunition or sub-machine guns would sometimes disappear in transit. This was forbidden under the direst penalties, but life was stronger than orders.

After the new arrivals had handed over their money and

---

[26]) In France, on five occasions the parachutists jumped straight into the arms of the Germans, who had manned the dropping zones.

personal arms, and the equipment had been collected and loaded on to carts, the next stage followed immediately. The carts set off into the night, guarded by members of the reception centre or in later times by a partisan detachment, and the newcomers proceeded on foot or horseback to a hiding-place at a safe distance, where they were given food and a chance to rest. Some days later, when local intelligence reported that the coast was reasonably clear, they were divided into pairs, given occupation zlote and sometimes fresh personal papers, and sent off by rail to Warsaw under the care of a "liaison girl". They often travelled by the same train, but never together. Once in Warsaw, they were supposed to make their own way to the contact addresses they had been given in Britain.[27])

As already explained, the reception of both men and supplies was organized on a central basis and carefully supervised. A special department for the purpose was set up at headquarters in Warsaw. It was divided into three sections dealing respectively with reception (this section appointed the representative who attended at the reception centre), evacuation of supplies and evacuation of personnel. Milewicz, whom we have already met, became head of reception in 1943. The second section was responsible for the storing and distribution of equipment and the third for looking after the parachutists on their arrival in Warsaw, when they were boarded with ladies known as "aunts". Both the women who successively ran this section perished in the war.

Naturally the organization thus outlined came into existence slowly, through long months of experience, trial and error, success and failure. The same was true of the reception stations. At first there were only a few of these, all near Warsaw; later they became much more numerous, and were located in the areas of Radom and Kielce south of Warsaw, Lublin and Zamosc to the south-east, and Cracow and even Lodz to the south-west. In all they numbered several hundred, and there were nights on which dozens of them were simultaneously alerted. As drops too became more numerous and better organized, it was laid down towards the end of 1942 that on any given occasion a reserve station should be alerted as well as the principal one, so that if the navigator could not find the site he was looking for he would not have to return to base and waste a night of suitable weather, or

---

[27]) It happened several times that parachutists (known as "birds" in Poland) who did not know Warsaw asked the liaison girls to take them to where they had to go and told them the secret addresses. This was very careless and contrary to orders. The liaison girl, going back to her own area, could be arrested and forced under interrogation to betray a valuable address in Warsaw.

make a blind drop with its attendant risks. There were many stations which, although alerted, never actually received a drop or experienced the thrill of meeting parachutists or collecting supplies.

In the first year or two the stations were wholly clandestine and possessed no defence force, but towards the end of 1943, when partisan activity had expanded greatly, they were placed on a combat footing. Each station was guarded by anything from 25 to 100 partisans, summoned for the period of the alert by the local Home Army commander. Sometimes the number was even greater. One night in September 1944, during the period of operation "Tempest" in which large units of the Home Army were mobilized, a major drop in the region of Sandomierz in southern Poland was guarded by 800 soldiers. This was necessary, because the area was swarming with German troops retreating from the east. In general, the drops had to be protected not only from occupation troops or the local police, but also from units specially formed by the Germans to combat parachute activities.

The first stations were small and could only handle one plane load on any given night. Later, larger ones were formed named "bastions", which could cope with two or more loads. At first it was laid down that these should be taken off the rota as soon as they had performed their function, but later this was modified. "Bastions" which could handle drops for several nights in succession were known as "permanently alerted stations".

Eventually, despite the distance between Poland and the bases concerned, it became possible for military aircraft to land there under cover of night. But this two-way operation, known as "Bridge", did not become possible till much later.

Towards the end of the war, the principle of centralizing deliveries underwent a change. While the Warsaw rising was in progress the rest of the country (in so far as it was not occupied by the Red Army), where operation "Tempest" was in full swing, felt a severe shortage of arms. Everything possible was done to supply the capital, but some drops were made elsewhere and these supplies became the property of local units. There was no alternative, since Warsaw was cut off from the rest of the country by a ring of powerful German forces and no access to it was possible.

After the rising, the control of air drops in Poland became the responsibility of district commanders. This included wireless liaison with the base in Italy and the organization of alert periods. All supplies dropped in a given district became the property of the local Home Army forces. Despite the gloom caused by the defeat of the rising, dropping operations continued to be carried out efficiently. A reception station near Zamosc was able to send a wireless message confirming the receipt of a drop, so swiftly that the plane in question had not yet regained its base.[28])

All these nocturnal adventures, secret radio signals, reception stations, guard detachments, evacuation and cover arrangements were the subject of precise and well thought-out instructions. As a rule these were scrupulously observed, but no human arrangements are perfect. There was not always a man from Warsaw headquarters to check reception; the stations did not always function as they should, the navigator did not always guide his plane correctly. Nor must it be thought that all concerned in these difficult and risky operations were among the noblest specimens of the human race. Money-belts which fell outside the dropping zone sometimes fell into thieving hands, if not into the Germans', and were lost without trace.[29])

In addition, the utmost care was not always proof against the malevolence of chance. Life, as usual, took little heed of human plans. There were many surprises, many fantastic and hair-raising situations. One group of parachutists landed in the very place where a German division was billeted, another on a police station; on another night, a navigator mistook the lights of a railway station for those of the dropping zone. Men were landed in trees, in the icy waves of a river or on the roof of a peasant's hut. Sometimes the parachutes failed to open; on other nights the heavy containers, dropped from too low an altitude, fell on sleeping villages with fatal results.

There were losses and casualties, but these were the fortunes of war. The needs of those who were fighting it grew day by day, and so did the frequency, range and scale of the clandestine flights.

VII

According to a view which has been widely held in the course of history, the British prefer in time of war to avoid a head-on conflict with the enemy, relying on foreign troops

[28]) H. T. Willetts (Proceedings of a Conference on Britain and European Resistance, 1939-1945, St. Antony's College, Oxford, 1962).

[29]) The honesty of those people who were officially responsible for the whole organization of the drops and for their safety was of a very high order. Nevertheless there were two cases of theft of the money sent from the West. Once this was perpetrated by an officer on duty at the dropping zone, the second time by a man to whom the money belts had been entrusted temporarily. Both cases were tried by the Special Military Court. There exists a despatch from Poland confirming the passing and carrying out of the death sentence in the first case. There are no papers relating to the second case, but it can be assumed that the court's verdict was the same and that the sentence was carried out.

to do the fighting, and themselves providing money and equipment in lieu of blood. It was understandable that this view was held by some of Britain's allies in the second world war. But no nation with a proper regard for its own future can afford to squander human resources, which take a long time to make good, and the British cannot be blamed for exercising caution in this respect. They had, after all, gone to war for the sake of their own political interests and not other people's.

However, the course of the Western campaign knocked the bottom out of British calculations, and the unprepared islanders found themselves face to face with the formidable power of Nazi Germany, intoxicated with success and supported by Soviet Russia. In this tense situation, events were measured not by months but by days. The world held its breath as it contemplated the fate of the lonely island. Many, perhaps most, expected it to yield on more or less humiliating terms.

Then Churchill came to power, and his voice rang out like a great bell as he proclaimed that his country would fight on and would never surrender. This meant that Britain was now taking upon herself the whole burden of the war, and that her sons would have to perish in the defence of their homeland and of the whole free world. If Britain had been occupied or had patched up an agreement with Hitler to divide the world into spheres of influence, it would have meant the end of Europe and of the way of life which hundreds of millions of free men desired to go on living.

The Poles — along with the Dutch, Belgians, Danes, Norwegians, Czechs and Free French — were Britain's allies, but their countries were occupied and their forces in the British Isles, other than pilots, did not amount to very much. What was more, they had no equipment. Thus Britain stood almost alone against the Nazi fury, and did so for twelve months until, on June 22, 1941, Hitler committed the lunacy of opening a new vast front by attacking Russia.

It is well to recall these facts by way of countering certain derogatory opinions sometimes expressed, if the picture of the war is to be a true one. For instance, the valour and skill of the US forces are frequently disparaged. Yet many facts refute this attitude. During the battle of the Midway Islands,[30] 40 fighters took off from a single American aircraft

---

[30] This battle, one of the biggest in history, was fought from June 4-6, 1942 and was a turning point in the war in the Pacific. The American fleet, commanded by Admiral Nimitz, defeated a Japanese fleet twice its size, thanks to superior command and the courage of the American sailors and airmen. This marked the end of the long era of the supremacy of large warships. The Japanese had 11 battleships at Midway and the Americans none, but it made no difference to the results. The Japanese were so afraid of the effectiveness of the air attacks that they did not bring their battleships into action.

carrier, of which only two returned: a 95 per cent casualty rate. It would be difficult to parallel this from any other theatre of war.

At all events, after the fall of France Britain was virtually the only source of supplies for the Polish forces in the West. Negotiations were carried on with the Americans and led to some results, but only by way of supplementing what was being obtained from the British. Moreover, from the beginning of 1943 all requests for aid from the western hemisphere had to be endorsed by the British military authorities, as by virtue of an Anglo-American agreement Poland fell within their area of responsibility.

This dependence on Britain for supplies had far-reaching consequences. An independent Polish government sat in London, along with the General Staff and the naval and air force chiefs, but all Polish units were "under British command". In theory the Polish forces in the West formed a single entity under the control of the Polish government and commander-in-chief; but in practice, both because of dependence in the field of supplies and for other reasons, they never acted as a coherent whole [31]) or at the unfettered discretion of the Polish authorities.[32]) At times this led to unpleasant complications and almost insoluble crises.

From this point of view the governments of the other occupied countries were in a much better position than the Poles, though their contribution to the war effort was in many ways less great. The Norwegians possessed a huge merchant marine of about two million tons, nearly the whole of which escaped German hands and provided a valuable source of revenue. The Dutch, though their home country was occupied,

---

[31]) Para. 10 of the report presented by General Kopanski as chief of staff to General Sosnkowski states that: "To ensure constant participation in war, the whole of our armed forces should never be engaged in one campaign, but only the smallest possible part and for a limited time and range." (S. Kopanski, War Memoirs 1939-1945, in Polish, London, 1961). These remarks referred, of course, to Polish armed forces on foreign soil, where there were no replacements and which in the General's opinion were to some extent of a symbolic and propaganda character.

[32]) In the spring of 1944, when intensive preparations were being made for the invasion of the continent, the British authorities asked the Polish Government whether they would allow the Independent Parachute Brigade to be used. They could have refused in the hope that the moment would come when the brigade could be used in Poland, but this refusal would have brought about a suspension in the equipping and bringing up to strength of the brigade. In practice, it would not have been fit for active service. The British authorities made no secret of the fact that if the Poles refused they would have to form their own unit of the same type quickly, and that it would receive priority in every respect.

still controlled the vast resources of Java and their other colonies in the Far East.

The Polish armed forces were supplied by the British on the basis of an agreement of August 5, 1940,[33]) under which all items were charged against a loan. When the Lend-Lease Act came into force, supplies to the Poles were brought within its scope.[34]) These arrangements applied to the material sent by air to Poland, through the Polish section of SOE to which the Sixth Bureau submitted its requirements in the form of money and equipment.

All this would have been simple enough if the British had had plenty of equipment to spare and if the presentation of shopping lists had been a purely administrative matter. Unhappily this was not the case. British war preparations were complete only in a few narrowly defined sectors, and industry was only just going over to rapid and large-scale military production. Raw material supplies were running out, and could only be replaced by cargoes proceeding in slow convoy by long, roundabout routes infested with German submarines.[35])

The Polish section of SOE was extremely friendly and did its best to meet the Sixth Bureau's requirements, but this good will was not enough. It became necessary to go outside official channels and try to obtain the necessary equipment from private sources. This makeshift procedure had its effect on the quality of the material dropped in Poland in the early stages. The recipients of ill-assorted and unusable equipment cursed their countrymen for negligence, not knowing that the latter were all too well aware of its shortcomings.

---

[33]) It is worth studying the figures to get some ideas of this effort. For instance: the whole cost of the upkeep and operations of the Polish Air Force in Britain (personnel, aircraft, airfields, armament, ammunition, repairs etc.) from 1939 to 1945 inclusive came to £107,650,000.

[34]) On March 11, 1941 the Congress of the United States passed a bill, empowering the President to direct that any article should be sold, leased or otherwise made available to any state whose defence he might regard as essential to the defence of the United States. Thus, very shortly, the principle of Lend-Lease may be described. Thanks to this bill the Americans could send huge supplies to the countries fighting against Hitler without asking them for payment. Debts were to be settled after the war, with the basic proviso that the United States took into account everything they received from their debtors in various forms, such as services during the war etc. In the first phase the chief recipient of American aid was Great Britain, later she herself began to help others in the same way and according to the same principles. Poland also profited by Lend-Lease: an agreement to this effect was reached with the United States on July 4, 1942.

[35]) During the first years of the war the Suez Canal could not be used, although it was controlled wholly by Great Britain, and convoys had to be sent round the Cape of Good Hope as the Mediterranean was at that time too dangerous.

Although the United States were not in the war till the treacherous Japanese attack on Pearl Harbor in December 1941, that great country, the home of men who crossed the ocean in search of freedom and livelihood, has never been backward in extending help to victims of aggression and persecution. Failing to find the supplies they needed in Britain, the Poles turned their eyes westward, as they had done in the matter of long-range aircraft. Sikorski visited the States in April 1941 and had several talks with Roosevelt in which he raised *inter alia* the question of war material and other supplies needed by occupied Poland, such as automatic weapons, equipment of all kinds for sabotage and irregular warfare, and also printing machinery, duplicators, typewriters etc., for purposes of underground propaganda. The home country also needed cameras for intelligence purposes, wireless and medical stores. At first, efforts were directed towards securing permission to buy these for cash on the open market; later, towards obtaining specified types of articles under Lend-Lease.

The Americans readily agreed to make supplies available. On the Polish side, these matters were handled after September 1943 by Colonel Leon Mitkiewicz, who was Deputy Chief of Staff to the C-in-C and the latter's representative with the Anglo-American Combined Chiefs of Staff.[36])

But, in spite of good will, purchases were slow, a good deal too slow for those waiting in the home country. Once the equipment was bought it was sent to Britain generally by

---

[36]) In 1942 the Americans, seeing the success of SOE, formed their own organization of a similar type: the Office of Strategic Service (OSS), under Colonel Donovan. Its agencies operated from Great Britain and later, when in November 1942 the Allies landed in North Africa, from that area also. Its task, like SOE's was to aid sabotage operations in Europe.

Colonel Mitkiewicz, who on behalf of the Polish C-in-C handed a memorandum to the Combined Chiefs of Staff in the summer of 1943 on the use of the Home Army in Allied operations in Europe, received an evasive reply to it on Sept. 23, 1943. At the same time he was told that the commander of the 8th Air Fleet, stationed in Great Britain, would receive orders that one of its heavy bomber squadrons should commence flights to Poland with supplies for sabotage operations. Later it was to be reinforced by a second squadron.

There is information from other sources that the Americans anticipated a fairly large number of flights to Poland, since the help sent by them was to amount to 25% of the help sent to the whole of occupied Europe.

As the American airmen did not know the technique of navigation for drops, a number of their crews underwent training in 138 Squadron.

Unfortunately all this ended with promises only. Probably political considerations were the reason for OSS giving no help to Poland. The big flight of 110 aircraft with supplies for the Warsaw Rising (Sept. 18, 1944.) was an exception to the principle previously adopted.

sea,[37]) or if specially urgent by air, and was stored by SOE before being finally transferred into packages and containers for despatch to Poland.

However, this process ran into the same obstacles as had the procurement of aircraft from the US. At the beginning of 1943 the British authorities raised objection to direct contacts between the Polish General Staff and the Americans, and much argument took place before a mutually satisfactory solution was reached. This took the form of a proposal by SOE according to which the desired equipment was divided into three categories: (1) war material furnished to the Poles by SOE from its own stocks; (2) war and other material which was not available in Britain and which SOE was to obtain for the Poles from the US; and (3) various items which the Poles were free to seek from the US on their own account. This arrangement worked fairly well until the whole system of air drops began to be overshadowed by politics.

The first trial period of drops in Poland was succeeded by another with the code name "Intonation", which lasted from August 1, 1942, to the end of April 1943. The initial difficulties had been surmounted, improvisation was a thing of the past, and air supplies to the underground had been placed on a regular and efficient footing. Apart from the acquisition of experience, this was due to the fact that British industry was working at full capacity, more planes were available, and the underground authorities were precise in stating their requirements. These were conceived partly from the point of view of current needs and partly from that of a general rising.

In 1942-3, current needs consisted mainly of sabotage and clandestine operations. Here and there partisan units had sprung up, but they did not come into existence on any scale until the second half of 1943.

After some experimentation an outfit was evolved comprising equipment for "mining and diversionary" purposes (known as "MD"). This was intended to serve for the accomplishment of one major act of sabotage and several minor ones, and also for the armed protection of those carrying them out. Each outfit weighed about 12 hundredweight and was divided

---

[37]) Polish orders for supplies from the USA were often consigned in Polish merchant ships. For instance in February 1943 *SS Morska Wola* carried 54 crates containing hectographs, soap, thread, tea and chocolate; in March 1943 *SS Lechistan* carried 52 large cases, in April 1943 *SS Wisla* a considerable transport of photographic equipment. These ships crossed the Atlantic in convoys, which also delayed the American deliveries.

among six containers.[38]) If a plane was carrying supplies only it could take two outfits, but if parachutists were aboard it usually took only one.

However carefully the containers were packed, there were usually empty corners which were filled with uniforms, warm underclothing, chocolate and cigarettes.[39]) The containers and packages were of course dropped by parachute.

In the context of preparations for a general rising, another outfit was devised known as "OW" [40]) (from the Polish for "fighting area"), to enable ten platoons or about 500 soldiers of the underground movement to go into overt action. These outfits were to be stored until the time came for a country-wide insurrection. Such a rising was in fact never proclaimed, and the "OW" outfits were eventually used for partisan activities, operation "Tempest" and the Warsaw rising.

These two basic types of outfit did not, of course, exhaust the manifold requirements of the Polish resistance movement. Besides arms and explosives there was a crying need for signals equipment of all kinds. In 1943-4, in less than a score of months 877 radio sets of Polish make were dropped in Poland.[41]) Requirements also included the necessary material for forging passes, invisible inks, reagents, books etc., together with a large quantity of medical supplies.

Many types of container were also tried out before two were selected as the most efficient in the light of SOE's experience in all territories. The first, denoted by the letter C, looked like a huge tin cigar, nearly six feet long; it contained three metal boxes and when full weighed over two hundredweight. It was convenient for packing but less so for the recipient, as it had to be retrieved and carried as a single object. In view of this disadvantage a different type was

---

[38]) Equipment in load "MD": 509 lbs. explosive, 10 Stens plus 3,000 rounds of ammunition, 27 045 mm revolvers plus 775 rounds of ammunition, 20 Mills bombs, 8 anti-tank grenades, 15 anti-tank detonators, 13 railway charges.

[39]) After the United States came into the war there was a project to make cigarettes similar to those smoked in occupied Poland ("Sport", "Möwe"), identical in packaging, excise band, paper and brand of tobacco, and to drop these in packets containing or bearing propaganda slogans. There was a similar project concerning matches. Dropping leaflets was also considered. The military authorities at once stipulated that these propaganda drops must not be made by the operational aircraft carrying parachutists and supplies, since it would have disclosed the flight paths and dropping zones. As far as is known these American plans were never carried out.

[40]) Equipment in load "OW": 2 Brens plus 2,520 rounds of ammunition, 18 Stens plus 9,400 rounds of ammunition, 27 045 mm revolvers plus 575 rounds of ammunitions, 40 Mills bombs, 76 anti-tank grenades, 27 anti-tank detonators, 206 lbs. explosive.

[41]) Details in the author's book *Between London and Warsaw*.

devised by a Pole whose name has not been preserved in the files.[42]) This, the H type, consisted of five cylindrical canisters held together by a pair of metal rods and each weighing 45 lbs. or so: the rods could easily be severed and the cylinders carried separately.

The containers were loaded into the bomb bay of the aircraft, while packages weighing up to a hundredweight or so were kept in the main part of the hull, to be thrown out by the dispatcher. These contained lighter and less easily damaged equipment. At first cloth coverings were used, reinforced with straps, but these proved too liable to damage and were replaced by strong rubber or fibre.

The rapid development of night flying and parachute drops caused a crisis in parachute production. Silk was in short supply and an ersatz material had to be found. A very fine type of cotton was used, but parachutes made from it were less reliable in opening and were only used for dropping stores.

If it were possible to see the past and display, after the fashion of a television documentary, the whole apparatus of nocturnal flights and secret drops, the great majority of spectators would be fascinated by the parachutists, pilots and aircraft, the elaborate technique of the expedition and sudden, dramatic encounters with the enemy. Few would be interested in the storehouses and the anonymous civilians in shabby rooms who filled the containers and packages and looked after the meticulously folded parachutes. But this would be a mistake, for a very great deal depended on those unknown men and women, who were never mentioned in dispatches or newspaper stories and received no decorations. The slightest lack of care, an insignificant crease in a folded parachute might mean the loss of vital stores and the calling off of a military operation.

Cases of negligence and shortcomings in this seemingly humble sector were, relatively speaking, extremely few. The beginnings were difficult for lack of experience and proper implements, but in the second period of dropping operations things were much better. The packing stations, which worked for SOE as a whole, developed a high degree of efficiency and an *esprit de corps* such as one would expect to find in a separate branch of the armed forces. Naturally, as the flights depended on a variety of factors and were often much delayed, equipment often failed to reach the home country in time, and above all there was never enough of it. The demand for arms, ammunition and plastic explosives was never satisfied, but

---

[42]) This detail is given by Michael Foot in his excellent book *SOE in France*.

that was a general complaint and was no fault of those who filled the containers. The packers, among other things, attained such a degree of perfection in the art of using space that experts found it impossible to repack into a container all the objects that had come out of it.

It should be added, though perhaps it will have been guessed, that the majority of the packers were women. They are generally neater and more patient than men, and also have the great merit of being able to work hard and devotedly in obscure surroundings, away from the shouting and limelight.

NIGHT AND VENGEANCE

I

Major Rémi Grocholski pushed back his chair, rose and began to pace about the narrow room. He was a huge, tall, robust man with powerful shoulders and a large head covered with curly grey hair. He had a broad face, a grizzled moustache and blue eyes full of alertness and courage.

It was contrary to security for a man's code-name to suggest in any way his origin, appearance or real surname; but Grocholski made light of this and, in obvious mockery of the Germans, had chosen the name *Goliath*. This in itself might not have mattered so much, but the irrepressible major, who had been a dashing cavalryman in the twenties, conducted all his secret activities in the same style. He had embarked on these immediately after the September campaign, and his mode of action would long ago have landed anyone else in prison. Although he was a head taller than those about him, was so burly that he could hardly negotiate the doors of a tram, and had a voice that could be heard many yards away, he threw himself into every kind of danger, despised all difficulties and tempted Fate time and again — and yet he survived unscathed for more than two years of the occupation period.

As a result, he came to be known not only as a brave man but as a lucky one. Perhaps for this reason as well as for his qualities of mind and character, he was entrusted by the Home Army commander with an important and difficult task, namely the large-scale organization known as "Fan" ("Wachlarz"), whose first commander, Major Jan Wlodarkiewicz, had died suddenly at the beginning of 1942.

Within a few weeks of Hitler's attack on Russia, the German armies not only swept over the eastern Polish territories which Stalin had occupied, but advanced far into the Soviet Union itself, thus opening up a vast area extending from the Baltic to the Black Sea. The Home Army command were quick to see the possibilities of this, and before the end of

101

1941 a plan had been worked out to infiltrate saboteurs and agents into the newly occupied territory. Their main duties were twofold. The first was to organize a simultaneous widespread attack on bridges, roads and railways which would, after the Germans were defeated in Russia, hold up their retreating forces for forty-eight hours while they were still east of the Polish frontier, and so clear the way for a general insurrection in Poland. As we know, the situation developed otherwise and no general insurrection took place.[1])

The second duty of the Home Army personnel was to harry the Germans' tremendously extended communication lines by which supplies reached the eastern front. Both duties were entrusted to the "Fan" organization, which was responsible to the Home Army command in Warsaw for all subversive operations in the eastern territories.

Goliath returned to his desk and bent over the outspread map, on which he had marked in red pencil five sectors where subversive centres had been organized and were already in operation.

The most southerly of these sectors, based on the Black Sea and directed towards Lwow and Ploskirov, was of minor interest at the moment, as it had not been possible to do much there. Nor did he spend much time on the portion of the map which included the Baltic and the fifth sector, north of Wilno, in the direction of Dvinsk and Polotsk. Here too there was not much going on, and the Major had less taste for organization and preparation than for aggressive action. His gaze fastened on the three central sectors: the second, towards Rowne and Kiev, the third opposite Pinsk and Kalinkovichi, and the fourth, covering Baranowicze, Minsk, Borisov and the Slutsk-Bobruisk highway.

In these extensive areas something was clearly afoot, for the Major pored over the map and made six blue-pencil crosses on it, some of them close together. He paid close attention to the railway lines, main roads and signs indicating bridges, and carefully measured several distances with a ruler. Then he stood up straight, stretched himself, rubbed his weary eyes and walked across to the window. A few floors below, he could see the busy Warsaw street and hurrying pedestrians.

'I wonder,' he muttered to himself. 'I wonder.'

The day before, he had had a conversation with General Rowecki in which he had asked for trained saboteurs, mining equipment and explosives, and had been assured he would get them all. 'As you know,' Rowecki had said, coming closer and speaking as low as possible, 'our young fellows are being

---

[1]) Instead of a general uprising operation "Tempest" was authorised.

trained in Britain and flown over to us. Some have already arrived. Before long there will be a lot more, and all the kinds of supplies you need will be parachuted in as well. They've promised us.'

The Major walked heavily back from the window to his desk, folded the map carefully and took it to a corner of the room where he prised up two loose pieces of the parquet floor. He stowed away the map in its hiding-place, and once more paced about the room.

There was no sound to be heard, but he felt uneasy. He well knew the difficulties of his task; he could say exactly how many soldiers he had and how many more he needed, and he realized that little could be done without adequate supplies; but these were not his chief worries. From intelligence reports he knew that secret Soviet agents had already begun to appear in German-occupied eastern Poland. Some had been parachuted, others were political commissars from routed divisions who had escaped capture by the Germans and gone to ground among the population.

Although on a modest scale, the Soviet underground had already gone to work. Clearly the men of "Fan" would come up against the Soviet agents sooner or later, and what would happen then? How would the Russians react, and what would their orders be? Would they be prepared to co-operate in good faith?

The Major was himself a man of the eastern provinces, he knew the Bolsheviks and did not trust them. His brow furrowed as he pondered anxiously on the future of the historic lands of the Polish Republic.

II

For Klimowski, the period of "acclimatization" in Warsaw was an irksome one. After the long wait at the holding station near London and the emotional impact of finding himself once more on Polish soil, his overstrained nerves demanded the relief of action; yet here he was, condemned by stern regulations to three weeks of idleness. Although living in the city, he had hardly yet seen it. He raged inwardly and cursed the bureaucrats with their pettifogging rules but managed to keep his self-control and to behave calmly.

His impatience was in large measure disarmed by the tactful and friendly care of the "aunt" with whom he was billeted. This middle-aged woman with two teen-age children, whose husband was a prisoner in German hands and who sent off parcels to him regularly, treated Klimowski as a member of her own family. Indeed she did more for him than this, since apart from full board and shelter she provided all the assistance he required during the "transition" period. In the course of those three weeks he was required to change his skin, to transform himself from a uniformed officer enjoying every privilege into a citizen of an occupied country, a secret agent who had to watch his every step. Gradually she introduced him to a way of life which was already quite familiar to her but which, to a newcomer from Britain, was a jungle full of death-traps and surprises.

The first few days he spent resting and getting used to his immediate surroundings. His hostess was not only a woman of experience but had a friendly, natural manner. As soon as they had exchanged passwords and she was sure of his identity, she gave him a smile which disarmed his somewhat stiff and reserved attitude.

'We'll say that your name is Janek and that you are a distant cousin whom my children haven't met yet.'

'Certainly.'

'And now, Janek, you must put up with being under my orders.'

'I've no objection whatever.'

They laughed, and the ice was already broken. Two days later, she took him out of doors for the first time to have some passport photographs taken, so that the underground authorities could provide him with fresh papers: those he had brought from Britain could no longer be used.

Klimowski looked about him with astonishment. This was a completely different city from the Warsaw he had known before the war. Not because of the ruins everywhere, or the German soldiers they passed at every step, for these were to be expected. But the whole rhythm and atmosphere had changed: even the smell of the streets was different.

He came home full of confused and indefinable impressions, and the two of them talked late into the night by the light of a carbide lamp. He asked question after question and received a brief reply to each which enabled him to clarify his thoughts. After this first outing he demanded more, which his protectress allowed him from time to time as one might to a convalescent. There was a hard frost, and they used to sit in cafés to keep warm. They would go into shops, study prices and perhaps buy something or other, and occasionally they rode in trams. As the days passed, Klimowski felt that he knew enough about life under the occupation: he wanted to rush off and report for work, and demanded the

Wladyslaw Sikorski

Kazimierz Sosnkowski

Stefan Rowecki

Tadeusz Bor - Komorowski

Colin Gubbins

John Slessor

H. B. Perkins

Henry McLeod Threlfall

Leopold Okulicki Kazimierz Iranek-Osmecki

Jozef Hartman Maciej Kalenkiewicz Tadeusz Klimowski

Adolf Pilch *Ponury* Zygmunt Milewicz

Halifax in Brindisi. Only two engines are visible.

Polish airmen in Brindisi, at the time of the Warsaw Rising.

name of his next contact; but his hostess only smiled meaningly and glanced at the calendar.

During the second week they went to the open-air market at *Kiercelak*[2]) and narrowly escaped being caught in a police raid. Another day they stood outside the ghetto walls at Leszno: the police were too numerous for comfort, and they returned home in silence. At the gate they were stopped by gendarmes who demanded to see their papers, and for a moment it was uncertain whether they would be arrested.

That evening Klimowski resolved firmly that although devoured by impatience he would obey the rules and not seek to shorten the prescribed period. The regulations which had seemed nonsensical now took on a different aspect.

Meanwhile, he spent his evenings reading the underground press, which furnished material for further questions and arguments. By degrees he was becoming familiar with the new world in which he found himself. He began, too, to realize that the Germans were not simply soldiers whom one met in battle. He had known all this before, but it had not sunk into his imagination. What he now experienced was a far cry from what he had expected during the long period of training in Britain. He felt himself changing inwardly, becoming a different man not only on paper but in reality, in his thoughts and even his physique.

III

Rowecki's promise had not been an empty one. Young men of decisive bearing and bold appearance began to appear at Grocholski's headquarters. The Major spent long hours explaining the situation to them and answering their questions. Together they studied the map of the eastern territories and debated courses of action. The huge front, extending over more than a thousand miles and as yet thinly manned, began to assume fresh significance.

Among the first to report was Lieutenant Klimowski. The Major had a difficult time with him, for the newcomer took his duties seriously and was not always satisfied with the answers to his questions. He was offered the command of the second sector, from Rowne to Kiev, an area about 200 miles wide and the same distance in depth. On asking what had been set up there already, he was told: nothing. Asking further what resources he would have to draw on, he was

---

[2]) A popular market in Warsaw, destroyed during the second half of the war.

told with equal frankness and brevity: money and his own ingenuity. Materials would come later.[3])

Klimowski asked for a week in which to think things over, after which he accepted the assignment subject to one basic condition. This was that the first purpose of "Fan", namely that of holding up the retreating Germans for forty-eight hours, should be the principal one and should take precedence of current sabotage. The Major, who was eager for action, at first objected to this, but yielded after some hours' argument. He could hardly expect prompt results in the form of sabotage from an almost singlehanded officer, despatched to an unknown territory and furnished with no local contacts.

While Klimowski was in the process of choosing his immediate staff and making preparations to leave, another parachutist reported to *Goliath*. This was an officer with the code-name *Ponury* (Grim), who radiated qualities of leadership so strongly that the Major changed his mind and offered him the second sector, transferring Klimowski to the first. *Ponury* collected a band of followers and made off eastwards with all speed, but was captured almost at once by the Germans. He escaped and returned to Warsaw, but Klimowski, who had been reinstated as commander of the second sector, was now ready to set out, and no further change was made.

After arriving at Rowne, Klimowski set up a secret depot with some difficulty and proceeded further east. He soon found that the Major had described the situation correctly and that little support was to be found in this war-torn area, ravaged by two occupations. Matters were not quite so hopeless on Polish soil, though the Ukrainians were hostile and were banking on a German victory; but in the Soviet Ukraine conditions were catastrophic. The terrible years of Bolshevik government, in which millions of inhabitants of the richest lands in Europe had starved to death and millions more had been sent to hard labour in Siberia, had destroyed hopes of any change or of a better future. When the Germans came, they turned out little better than the Bolsheviks. The secret agents who were now appearing from the West told the natives that they were fighting the Germans and needed help, but was it safe to do what they asked? Sooner or later the NKVD

---

[3]) These supplies generally came from drops. While the aircraft were flying from Britain, their range was no farther than Lublin (about 100 miles south-east of Warsaw), so that "Fan" could not get its supplies straight from the air. When they began to fly from Tunis — the first flight was on Dec. 18, 1943 — and from Italy at the beginning of 1944, and when, thanks to this, the southern and eastern areas of Poland became accessible, "Fan" no longer existed.

would come back and demand an account from everyone. What if the newcomers were provocateurs? In short, it was easier to find a spring of water in the Sahara than to be given shelter amongst this race, which had once been proverbial for hospitality.

A curious incident befell Klimowski in a village near Zhitomir. Here, thanks to an involved series of contacts, he found an isolated Polish family living in a tumbledown cottage, who by some miracle had survived the tribulations of those appalling years and who agreed to shelter him for a few nights. They were sitting by candle-light, puffing at cigarettes of cheap tobacco and sipping moonshine liquor, when a knock was heard and a stranger came in. Seeing Klimowski he was about to withdraw, but on being reasured by the host he drew a small packet from under his coat. It was a copy of *Pan Wolodyjowski*[1]) dating from before the first war, so thumbed as to be almost illegible, and so dog-eared that it was almost circular in shape. Circulating in secret around the few, widely scattered Polish families of those parts, it completed its round every two years and was now starting once again. Klimowski was struck dumb and could hardly conceal his emotion. He held in his hand, like a sacred relic, the last weapon of Polish culture in those outlying lands.

Having examined the situation on the spot, Klimowski realized that he would never achieve anything unless he and his men could find some way of establishing themselves in the area. He resolved to penetrate the occupation administration, thus living among the Germans instead of alongside them.

He began with the German building firms, into which he first infiltrated one of his officers as a cook. This modest function enabled the officer in question to make contacts and acquire influence to such an extent that in a few months he was virtually in charge of the movement of workers within the Ukraine, and could install Klimowski's men in a variety of positions. In this way clandestine groups of up to platoon strength came into existence at Kiev, Zhitomir and Shepetovka.

Another opportunity for infiltration was offered by the signals organization. The Germans set up posts to defend the army's telephone system and provided those who worked in them with quarters, arms, uniforms, food and pay. A Polish engineer named Wroblewski, who worked at one of these, succeeded in bringing into the service 120 soldiers of the

[1]) A historical novel by the Polish writer Henryk Sienkiewicz, author of *Quo Vadis?* and Nobel prize winner.

underground army and three officer-parachutists, including Klimowski himself. This was an ideal situation. The patrols guarding the telephone lines, which consisted almost entirely of Home Army soldiers, were able to station themselves openly at key points; they moved about the country on German transport, listened in to conversations and could send warning messages at any time — a perfect background for sabotage.

They also needed transport of their own, and so two men were infiltrated into a German forwarding establishment at Kiev. Cars belonging to this firm often travelled westward as far as Warsaw, and in this way reports were sent back to *Goliath*.

The base for all these operations was at Rowne, and its commander from the supplies point of view was Lieutenant *Zagiew* (Fire-brand).

After these organizational problems had been solved it was possible to think of sabotage. Small patrols would slip off for short periods, blow up a bridge or railway line and return to their quarters under the very noses of the infuriated Germans. Sabotage of telephone lines was even easier, since they were almost entirely "guarded" by members of the underground. Delicate apparatus was put out of action, and repairs were spun out as long as possible.

Subversion became more widespread, but was still hampered by lack of gear and explosives. *Goliath* promised to send a carload to the sector, but this never materialized. Parachute drops were still all too few, and the underground in all parts of the country was clamouring for supplies. Clearly it was not enough to ensconce oneself among the Germans: the next step was to seize weapons of war from their magazines.[5]) A day came at last when it was possible by this means to set up a well-armed partisan unit for the first time.

* * *

In the fourth sector, based on Minsk and covering Polotsk, Nevel and Vitebsk, work began in the same way as in the second, namely by infiltrating the German administration and building firms. The commander was a local man, Major Zygmunt Reliszko, who knew the area well, but nearly all his subordinates were from Warsaw or central Poland. Many of them were parachutists, who brought with them a number of young soldiers whom they had trained in the arts of sabotage. These men provided the core of the enterprise, and

---

[5]) Once a case of pistols was stolen which, when examined, proved to be useless. The firing pin was a fraction of a millimetre too short and did not hit the hammers. A fine example of precisely carried out sabotage.

members of the local population were only taken on with the greatest caution and for auxiliary jobs.

The movement of men and equipment was a complicated matter, for the Germans had divided up the occupied area into districts (*Bezirke*), the boundaries of which were closely guarded. Fortunately several German firms engaged in building roads, airfields, hangars and barracks had their headquarters or branches in Warsaw. The Home Army kept a close watch on these from the outset and took every opportunity of infiltrating its own men. The firms were in constant need of labour, for the eastern front grew steadily longer and more distant and more and more military establishments were built in the rear area. Underground soldiers with their papers in perfect order would report to prearranged contacts, be given jobs and set out eastwards as soon as possible. They usually travelled in lorries, often military ones driven by German soldiers, and crossing the various borderlines was relatively safe. The vehicles were also loaded with building materials, and there was often a chance of smuggling in plastic explosives, mines, arms and ammunition. The fourth sector was better off in this respect than the second, and did not have to rely wholly on equipment captured from the enemy.[6])

To expedite these activities, the whole sector was divided into two triangles. The apices of triangle A were at Minsk (where its headquarters were), Smolensk and Gomel. It was commanded first by Captain Tadeusz Naturalista and later by Captain Bohdan Piatkowski (*Mak*), who skilfully succeeded in a fairly short time in planting his men in key positions, equipping them and launching subversive activities, especially by means of patrols which attacked German lines of communication. He was aided by Lieutenant *Mira,* who had attended courses with him in Britain, and several other parachutists.

Triangle B was bounded by Polotsk, Nevel and Vitebsk and was under the command of Lieutenant E. Banasikowski. He had a more difficult task, as it was not possible to settle in any of the three towns for long. The solution found was to reconnoitre the terrain and then send in patrols from Polish territory, which would carry out their mission and return swiftly to base. They were mainly employees of various German firms, housed in barracks and closely watched. If they did not turn up for work, a check was immediately made to see if they were sick or absent. Consequently it was

---

[6]) It appears from despatch No. 118 from the Commander of the Home Army, that in the earliest stages of the drops, up to March 1942, only 200 lbs. of explosives were received and this was all handed over to "Fan". To this was added 3,000 lbs. of explosives made in Poland.

hard to get away overnight except on the pretext of travelling on the firm's business, for which excuses had to be found and passes obtained. Those who were allowed off work on Sundays would slip away on the previous evening (without sleep, for the operations took place at night), and in general the German overseers were fooled in every possible way.

Another difficulty in the field of organization was the standing order forbidding members of "Fan" to contact the local Home Army network in any sector. This was a sound rule, since "Fan" had to be kept extremely secret in view of the extent to which it had penetrated the German organization; but it involved working in watertight compartments and made it harder to gain a local foothold. It also led to misunderstandings, some of them tragic. In the fourth sector a member of the "Fan" organization was shot by a Home Army soldier who took him for a provocateur.

Apart from patrol activities which were self-contained and not part of a single plan, major operations were sometimes mounted, involving the whole sector. In one of the most successful of these, the Minsk railway junction was put out of action on the night of May 31 / June 1, 1942, when several bridges and sections of track surrounding the town were blown up.

* * *

The organization of the third sector (Pinsk - Kalinkovichi) was easier in that the Polesian area had been less affected by Soviet deportations [7]) and, lacking good roads, was an unsuitable theatre for large-scale warfare. The local population were more numerous and less terrorized, and it was possible to find some support among them.

The commander of this sector was another parachutist, Captain Alfred Paczkowski, who set up his headquarters at Brest Litovsk in the early spring of 1942. He selected a dozen or more locals with convincing papers and a good knowledge of the area, and began to create a subversive network. Himself an expert with explosives, he trained his men and set about planning attacks on German rail communications. Thanks to the transport firms' organization he kept in touch with headquarters in Warsaw and received from there arms, stores and recruits for his meagre forces. Towards the end of autumn he was joined by another para-

---

[7]) During the period of close co-operation between Hitler and Stalin, from Sept. 1939 to June 1941, about 1,250,000 people were deported from the eastern territories of Poland into Russia, mostly to Siberia. This cruel proceeding comprised above all intellectuals, soldiers, civil servants and persons active in politics or welfare work. It was not strange that the soldiers of "Fan" had so much difficulty in establishing themselves in this area.

chutist, Lieutenant Mieczyslaw Eckhardt (*Bocian* - Stork).[8])

In November, after a series of successes in the shape of blown-up tracks, destroyed locomotives and derailed transports, Paczkowski (whose code-name was *Wania*) went with *Bocian* and a locally contacted soldier *Azor* to the Dawidgrodek area east of Pinsk to carry out a further raid. Unfortunately he broke a leg when crossing over the frozen river Horyn, and this accident had serious consequences. His comrades left him in the forest in the care of a pitch burner and went to Dawidgrodek to get help. There they were captured by the Germans, who, on finding that they were armed and carried explosives, organized a wide-ranging hunt: they found *Wania* and also his deputy *Rys*, whom they arrested. *Bocian* was interrogated so brutally that he died twenty-four hours later at the Dawidgrodek gendarmerie post.[9]) *Wania*, despite his broken leg, stood up well to the beating he received and survived the interrogation. Before Christmas he, *Rys* and *Azor* were transferred to prison at Pinsk.

The news of *Wania's* capture reached Warsaw fairly quickly, but it was not until after his imprisonment at Pinsk that headquarters knew where he and his companions were. As soon as they did, General Rowecki gave orders that the three men were to be rescued.

Luckily the commander of "Fan" had *Ponury* at his disposal in Warsaw: the latter had escaped from gaol at Zwiahel and had not yet received a fresh appointment. On New Year's eve *Goliath* ordered him to rescue his comrades by any means he thought best, whether bribery, trickery or an armed attack: he could have any troops, arms and transport that he wanted.

Together with a friend and fellow-escapee from Zwiahel *Czarka*, who was also a parachutist, *Ponury* set to work. On the day of receiving his orders he sent off a messenger urgently to contact the prison warder who had sent word about the three men, and who was himself a member of the Home Army. Meanwhile *Ponury* drew 60,000 marks from official funds, arranged for the use of a car and two lorries and speedily formed a commando group consisting, besides himself and *Czarka*, of two parachutists, *Kawa* and *Kra*, and three first-class Home Army men whose *noms de guerre* were *Edek-Monter*, *MSZ* and *SS*.[10]) *Edek* and *MSZ* were to act as drivers. Besides money, the group drew arms and explosives and the uniform of an NCO in Hitler's SS.

[8]) Altogether 32 parachutists were sent to "Fan".

[9]) One version says that *Bocian* hanged himself in his cell for fear that he would break down and give the Germans information.

[10]) The code-names *Czarka, Kawa, Kra* etc. mean respectively bowl, coffee, ice-floe, Eddie the fitter, Foreign Office and, of course SS.

Arriving at Brest, the headquarters of the third sector, on January 2, *Ponury* left *Czarka* with a supply of arms to recruit further members of the group, and himself went on with *MSZ* to Pinsk to find out what his messenger had achieved. This proved to be a great deal. In barely two days he had contacted the prisoners through the warder and knew the numbers of their cells. *Ponury* found a hiding-place on the outskirts of the town and made this his base for the operation. His next problem was to find the answers to a number of important questions about the composition and strength of the German garrison, the lay-out of the prison, the wardens' duties, what sort of men they were and so forth; also whether there was any chance of achieving his objective by bribery. It soon turned out that there was not; this was no surprise to *Ponury*, who from the start had based his plan on the idea of an armed raid.

The next few days were extremely active. *Czarka* selected nine men of the local Home Army organization and kept them in a state of alertness. He also organized a reception point for the escapees in a country house outside Brest, with a sick bay attended by a nurse and a doctor with surgical instruments. Meanwhile *Ponury* returned to Warsaw and, in a car driven by *Edek*, brought *Kawa* and *Kra* to Pinsk; he also made several trips to Brest to collect information and organize details of the raid.

It turned out that the Pinsk garrison consisted of 3,500 men and was connected with Brest by three telephone lines, while the gendarmerie had five wireless stations which could communicate with Luck to the south and Kobryn to the west. *Kawa* prepared an exact plan of the prison, to which were added full details about the guards, their schedule of duties and other activities, their individual characteristics etc. Constant liaison was kept up with the prisoners themselves. *Wania* was pressing for urgent action, as he feared that the Gestapo might finish them off any day, or else get wind of the rescue preparations and move them to another prison.

At last it was decided to carry out the attack on January 18th at five in the afternoon, when it would be nearly dark and the warders would be least on their guard. The day before, the whole assault party were brought from Brest to Pinsk in a Ford lorry driven by *Edek* and an Opel driven by *MSZ*, and were led cautiously in groups of five to *Ponury's* hideout. Here for the first time he told everybody the object of the preparations: till then, those in the know were only *Czarka*, *Kawa*, *Kra* and *MSZ*.

The sixteen soldiers were divided into three parties of four plus two patrols of two men each. *Ponury* explained the plan in detail, assigned each group its duties, ordered them to hand in their personal papers, paid each man a sum of money and forbade them to leave the hiding-place. As German reprisals were to be expected, they were to pose as Soviet partisans: any talking during the raid must be in Russian or German, and those who did not know either language were to keep silent. In case they were pursued by dogs, a decoction of tobacco was prepared to destroy the scent. The men were shown a map of the town and given the location of meeting-places to which individuals could retreat in case of need. The telephone connections were taken care of: one of the local men organized patrols to cut the wires immediately before the action.

Ponury, with three of his own group, made a last reconnaissance, and arms were issued on the following morning, a few hours before the attack.

At exactly 5 p.m., in pitch darkness, a small camouflaged car drew up before the prison gates. It was the Opel driven by *MSZ*, with *SS* (appropriately dressed in German uniform) in the passenger seat beside him, and *Ponury* in the back with a comrade *Motor*. The car remained stationary with its engine running; the door half-opened and the "SS man" leant out, shouting and making angry signs. The warder on duty looked through his spyhole, heard the German voice and unsuspectingly began to open the gate. As soon as there was enough room to pass, *MSZ* stepped on the gas and the car shot in. *SS* and *Motor* jumped out and ordered the warder to open the inner gate leading to the prison yard. The man became suspicious at this and reached for his rifle, but *Motor* was quicker and laid him low with a pistol-shot. The sound was almost inaudible owing to the roar of the car's engine and the noise of voices from the street outside (five hundred German soldiers were quartered a few dozen yards away). Two members of a covering patrol dashed in and shut the gate, after which they took possession of the sentry-box. The whole operation so far had taken not more than a minute.

SS and *Motor* jumped back into the car, which made for the inner gate. Here the stratagem was repeated, except that as soon as the warder opened up he was bound and disarmed. Only an iron grille now separated the attackers from the prison itself.

Meanwhile two other groups, armed with ladders and led by *Czarka* and *Kawa* respectively, had scaled the outer wall at different points. *Czarka* captured the administrative office and proceeded from there to the second gate, while *Kawa* raided the prison officers' quarters where, as he had hoped, he found the commander and his deputy, Hellinger and Zelner. His object was to get the keys of the cells so that it would not be necessary to break down or blow up the doors. The

Germans resisted, and were polished off with Sten guns; then *Kawa* seized the keys and led his men through the watch-tower into the inner yard. Here he overpowered the guard and opened the grille with his key.

Thus within a few minutes all three groups, which had suffered no losses, joined forces in the midst of the prison. Some of the men occupied the offices, other looked after the prostrate warders, while *Ponury* dashed to the male prisoners' section and the cells were thrown open. *Wania*, *Rys* and *Azor* were found and at once taken to the car; the first-named, suffering from the effects of beating and with his broken leg, had to be carried. *MSZ* once more stepped on the gas and they disappeared into the darkness.

Altogether over forty men [11]) were set free, including seven Soviet partisans. A member of the attacking force spoke to the whole group in Russian, advising them to take refuge in the woods and form themselves into a fighting unit. The warders were jammed into a cell and told that hand-grenades would be thrown in if they gave the alarm.

A threefold whistle was heard. The soldiers rushed to the main gate, where *Edek* was waiting with his Ford lorry. *Ponury* counted the men as they jumped aboard; a moment's wait for the last two, and they were off at full speed for Brest, dropping goads behind them to puncture the tyres of any pursuers.

Despite minor hitches and although the Opel had to be burnt, as it burst a tyre and its engine caught fire, the escape was a triumphant success. On January 20th, the three liberated officers reported to their superiors in Warsaw; next day *Ponury* did the same, having stopped in Brest to discharge the local men recruited for the operation.[12])

[11]) The women's wing was not set free, as keys could not be found and there was no time to break down or blow up the doors.

[12]) Breaking into the prison in Pinsk and freeing three fellow-soldiers, among them the commander of the third sector of "Fan", was a great personal success for *Ponury* and his men and a fine achievement for the Home Army. Pinsk is 210 miles from Warsaw, was separated from it by a well-guarded frontier and had a garrison of 3,500 soldiers. The "Information Bulletin", the official clandestine organ of the Home Army, advertised the operation widely, printing Gen. *Grot's* orders and a short account of the successful raid. It was a classic example of the tactics of a small commando group, led by well-trained and selected parachutists, equipped with modern weapons. It was also of real political significance. The release of the prisoners took place at a time when Soviet Russia had already shown her cards and was demanding the Polish eastern territories; yet it was not the soldiers of the Red Army who came to the help of their partisan comrades. They were freed by Polish parachutists and local underground soldiers who went to the help of their own comrades. The commando group came not from Moscow but from Warsaw.

* * *

At the same time as the Germans captured the commander of the third sector and his immediate companions, the fourth sector, which was working successfully, underwent a reorganization with important consequences, due to the fact that Major Reliszko fell seriously ill and could no longer carry out his duties. In his place Warsaw sent out Major Tadeusz Sokolowski, known as *Trop* (Trail), who had been parachuted into Poland on March 31, 1942 and had performed one or two urgent tasks since his arrival and acclimatization. *Trop* proceeded to Minsk and took over command from Captain *Mak*, who was temporarily acting for Reliszko.

The new commander was a cavalry officer, slim and below average height, who had been a crack rider before the war. He was a brave man, full of energy and prompt in decision, but too fiery and impatient to be suited to the difficult conditions of underground warfare. Before a few weeks were out he had given away the network of subversive activities which had been created with immense care, and had laid it wide open to German attack. By December 5th he and many of his subordinates were in prison, including the parachutists *Mak* and *Ryba* (Fish) and, the engineer Kisielewski, who had been a key member of the sector's staff. In three days, no fewer than 75 members of the "Fan" organization were arrested and the arduous work of many months was all but ruined.

Lieutenant *Mira* escaped being arrested in the first batch, as he had set out for Slutsk a few days before. Within a month he was arrested there, but escaped from gaol and returned to Minsk. Finding out what had happened to his comrades, he went off to Warsaw to organize help. His arrival coincided with *Ponury's* success, and Rowecki, encouraged by the latter and feeling bound to attempt something of the same sort at Minsk, agreed to let the local commander see what he could do. Armed with 40,000 marks, *Mira* returned to Minsk with three companions who, like him, had escaped arrest there in December. The would-be rescuers were led by the "Fan" chief of staff, Captain *Tumry*, the only officer who remained unidentified in the Minsk area.

It was practically impossible for the tiny group to achieve anything, as nearly all their comrades were behind bars and they could not safely show their faces in the town. The local population could not be relied on, with the exception of the very few Poles who might be found amongst them. The group had perforce to disobey the ban on contacting the local Home Army intelligence network. They found that a member of the latter, a woman known as *Grazyna*, was already in touch with the prisoners, and through her they communicated with *Trop, Mak*, Kisielewski and others. They were able to send in some food and give warning of the escape plan, and to receive from their comrades a plan of the prison showing the position of their cells. Just before the attempt, they managed to smuggle in four Colt revolvers.

Grazyna explained at once that it was hopeless to think of bribery, which would at best only secure the release of one prisoner. The idea of a ruse was not promising either, which left only armed attack. The necessary stores were to hand, as the Germans had not succeeded in discovering the local cache of arms, ammunition and bombs, but how could a group of only five officers make use of these? In their dilemma, *Mira* put forward a plan to which *Tumry* agreed. In the course of the December arrests the Gestapo had laid hands on almost the whole Central Committee of the Byelorussian Communist Party, which was functioning clandestinely in Minsk. The arrested members were in the same prison as the Poles, and presumably those of their Committee who were still at liberty would be interested in mounting a joint rescue action.

There was as yet no liaison with these people, but it was not hard to organize, as the woman who was sheltering the group from Warsaw, a communist of Polish origin named Katya, was responsible for the Committee's links with the Soviet partisans who were operating in the Naliboki forest. She arranged a meeting between *Tumry* and three of the communists, who eagerly accepted his proposal; they promised to provide an unarmed assault group and two cars for the escapees and to ensure their protection as far as beyond Stolpce. *Tumry* in return furnished arms for their group and paid them 10,000 marks. It was agreed that the attackers would assemble at Katya's house, which was a few hundred yards from the prison and abutted on a store of military cloth. The plan was that the two cars would arrive there at 6 a.m.: the Polish and Russian group would each get into one and drive to the two prison gates. The Latvian on guard at the main gate had already been bribed, and the party which arrived at the back gate, where the kitchen was, would drive in on the pretext that they had come to collect potato parings for pig food. The operation itself was to take place at 7 o'clock.

On the day before the attack Katya went off on one of her secret missions, leaving her two small children at home. The five officers slept little that night, and were up and ready well before six, but no cars appeared. Instead, at 6.30 a tank rolled up, together with a German infantry patrol.

'They've double-crossed us,' said *Tumry*. 'Get under the windows!'

The trapped officers opened fire, but they had no chance against a tank armed with a flamethrower. Three Germans fell, but two of *Mira's* group were killed by submachine guns and *Tumry* was mortally wounded. Katya's home and the storehouse were in flames.

'Run for it,' whispered the captain to the two others. At the last moment, they escaped by way of the storehouse attic, leaving behind their three dead comrades and the children, who perished in the flames. A few days later the Germans, fully informed of the plot, executed the prisoners whom it was intended to rescue.[13])

IV

These events in the fourth sector were a faithful reflection of the current political situation. In theory Russia was a member of the alliance to which Poland had belonged from the first day of the war, but in practice she had once more become an enemy. Scarcely had she warded off the deadliest blows of the German invader when she began putting forward claims to Polish lands which had been hers at various times in the past thanks to robbery and violence.

Unfortunately the Western allies, to whom Russia's aid was of immeasurable value, accepted the plea that she must advance her frontiers westward to guard against a future German attack. This was an absurd argument on the part of a state which extended for 6,000 miles and which, moreover, had helped the Germans to unleash the present war; but in politics might is right, and no-one was prepared to listen to voices on the other side.

The Polish political and military authorities realized that the position was serious, but what could they do? If they had withdrawn their troops from the Western theatre of war and disbanded the anti-Nazi resistance movement in Poland, they would have been playing straight into Stalin's hands and vindicating his contention that the Poles were secretly on Hitler's side and that their Home Army was a sham. This would have meant an end to Poland's unshakable position, her national aspirations and moral right to independence.

The situation was extremely difficult, but there could only be one decision: to go on fighting the Germans and to build up the armed forces in the West and the military underground in Poland.

[13]) The execution of a large number of soldiers from "Fan" took place on February 6, 1943, though this date is not absolutely certain. Captain *Mak* lived longer, as at the time of the execution he was lying wounded in the prison hospital after an earlier unsuccessful attempt to escape. When partly recovered, he tried to escape a second and third time. The third time he was shot in the chest and died shortly afterwards.

The spring of 1943 marked the end of the second annual period of flights to Poland, known by the codeword "Intonation." Since the flights began, 167 parachutists and 50 tons of supplies had been dropped. Seven planes had been lost, with one British and three Polish crews, and six parachutists had been killed: three in a plane destroyed over the North Sea, one on landing and two in a fight with Germans after an unsuccessful drop. The remaining parachutists joined the ranks of the ever-growing Home Army, and by the end of spring nine of them had given their lives in active service.

The second period was marked by a new aspect which is worth attention. The Home Army commander frequently urged in his reports that bombing should be carried out in reprisal for German crimes in Poland, and suggested suitable targets. The allies, of course, dropped thousands of bombs in strategic night-time raids aimed at destroying Germany's industrial resources; but these raids had no direct connection with what went on in German camps and prisons on Polish soil, the police raids and the mass graves at Palmiry and Auschwitz (Oswiecim).

The British considered the Polish suggestions, but eventually turned them down for fear of political complications. Then a proposal was put up for bombing the camp at Auschwitz, which was located in Poland but whose inmates came from all over Europe. A successful attack might destroy the whole monstrous complex; some SS-men at least would be killed, and some prisoners might escape. A great blow might be struck for morale in the occupied countries. But, for sound reasons, this plan too was rejected. To be effective, it would have had to be carried out by a vast number of planes; the prisoners in their crowded huts would suffer huge losses, and what would become of any who managed to escape in the confusion? The Polish underground could not have absorbed thousands of ex-prisoners of every nationality in Europe.

Despite British objections, the Poles in London and Warsaw continued to think in terms of retaliation raids. Possibilities were examined, telegrams exchanged and finally a plan was evolved which came close to being put into effect.

On the night of October 29/30, 1942, Fl.-Lieutenant S. Krol, an experienced navigator who had already been over Poland several times, flew an adapted twin-engine Whitley on a mission with the object of bombing the Gestapo headquarters in Aleja Szucha, Warsaw. He knew the city thoroughly and was confident that he could locate the target and take revenge on those who were terrorizing the country and torturing prisoners with impunity. He reached Poland without difficulty and visibility was good, but it became clear that the target was too small and too close to other houses: he would most probably have missed his aim and brought death to many innocent people. So the bombs were dropped on the Okecie airfield and the disappointed crew turned back. The plane came down off the Norfolk coast near Sheringham; it was early dawn, and they were sighted by a lifeboat which rescued them from the icy waves.[14])

During the period when flights to Poland were suspended owing to the shorter nights, fresh blows fell upon the country which made its lot still harder. In April 1943 the Germans discovered the graves of the murdered Polish officers at Katyn;[15]) they gave immense publicity to the affair, and the Polish Government for their part appealed to the International Red Cross at Geneva. Moscow used this as a pretext to break off diplomatic relations with the Poles. Thus when, after three and a half years of war, the scale was at last turning in the allies' favour, our country's plight was becoming more and more tragic from the political point of view.

Difficult, complicated and dangerous situations call for outstanding leaders — men of strong personality, authority, decision and courage. In Poland itself we possessed such a man in Rowecki, the commander of the Home Army, and in

[14]) The fact that this flight took place is confirmed by the coded despatch No. 4591/VI of Oct. 30, 1942 sent by *Rawa* (Lt. Col. Protasewicz's code-name for correspondence with Poland) to *Kalina* (Gen. Rowecki's code-name for correspondence with the West). It is also mentioned in Jerrard Tickell's book *Moon Squadron*.

[15]) When, after the signing of the Sikorski-Maisky pact in July 1941, a Polish army, under the command of Gen. Anders, began to be formed in Russia from Poles deported during 1939-1941, it was found that several thousand Polish officers were missing. They had been taken prisoners by the Russians in 1939 and held in the POW camps of Kozielsk, Starobielsk and Ostaszkow. Gen. Anders asked Stalin about them several times but he never got a straight reply. In April 1943 the Germans made known that outside Katyn near Smolensk they had uncovered mass graves in which lay the bodies of several thousand Polish officers. A German medical commission, working with representatives of other nations, stated that the officers had been murdered by shots in the back of the head, that the murders had been committed in the Spring of 1940, when that territory was in Russian hands, and that the officers came from the camps in Kozielsk and Ostaszkow. The commander of the Home Army, Gen. Rowecki, sent his own secret agents to Katyn and they confirmed the above. Everything pointed to a Soviet crime.

After the Russians had retaken the territory from the Germans in the second half of 1943, Stalin appointed his own commission, which placed the blame on the Germans.

During the Nuremberg trials of war criminals the Russians brought up this case, but the court did not bring in a verdict of guilty against the Germans. Details in the book *The Crime of Katyn* (Polish Cultural Foundation, London, 1965).

London Sikorski as premier and commander in chief stood head and shoulders above his rivals. But now suddenly a cruel fate bereft us of both. On June 30th, Rowecki was arrested by the Gestapo in Warsaw, and four days later Sikorski was drowned in the air disaster at Gibraltar.

V

It had been a cold, rainy night, but at dawn the sky cleared and a warm summer sun caused a light vapour to steam up from the wet streets.

Lt.-Colonel Michal Protasewicz emerged from the tube station at Victoria and made his way briskly towards the Rubens Hotel, where he was due to report to the new chief of staff, General Kopanski. It was the second fortnight in August 1943; within a week or two the third season of regular flights to Poland, known as "Riposte", would be beginning, and the general wanted to be briefed on the preparations, plans and difficulties. He had become chief of staff early in August in succession to General Klimecki, who had perished with Sikorski. The period was a difficult one not only politically, but organizationally as well. In London it had been necessary to appoint a new premier and a new commander in chief (Mikolajczyk and Sosnkowski respectively); in Poland Rowecki was succeeded as Home Army commander by General Komorowski (*Bor*), who was at that time scarely known in the West.[16])

Colonel Protasewicz had been head of the Sixth Bureau since April 1942. Today he was about to submit to his chief a new plan of action which required a quick decision and even quicker action. A few days before he had had a talk with Colonel Perkins, who had once more brought up the idea of transferring the base for the parachute operations to Italy. The allies had had a run of success in the peninsula: the southern part of the country was free; Mussolini had been arrested by order of the new head of government, Marshal Badoglio, and was interned at the top of the Gran Sasso mountain. If the flights to Poland were mounted from Italy it would increase the quantity of supplies that could be sent, and would open up the southern provinces which were inaccessible from Britain. The plan was a good one in itself, but it required a lot of organization and had the drawback that it would mean interrupting the drops for a period, including those of parachutists.

---

[16]) He was at that time second-in-command to Gen. Rowecki.

This was not the only serious problem that Protasewicz was on his way to discuss.

Since the Western allies had acquiesced in Russia's political and territorial claims, they had begun to adapt their strategic plans accordingly. In the first half of 1943 it was already on the cards that Poland would be excluded from the British theatre of war and regarded as belonging to the Russian sphere of influence.[17]) There were as yet no clear indications of this, but it could be felt that changes were in the air.

For the Poles, the basic objective was still that of a general insurrection against the Germans, without prejudice to immediate, relatively minor operations. For the British, all that mattered was to defeat Germany and end the war as soon as possible. The underground was crying out for arms, ammunition and explosives; SOE and the London Poles did their best to collect supplies and send them out as fast as they could, but the tacit condition on the British side was that they should be used at once for sabotage and guerrilla warfare.

Furthermore, as the British political leaders had accepted Russia's claim to the eastern parts of Poland, it was difficult to organize drops east of the Curzon Line.[16]) War material dropped in the east could be stored and used against anyone who might seek to wrest those territories from Poland. The British had no desire for such complications; on the other hand, they were in a position to know Polish plans and forecasts.

Hitherto the problem of flights to eastern Poland had solved itself owing to the limited range of the aircraft involved. But now that Liberators were about to be brought into use and the bases might be transferred to Italy, the conflict of views might lead to grave complications. These it was vital for the Poles to avoid. Their dependence on the West for supplies was such that any protest on their part was likely to result in less equipment being sent rather than more. Their

---

[17]) Later, in August 1943, by an Anglo-American decision, Polish territory was excluded from the allied invasion plans. The Polish political and military authorities were not informed of this.

[18]) In 1920, when the Soviet armies under Tukhaschevsky's command marched against Poland, intending to take Warsaw and set up a Communist government there, Lord Curzon, the British Foreign Secretary, in an attempt to mediate between the two combatants, proposed a demarcation line, running more or less along the present frontier of Poland and Russia. His proposal was not accepted by either side; the Bolshevicks almost reached Warsaw and there on August 15, 1920, they were routed by the Poles led by Jozef Pilsudski. The Peace Treaty of Riga gave back to Poland part of her historical territory including Lwow and Wilno.

best hope lay in maintaining a tactful attitude, backed by firmness and consistency.[19])

Apart from political difficulties there were many troublesome technical problems, but these were easier to solve thanks to SOE's undoubted readiness to help.

From the very beginning of the flights, the main obstacle had been lack of an independent air force, together with insufficiency of equipment. A Polish flight had indeed been formed within 138 Squadron, but it was never directly under the control of the Polish military authorities. Similarly, although the Squadron as a whole was used almost exclusively for SOE purposes, it never belonged to the latter's organization, large as that was, but remained under the Air Ministry. This led to endless complications, conferences, compromises and delays. SOE tried more than once to break the Air Ministry's monopoly, but the Chiefs of Staff took the view that while guerrilla warfare was important it must in the last resort take second place to global strategy.[20])

As there was no chance of the Poles obtaining a special flight under their exclusive control, the problem was approached in another way. On May 18, 1943 Sikorski, who had given much thought to it, laid down regulations which would have enabled the flight to be expanded into a squadron. Soon after Sosnkowski became Commander-in-Chief he took up this idea, and on August 18th made an official proposal to the Air Ministry for the reorganization of the flight, but was met with a refusal on two grounds. In the first place, there was still a shortage of aircraft for strategic bombing purposes. The second reason was linked with a basic weakness of the Polish military effort. In order to create a special

---

[19]) Only one instance is known of a drop being carried out to the East of the Curzon Line. On the night of April 8-9, 1944, which was Easter Eve, the 27th Infantry Division of the Home Army received two drops of containers with weapons (mostly small-arms), some anti-tank guns, ammunition, a radio station and several uniforms and pairs of boots. The division was in direct radio contact with the base in Italy and was several times informed of intended drops. The drop was carried out on a dropping zone three-fifths of a mile north of Wladynopol, near the H.Q. of the division, and one and a fifth miles north-east of Stezarzyce. The division was informed by radio that 6 aircraft were to fly over. Only 2 four-engined bombers, probably Liberators, arrived. These details are given by T. Sztumberk-Rychter, the former temporary commander of the division, in his book (in Polish) *A gunner foot-slogging*. The fact that the drops were received is confirmed by the former Chief of Staff of the division, T. Klimowski. There are no details of this operation to be found in the archives of the Sixth Bureau.

[20]) SOE's lack of independent aircraft was much felt during the preparations for the landings in N. Africa in November 1942. There was such a need for transport aircraft that even Halifaxes from 138 Squadron were taken. This had an immediate effect on flights to Poland. Between Oct. 29, 1942 and Jan. 25, 1943 not one parachutist was dropped, although the nights were the longest of the year.

flight, 301 Squadron had had to be disbanded. Where were the trained pilots, mechanics and navigators now to come from? There are no "passengers" in a modern air force: everyone is a specialist. And these were especially difficult long-range night expeditions, for which extra skill was required.

Again, it was impossible to secure any change in the rule whereby any aircrew in 138 Squadron could be directed to whatever destination seemed best on the night in question. Decisions under this rule were taken at a higher level than the Sixth Bureau or the Polish section of SOE, which always defended our interests to the best of its ability. There was some justification for the arrangement, but it did not work out to Poland's advantage. During the "Riposte" period, from August 1, 1943 to July 31, 1944, Polish crews flew 206 times to Poland and 474 times to other countries, while British crews flew to Poland only 74 times.[21])

Apart from these problems there were others of a purely internal, Polish character, but which could not be ignored. A minor one concerned the selection and training of parachutists. The Home Army commander had reported several times that, while the men sent over were admirable from the point of view of training and morale, they were not well suited to underground life. There were too many cases of carelessness, idle talk and disregard for security. Several avoidable arrests had taken place, involving a wide circle of people and jeopardizing important secrets connected with air drops and liaison with the West in general.

There were also cases of insubordination. Some parachutists refused on landing, to take orders from the reception station commanders and insisted on keeping their own weapons. Others brought with them stockings, shirts, sweaters and even small radio sets, in addition to their proper equipment. Trouble also sometimes arose over the continuance in Poland of the pay and allowances they had received in Britain.[22])

[21]) This proportion changed when assistance was being given to fighting Warsaw. It must also be remembered that the flights to Poland were the longest and the most difficult and that they required suitable weather over the whole, long route.

[22]) Each parachutist before take-off received 6 months' pay in dollar bills, or sometimes 5 or 10 gold dollars. On landing in Poland they became soldiers of the Home Army and received the same pay as the small number of officers in Poland, who devoted all their time to underground service. Some parachutists complained that they being badly done by; however, no other solution was acceptable either morally or financially. For instance: at the beginning of 1943 a lower-ranking Home Army officer in a position of command received 1,275 zlote monthly (2 lbs. of pork-fat cost 400 zlote in Warsaw at that time). Since the value of a dollar bill was round about 120 zlote, his pay was worth 10 dollars. A parachutist, with the rank of Second Lieutenant, received before take-off over 600 dollars, i.e. 100 dollars a month viz. 10 times as much.

All these problems were human and understandable, but required firm action. Any departure from the rules which had been carefully worked out increased the already considerable risk of each operation.

A more difficult Polish internal question had come to light in the past week or two. In a despatch dated August 5th, the Home Army commander had reported indications that the Polish Ministry of Home Affairs in London intended to organize drops of its own, the reception of which would be entrusted to members of the Peasants' Party. The commander took exception to this proposal, which raised delicate issues. Ever since the drops had begun, they had been dealt with in all their aspects by the military; in Britain by the Sixth Bureau in consultation with SOE, and in Poland by the Home Army command. The Polish military acted as intermediaries between their Government in London and the political side of the Polish underground, and they carried out their duties in this respect very scrupulously. The parties of trained parachutists included political couriers carrying money-belts and mail for the *Delegatura* in Warsaw. At the reception stations it sometimes happened, in the dark and haste, that sums of money got mixed up, and the political leaders complained that they were not receiving what was due to them. Many telegrams were exchanged on the subject and remedial measures taken, but some ill-feeling remained. It was known that Mikolajczyk, who was Minister of Home Affairs in Sikorski's government, had tried to secure a measure of authority over the air bases and courier routes; but so far the air dropping operations, calling as they did for special precautions and accuracy, had not been the subject of interference which might have had unfortunate consequences. Meanwhile the Home Army had succeeded in bringing under its control the Peasant Battalions which manned a majority of the reception stations, so that no further complications should have arisen at the Polish end; yet the commander was now reporting that the unity of control was being threatened.

His apprehensions may have been connected with the changes in London following Sikorski's death. Mikolajczyk's power was of course enhanced by his appointment to the premiership, and he may have sought to enhance it further by gaining control of drops into Poland.[23]

Protasewicz had belonged to Sikorski's immediate entourage,

---

[23] The commander of the Home Army, who was ready to fight to maintain the status quo, received the full support of the Commander-in-Chief. SOE too, did not want any change in the system of drops to Poland, and they remained under the exclusive control of the military authorities.

and the latter's tragic death was a great blow to him. He was operating in a difficult sector and needed every support from his superiors. Sosnkowski he hardly knew at all, Kopanski a little better, but only officially. This was the first time he had sent for Protasewicz, and for the latter much depended on securing the right atmosphere of harmony and co-operation.

The colonel paused for a moment and then walked briskly into the hotel lobby. The NCO on duty stiffened into a respectful salute.

VI

After his exploit at Pinsk, *Ponury* became at a stroke one of the foremost soldiers of the Home Army. His superiors had a high opinion of his qualities of leadership, and realized the importance of giving him a new field in which to exercise them. Administrative staff work or clandestine activity in towns were not in his line, and a return to the "Fan" organization did not come into question as it was being wound up: the Home Army command in the eastern territories had been reactivated and was taking over responsibility for sabotage in that area.

In spring 1943 partisan units were taking on increasing importance, and it was felt that they would provide scope for the warlike young parachutist. The Zamosc area south-east of Warsaw was considered, but the choice fell on the Radom-Kielce district to the south, which was *Ponury's* home ground and where the terrain was more suitable for forest troops. He set out from Warsaw in April with a small team including *Czarka* and *Motor*, his comrades in the Pinsk episode. They were not first in the field, as another parachutist named Captain *Nurt* (Current) had been operating in the area since the previous December, when he was sent there as district chief of staff of a body known as ZO — (*Zwiazek Odwetu*[24]) — the Reprisal Organization). When this was dissolved, *Nurt* was appointed to the Home Army's Diversion and Sabotage Command, known in Polish as "Kedyw", and set about organizing and expanding the partisan forces that had sprung up in the area, some of them independently of the Home Army.

Nurt and *Ponury* were of the same rank and had trained

---

[24] This was a sabotage organization formed by the commander of ZWZ, General Rowecki, in April 1940 and, for security reasons, enjoyed a considerable degree of independence. Its headquarters were in Warsaw and there were sections in the country, attached to each district. At the beginning of 1943 ZO was disbanded and its functions taken over by "Kedyw". Attacks on lines of communication, industrial targets and the German police were then renewed.

together in Britain, but *Ponury* had come to Poland some time earlier and had had much guerrilla experience including the Pinsk raid. He was therefore chosen as "Kedyw" commander for the district. *Nurt* willingly accepted the role of second in command, and they set to work together.

Of the several units already operating in the district, the largest, numbering nearly a hundred men, was led by a lieutenant in the reserve known as *Grot*. However, complications arose which led him to withdraw, yielding his command to *Ponury*. Thus, within a few days of arriving in the area and after reporting to Colonel *Daniel*, the Home Army district commander, *Ponury* found himself at the head of a large and fairly well armed forest unit.

He then showed fully what he was made of. Any fit man can be a regular soldier, but one has to be born a guerrilla fighter. Much has been written in the way of reminiscences, instructions and manuals of partisan warfare and sabotage carried on by small clandestine units, but no-one has yet caught the full essence of this highly specialized branch of the military art, or defined the exact qualities needed for success in it.

From the moment *Ponury* became a denizen of the forests, he behaved as if he had been one all his life. His unit had more than one exploit to its credit, but as soon as he took command it was as if transformed.

Ponury's project was the ambitious one of combining all the units operating in the district into a single force capable of undertaking military actions of more than minor significance. It was undulating, well-wooded country, which became wilder as one approached the Holy Cross Mountains, and, most important of all, the population was entirely Polish. It was only in such an area that irregular troops could maintain themselves and go on fighting, thanks to the absolute support they received from the surrounding villages, which gave them food, supplied their sons as recruits, sheltered them in the depths of winter and, not least, acted as a local intelligence service.

Apart from the unit which had been under *Grot's* command, there were several other armed groups which it would be worth while uniting in a single force. Sub-Lieutenant *Jacek*, an inspector of the Home Army sub-area at Bodzentyn, was in charge of 30 men and a radio station; Lieutenant *Jurek* had another 30; Lieutenant *Robot*, who had been parachuted into Poland together with *Nurt*, commanded 50, and a certain *Oset* (Thistle) had 60. Then there was Lieutenant *Habdank* of the NSZ,[25]) a good soldier with 30 men under his command,

---

[25]) NSZ — *Narodowe Siły Zbrojne* (National Armed Forces): units organized by extreme nationalist political group.

and a warrant officer named *Szort* of NOW [26]) with 20, well armed. In addition 20 Georgians were in hiding in the forest, having deserted from General Vlasov's [27]) force, and were thirsting for revenge upon the Germans. Last but not least, some of the "Jedrusie" (Andrew boys) [28]) were active in the vicinity, but they were not under Home Army orders at this period and kept themselves very much apart.

In all, eight units were operating independently in a fairly small area of the woods. *Robot* set up his headquarters on a well-covered hill named Kamen, and *Ponury* on a similar piece of high ground named Wykus. This site had been discovered by *Nurt*, and was so remote and convenient that the other commanders made their way to it and took up their quarters near by. This fact helped *Ponury* to assert his authority, and before long he had come to terms with his neighbours: *Habdank* and *Szort* joined the Home Army and the others too recognized *Ponury* as their chief, while remaining in control of their respective forces.

The new combined force assembled for the first time on the Wykus hill at the end of May. Arms and equipment, especially boots, were inspected, plans for raids in the immediate future were discussed and thought was given to longer-term problems of organization. The force at present numbered some 300 men, but it could easily be doubled if the necessary arms could be secured by attacks on German outposts. *Ponury* was confident of being able to expand his force, and realized that it would need to provide itself with transport. He decided to divide it into three parts to facilitate camping and occasional raids, without impairing its ability to combine for larger operations.

The reorganization into three sub-groups took place in the course of June 1943. The first was under *Nurt's* command. As it was high summer, recruits came flocking in, and his force numbered over 200 men in four companies commanded

---

[26]) NOW — *Narodowa Organizacja Wojskowa* (National Military Organization): units belonging to the National Party.

[27]) The Soviet General Andrey Vlasov (born in 1900) was taken prisoner by the Germans in 1942, went over to their side and undertook to rise an army from Soviet prisoners-of-war. Some of these enlisted of their own free will, others were driven by starvation and ill-treatment. At its peak this army numbered several hundred thousand. The Germans used it for auxiliary services and to fight partisans. Vlasov's men usually distinguished themselves by great cruelty and were noted for looting. Towards the end of the war he was taken prisoner by the Americans and handed over to the Russians. After a short trial he was hanged in Moscow in 1946.

[28]) "Jedrusie" — a famous partisan unit which grew out of a clandestine group formed in the autumn of 1939 in Tarnobrzeg (southern Poland) by a student Wladyslaw Jasinski (*Jedrus*).

respectively by *Grot, Jurek, Szort* and *Habdank,* together with a cavalry patrol under one *Tarzan.* They bivouacked on Wykus, where they built substantial sheds to house a field-kitchen and other necessary installations.

The second sub-group was commanded by *Robot* and had on its staff two more parachutists, *Czarka* and *Rafal.* It comprised over 100 men and took up its quarters in the Konecki forest. The third, in the Holy Cross Mountains, was under Second Lieutenant *Marianski* and consisted of some 150 men including the Georgians.

After the reorganization *Ponury* once more concentrated his troops and carried out manoeuvres, planned by *Nurt* and *Robot.* They had by now captured some quantities of German arms,[29]) and the forest troops were a force of which any district commander might have been proud. Colonel *Daniel* was in fact delighted with them, but his pleasure was mingled with faint doubts which grew with the passage of time.

A guerrilla force of 500-odd men naturally stood in need of maintenance. It could provide itself with arms at the enemy's expense, but it also needed boots, uniforms, linen, food and medicines. However, the district command received money from Warsaw and could obtain a good many things locally. Supply problems are common enough and the commander was not unduly exercised by them; his worries were of a different nature.

When *Ponury* reported to Colonel *Daniel* in April, the latter at once recognized his soldierly qualities, which he already knew by repute. It was at this time that "Kedyw" was being set up with the task of intensifying subversive action of all kinds. The colonel appreciated the need for this and realized that the fortunes of war were turning finally against the Germans. But his mind was occupied not only by qestions of troops, rifles and bombs but by the thought of towns and villages and the sufferings and sacrifices of the civil population. He was proud of *Ponury's* achievement in building up a guerrilla force in so short a time, but he was disturbed by the price that the surrounding villages had had to pay for its activity. He remembered the fearful reprisals that the Germans had exacted for the raids carried out by Major *Hubal's* force in the same area. Certainly activities were necessary, but must they be waged on such a scale, amounting almost to open warfare?

---

[29]) Only a small part consisted of stocks buried during the September campaign and later dug up. At this period the area covered by drops did not include the southern districts, and what was received in the neighbourhood of Warsaw was generally sent to "Fan" or, after the latter's dispersal, to points nearer the capital. *Ponury's* partisans only received a few English hand-grenades, a few Sten guns and later a radio station transmitter.

Ponury had been earmarked as the district commander of "Kedyw" and had been supposed to operate in an underground fashion, making use of the forest detachments but not expanding them prematurely. But in practice things had turned out otherwise. A first-class soldier and born guerrilla leader, he had in a few short months created a formation that would have done credit to a regular army. Its mere existence might well provoke the Germans to reprisals, since it is well known that partisans cannot live without the support of the local population.

Thus two conflicting points of view arose. The first, based on age, experience and deliberation, was in favour of caution and avoiding undue bloodshed and destruction of property: the time for open warfare, it was felt, had not yet arrived. The adherents of the second view, full of youthful energy and fighting spirit, were for an immediate onslaught on the Germans. They argued further that it was possible so to frighten the latter that they would be deterred from acts of repression.[30])

As yet, this conflict of views did not manifest itself in drastic form, by insubordination or the vetoing of activities. The dilemma was to be resolved by events themselves.

After a series of minor raids, chiefly for the purpose of capturing arms, and after reorganization as already described, *Ponury's* forces began to embark on larger activities.

On the night of July 2/3rd, they occupied a railway halt at Laczna near Suchedniow and, by changing the signals, stopped the Warsaw - Cracow express, the passengers on which were mostly Germans. Without firing a shot and without casualties they occupied each carriage in turn and collected several dozen small arms, after which they waited for the express in the reverse direction which passed through the station a few minutes later. They stopped it in the same way, but this time shots were exchanged with the armed guard of a mail van. A few of the raiders were wounded, but again they were able to capture some dozens of pistols and also rifles, amunition and money. After blowing up the engines and station building they withdrew, leaving behind them the corpses of several guards.

The Germans retaliated in bloodthirsty fashion. They surrounded the village of Michniow, set fire to it and murdered

---

[30]) In judging this matter one should ignore outside suggestions and pressures and think only of one's own nation. The Soviet partisans and parachutists who were dropped to carry out diversionary work on Polish territory did not care if, as a result of their activities, Polish villages were set ablaze and the inhabitants murdered. Their orders were based on the political principles of Soviet Russia: to weaken the national element in our country so as to subdue it more easily.

the inhabitants. Over two hundred innocent people perished, and only a few young men succeeded in escaping.

Ponury's response was to order *Nurt's* force to attack a German leave train. On July 12/13th the very next night after the destruction of Michniow, the partisans changed the signals at Ogonow station, held up a passenger train bound from Cracow to Warsaw and full of soldiers returning from furlough, and opened fire on it with sub-machine guns. The Germans, who were front-line troops and knew their business, took cover under the carriages and did their best to repel the attack, but in view of the surprise they had little chance. Nearly two hundred of them were killed, including a general and numerous other officers. The partisans destroyed the engine with bombs and blocked the track. Five of their number were wounded, including *Czarka* and a Second Lieutenant *Witek*.

German retaliation once more fell on the bleeding countryside, though less heavily than might have been expected. The gendarmerie returned to Michniow and burnt all the farms that were still standing.

Colonel *Daniel* attempted to summon *Ponury*, but there was no time to discuss the incidents, as the infuriated Germans had determined to crush the guerrillas once and for all. On July 17th, a large force of gendarmes appeared at Skarzysko, accompanied by members of Vlasov's army and an anti-guerrilla force from Radom. A few days later they were joined by A. A. units summoned in haste from Kielce, Ostrowiec, Starachowice and Wloszczowa. The total force amounted to over 4,000 well-armed regular troops.

The round-up operation began on the 19th. The Germans evidently knew that *Ponury* had concentrated his entire force on Wykus, since they advanced from the north directly towards it. They hoped to achieve surprise — naively, since the partisans had eyes and ears in every village. On the same morning, as soon as the grey-green uniforms began to advance, messengers brought word of the direction in which they were moving.

Knowing how far off they were, *Ponury* waited till afternoon before sending *Szort* with 30 men to the south-east to reconnoitre an area to which the whole formation might retreat. After dark, the main body set out. Over 400 men laden with arms, with a score of vehicles under the command of Lieutenant *Motor*, moved off as noiselessly as possible by way of thickets and forest paths. At dawn they reached the edge of the woods and pitched camp near a foresters hut. No-one struck a light and no cooking was allowed. They lay down in their tracks and slept, guarded by sentries.

At twilight they set out again, crossed a river and a railway line and reached the great Starachowice forest. This was a different place from the secluded retreat on Wykus. Its fine, perpendicular trees, broad clearings and avenues were no doubt a forester's dream, but to partisans they meant a threat of being discovered and surrounded. The men redoubled their vigilance.

After camping near a forester's cottage at Klepacze they turned north towards Ilza. Despite the long march and the men's fatigue *Ponury* intended to raid the gendarmerie post there; but while they were still in the forest the leading platoon under *Robot* was attacked by some German infantry and a skirmish took place. *Ponury* sent *Jurek* with his men to the rescue and withdrew with the rest of his forces into the depths of the woods.

There followed a series of arduous marches, in the course of which they fell upon fresh bands of Germans so constantly that it was hard not to believe that someone was betraying their movements. It came on to rain, and they began to flounder in mud as they wandered through the trackless undergrowth. The carts had to be abandoned and their loads transferred to the backs of men and horses. At last they reached the outskirts of the forest and could go no further. Dawn was breaking, the men were asleep on their feet and the horses were stumbling. *Ponury* ordered a rest in a coppice of young trees. They had run out of food, but had managed to obtain some precious water.

At nightfall they set off once more, crossed the Skarzysko-Szydlowiec railway line and finally shook off their pursuers. The men desperately needed food and rest, as *Ponury* well knew, but he also knew German psychology. Before finally withdrawing and allowing his troops to relax, he organized an ambush on the Skarzysko - Szydlowiec main road and, in broad daylight, held up several cars and relieved their passengers of arms, ammunition and uniforms. This done, he led his men back to the Osieczyn forest which they had left two weeks before, and ordered a spell of inactivity which lasted until August 8th.

After this escape from the German round-up, the young commander's fame spread far and wide. Every local village and settlement knew his name, and though the inhabitants were exposed to the invaders' wrath they regarded him with respect and pride, while the Germans themselves felt fear and admiration.

Colonel *Daniel* knew this, but he also knew of the burning of villages, murder of whole families and hanging of hostages, and his concern for the district entrusted to his care increased. He sent for *Ponury* and made him agree to leave his troops in the forest and go underground in order to direct "Kedyw" activities. The partisan unit was to remain in being but was not to accept further volunteers or provoke the Germans at this stage.

Ponury obeyed with reluctance and set about his new duties with indifferent success. He engaged in the production of Sten guns at which he had tried his hand earlier, picked candidates for minor acts of sabotage and took pains instructing them, but his mind and heart were with his forest comrades. He continued to plan operations, knowing that a partisan cannot bear to sit idle; he rejoiced in their successes and did his best to supply their various needs. Finally he could bear it no longer and rejoined them, concentrating his forces on Wykus as before.

It was the second fortnight in October, and mist lay over the fields and forest tracks. Although the men observed every precaution they could think of, the Germans had evidently got wind of their activity, for they at once organized another large round-up. This time, in addition to several thousand troops, they used reconnaissance aircraft.

The partisans were warned in time, but the enemy showed more boldness than usual. Contrary to their custom, the Germans entered the forest and scaled the Wykus hill. There was heavy fighting in which forty of *Ponury's* men were killed, but the rest managed to break away and escaped into the forest under cover of night. The Germans took possession of the encampment and destroyed the sheds and other installations. They then pursued the retreating partisans for three days and nights, during which the latter kept to the wildest parts of the forest in order to avoid contact and break out of the ring that was closing in on them. At Lysica they ran into the Germans and there were killed and wounded on both sides, but in the end the German attempt at encirclement failed.

When it was clear that the baffled and exhausted pursuers were resigned to defeat, *Ponury* led his men back by a roundabout way to the Osieczyn forest and set up a camp in which they could rest and recover.[31])

The men slept, but their commander was not in the mood for rest. After the second big round-up, from which they

---

[31]) Just at that time, when the unit was taking a well-earned rest, news came that the first drops in this area were expected and that the unit was to prepare dropping zones. This was done, but the drops did not take place, as flights were halted owing to the transfer of the base from Britain to Brindisi. It was not till the beginning of April 1944 that the soldiers of the Radom-Kielce district welcomed the first parachutists and picked up the first containers. In these parts the dropping zones were called "hampers".

had escaped as if by a miracle, it was quite clear that there must be a traitor among them who had kept in secret touch with the Germans. *Ponury* racked his brains and struggled with conflicting feelings. It was hard to have to suspect one of his senior companions, perhaps a friend; but the facts left no doubt that the informer must be someone in a responsible position, almost certainly an officer. He mentally reviewed the appearance, code-names and duties of his immediate followers. One of these men — hardened in battle, aware of what was at stake in the war, trusted without reserve by the lads under his command — was at that very moment their deadliest enemy.

As dawn broke, *Ponury* called a sentry and ordered him to fetch Captain *Nurt*, the second in command. The two senior officers talked the matter over for a long time.[32]

The partisans had once again eluded the enemy's snare, but they could not prevent the Germans from taking vengeance. A fresh wave of arrests, punishments and executions fell upon the neighbouring villages. *Ponury* was ill at ease, knowing that the district commander would hold him to blame for what had happened. For himself he believed in harrying the enemy without regard for consequences, but he knew that others disagreed and that he must take account of their views. His own impetuous temperament and brilliant qualities as an officer urged him forward regardless of obstacles; but the conditions of forest warfare, in which his followers' lives were his to dispose of, had weakened his sense of proportion and of discipline.

The Colonel for his part was in a difficult position. He could no longer shut his eyes to *Ponury's* insubordination, or there was no knowing what might happen. He knew that things could not go on as they were, but a false step might deprive him of an almost irreplaceable officer. With a heavy

---

[32]) The traitor turned out to be *Motor* (Jerzy Wojnowski) a lieutenant in the reserve, who had taken part in the Pinsk operation and been decorated with the Cross of Valour. *Ponury*, who trusted him completely, had taken him to the Radom-Kielce district and later brought him into the partisans. For a long time no-one had the slightest suspicion of him. It was only after the October raids that he was put under observation. *Ponury* refused for some time to believe the accusations brought against him. Apparently he was seen on Wykus in the company of some Germans who had climbed there to destroy the camp. Later, after *Robot's* death and *Czarka's* arrest, the head of "Kedyw", Colonel *Nil*, began to watch him. The evidence collected was sent to the Special Military Court which pronounced sentence of death. This was carried out on January 28, 1944 by *Nurt's* orders, after *Ponury's* departure. During the interrogation before his execution *Motor* confessed. The cause of his collaboration probably was that his mother had been arrested in Warsaw in March 1943 and he was being blackmailed by the Gestapo.

heart, but hoping that the situation might somehow change of its own accord, he decided not to give a direct order but to apply pressure by ignoring the young officer and withholding supplies of money and equipment. It was now November, and the partisans, with their boots in holes and no greatcoats for the winter, were encamped in sheds on the Holy Cross Mountains. The villages would have given them shelter, but this would have brought on fresh reprisals. *Ponury* fought against the situation and tried to contact the district command; he then went to Warsaw, ordered a partial demobilization of his forces, and appointed *Czarka* to remain in the capital and organize a supply base for the formation. But all this came too late. On the same day in January 1944 on which *Czarka* set out from Warsaw with a huge lorry laden with tons of supplies, *Ponury* received an order from General *Bor*, the Home Army C-in-C, relieving him of his command and ordering him to report to the capital.

On a dark, frosty afternoon in February, after settling one or two urgent matters, the young officer embraced *Nurt*, who was taking over from him, took leave of the rest of his staff and made his way alone to the railway station.

VII

Adolf Pilch was twenty-four years old when the war broke out. He was born at Wisla in Polish Silesia but educated in Warsaw, where he attended the Wawelberg technical college. He also did his military service in Warsaw, and was a corporal in the officer cadet corps when mobilization came.. By some mistake, due probably to his change of residence, he failed to receive his call-up papers. Feeling injured and disappointed he made his way towards eastern Poland, as did many other men in his situation,[33]) but turned back after reaching the Bug river which was the frontier of the Soviet occupation zone. Finding that Warsaw was under siege and there was no way of getting into the city, he returned to his native Silesia.

For a few weeks life there was tolerable, but the Germans then annexed Wisla to the Reich and began to deport young men for forced labour. Pilch talked matters over with his friends and decided that it was time to leave. Before Christmas a small group of them left for Hungary, and after the usual adventures arrived in Budapest on New Year's Day. With the help of the Polish Legation they moved on to Yugoslavia and thence by sea to Marseilles.

In France Pilch was again out of luck, as he was assigned

---

[33]) Orders were issued that all men capable of bearing arms, who had not been mobilised, were to make their way to the East.

to the 3rd Division, which failed to complete its organization and was not sent to the front. When the German invasion came, he and a few companions boarded a British destroyer at the small Breton port of Le Croisic and were taken to Plymouth.

In Britain he shared the fortunes of thousands of other young Polish soldiers: a longish wait in camp, a new style of uniform, his first appointment and training, and the gradual return to normal military life. He was tired of all these preparations and wanted to get to grips with the enemy, so he was overjoyed when he heard that volunteers were being accepted for special service in Poland. He sent his name in, was duly chosen and could at last look forward to training with some object in view.

However, Fate again interposed delays. After attending several courses and practice jumps he was sent back for further training, and the day of take-off seemed as remote as ever. When he finally reached the holding station in October 1942 he still wore the stripes of an officer cadet — his superiors evidently held no very high opinion of his military abilities.

It could surely now be only a week or two before he was called on to fly — but a fresh difficulty arose. The invasion of North Africa was being prepared, and all transport aircraft were requisitioned. 138 Squadron had to lend its Halifaxes, which put an end to all flights and jumps for the present. Pilch fretted his heart out as winter drew on — he had now been waiting nearly five months.

At last, on the night of February 16/17, 1943, he took off for Poland with three companions, jumped from the plane and felt the jerk of his parachute as it unfolded. The jump was not a fortunate one, as one of the group was killed on landing and Pilch and another were dropped far beyond the dropping zone. However, they found it next day, handed over their arms and money-belts and set out light-heartedly for Warsaw. At last they were on their native soil and could expect to see some action.

Incredible as it might seem, there was now a further hitch. Pilch had begun his period of "acclimatization"— he was quite prepared for this delay, irksome as it was — when, about three weeks after their landing, it turned out that all the official and private funds which the group had brought with them had gone astray between the reception centre and Warsaw. An inquiry was held, which meant that he had to stay in Warsaw for another five months. His long wait at the holding station near London seemed idyllic by comparison. Here he was in occupied Poland with German soldiers all around him, and yet he was obliged to go on counting the weeks in a state of almost complete idleness. True, he was given the task of lecturing to the secret military college about the Polish forces in the West and the organization of British armoured units, but was it for this that he had been parachuted into Poland?

At the end of August, 1943, four full years after the first German bombs were dropped, he at last found himself boarding a train for Baranowicze in the north-east. He had been appointed to the inspectorate of the Nowogrodek district of the Home Army, and his training in sabotage was expected to be of use to the local partisans.

When he arrived he found that a fellow-parachutist, 2nd-Lieutenant Rybka, was second in command of the Stolpce area. He reported to the district commander, made appropriate local contact and in a few days was sent to Lake Kroman in the Naliboki forest, near a village named Niescierowicze. Here the remains of the Stolpce partisan battalion were encamped, having been dispersed by the Germans in a recent round-up. Among the survivors were two parachutists, 2nd-Lieutenants *Grom* and *Ikwa*. Pilch, whose code-name was *Gora* (Mountain)), took command of the forty demoralized and almost unarmed men in the hope of reconstituting the routed battalion.

It soon appeared that the new leader, who had only been promoted Second Lieutenant on the strength of his successful jump, was completely at home in the forest and had no difficulty in handling the partisans and gaining their confidence. This calm, almost phlegmatic Pole from the borders of Germany, who spoke with a hard western accent and had never been in the eastern part of the country, got on splendidly with the local youths, who in turn made excellent soldiers. Calm, good-humoured and disciplined, never giving way to panic, always ready to carry out an order, respecting and trusting their superiors, they would never let down a leader who deserved their confidence. *Gora* was eminently such a leader, and relations could not have been better.

Within two months the bunch of demoralized ragamuffins had become soldiers again, and their commander had seen to it that they all had boots, uniforms and enough to eat. The group now numbered 400 men, divided into two infantry companies, a cavalry squadron and a small commissariat; however, there were as yet sufficient arms only for the cavalry and one of the two companies.[34]

---

[34]) The north-east areas of Poland never did receive any drops; transport from Warsaw was exceptionally difficult and in practice was restricted to explosives for "Fan", so the partisans had to manage as best they could. The first Home Army partisan unit, commanded by 2nd-Lieutenant *Dzwig*, was mostly equipped with Soviet arms, thrown away in panic by the Red Army and hidden in the villages. After *Gora's* arrival there was a preponderance of captured German arms.

While engaged in building up his forces *Gora* had also been acquainting himself with local conditions. As a result of questioning officers and men he had come to the conclusion that while the Germans were still formidable and might organize a large-scale round-up at any time, the partisans were exposed to an equal if not greater danger in the shape of Soviet forest units. There were many of these, each numbering several hundred well-armed soldiers to whom supplies were regularly dropped: they even had an airfield of their own, a clearing in the Naliboki forest on which small planes could land. Evidently these units were there for some important purpose, as they were so well looked after, yet they did not seem especially eager to fight the Germans. Every now and then they received visits by air from General Ponomarenko, the commander-in-chief of Soviet partisan units.

Although the purpose of the Soviet forces had at first been concealed, it was by now well known to the local population, who were to be its chief victims. The Russians regarded eastern Poland as their own property, and were doing their best to reassert possession of it before the Germans withdrew. The Polish element in the population was the main obstacle in their path, and they therefore sought pretexts to attack Polish villages and townships and murder the inhabitants. The usual technique for doing this was to demand large quotas of food and recruits for the Soviet forces and, if the locals hung back, to surround their villages, set fire to them and slaughter the male population. This happened to the small town of Naliboki in May 1943, when 120 Poles were murdered by partisans under Major Vasilevich. Earlier, Derewno and the village of Rubiezewicze were destroyed in the same fashion.

These murderous attacks appear all the more flagrant when it is recalled that the population of this very area had helped the fleeing soldiers of General Popov's army in 1941, when the Red divisions were broken by the German onslaught and the survivors dispersed over the countryside. It was from these soldiers, sheltered and fed by Polish villagers, that the partisan units were later formed, under the leadership of parachutists and commissars from the defeated armies who had escaped German hands. Irrespective of size the Soviets termed each of these units a "brigade".

The Polish partisans, whose sole concern was to fight the Germans and protect the population from banditry, did their best to achieve co-operation with the Russians, and *Gora* was no exception. He made contact with General *Dubov*,[35]) the commander of the combined Soviet brigades in his area, for the purpose of concerting attacks on German units and outposts. Russian officers paid frequent visits to the Stolpce formation; they made friendly gestures and promises of joint action, and took a close interest in the unit's arms, uniforms and supplies.

Despite their outwardly correct behaviour, the lack of good faith was manifest. Neighbourly relations might at any moment be superseded by guile and treachery. While still avoiding directly hostile action, the Russians sought to entice individuals from their allegiance. Warrant Officer *Noc*, in command of a cavalry troop, was offered the rank of a major if he would join the Bolsheviks, while his deputy, Sergeant *Dab*, was offered a captain's rank provided he would first shoot his commander. Attempts such as these were unsuccessful, but the Poles knew about them and mutual distrust increased rapidly.

A crucial moment occurred on November 11th, the anniversary of Poland's independence in 1918. Major *Waclaw*, who had taken over the unit at the end of October, *Gora* remaining as second in command, organized a celebration at Derewno, which had been partially rebuilt. Cover patrols were posted round about the town and many civilians were invited, together with the Soviet partisans. During the ceremonies Second Lieutenant *Swir*, the Home Army area commander, made a speech in which he declared that the Polish partisans were fighting for their native soil and that Poland would not cede an inch of it to anyone.

From then on the tension grew more acute. The Stolpce group planned an attack on the German strongpoint at Starzyna, where there were large quantities of arms, but the Soviet unit under Kurbanov refused. Other proposals for joint action and mutual support likewise came to nothing.

Towards the end of November a Soviet patrol brought the Polish command a letter from General *Dubov* inviting Major *Waclaw* and his officers to a war council on the 30th. *Waclaw* did not feel able to refuse, but he asked that the talks should be postponed till December 1st, as most of his officers were scattered about the countryside and it would take time to get them back.

Gora was deeply anxious. He knew the Bolsheviks by now and did not trust them, and the idea of all the Polish officers attending a meeting at the Red partisan headquarters struck

---

[35]) He was called Sidoruk, and during the Soviet occupation of eastern Poland was head of the NKVD in Iwieniec. There was not a single Polish family in the region that did not have cause to remember the part he played in the deportations to Russia.

him as most dangerous. He told the Major so, and persuaded him that he himself as second in command should remain in the camp together with some junior officers.

Early in the morning of December 1st, while it was still dark, *Waclaw* rode off with four other officers and an escort of eleven lancers. The Soviet camp was about twelve miles away. The Poles were still asleep; they numbered at most eighty men, as the second company was encamped at a distance of about a mile, while the first company and nearly all the cavalry were on operations in the surrounding country. Only *Gora* had got up to see his commander off.

About an hour later, a sentry appeared and reported that a Soviet patrol had arrived and was asking to see the officer in command. *Gora* stepped out of his dugout, saw a group of partisans and at the same time heard the tramp of several dozen feet. The Russians were advancing six abreast, with their automatic guns at the ready. Their leader was the same Major Vasilevich who had burnt Naliboki and murdered its inhabitants. Beside him stood Lieutenant *Lewald*, who had been in the group accompanying *Waclaw* and was now a prisoner.

Without losing a moment, *Gora* ordered the nearest Polish partisan to run off to the second company, commanded by Lieutenant *Grom*, and warn it of the danger. Then he jumped to one side and, under cover of some trees followed in the messenger's tracks. They arrived breathless, and *Grom* at once assembled his full company, together with twenty Home Army partisans from Molodeczno under Lieutenant *Maly*, who had been sharing their quarters.

Gora explained the situation and put forward two possibilities: they could either leave the camp at once, retreat into the forest and look for a safer place, or they could go to the main camp and try to rescue their comrades. They all chose the latter course, and the men set out in two columns. Unfortunately their arms left much to be desired.

They approached the camp and stood among the trees. In a clearing they saw their disarmed comrades, and in front of them a group of Soviet partisans with guns at the ready. Further off, a pair of machine guns were trained on the Polish ranks.

They hesitated for a few moments, wondering what to do. Vasilevich caught sight of them and threatened that if they used their arms he would open fire on their comrades.

It was hopeless to attempt a fight, and on *Gora's* orders all those of the second company who could do so escaped into the forest. Before doing so they saw the Russians battering their way into the huts and destroying them after removing everything of value.

A small party, including *Gora* himself, managed to escape from the surrounded camp, elude the sentries and set out across country, avoiding the roads, which were blocked by Soviet patrols. The temperature was below freezing-point, but the boggy ground gave no proper foothold. They sank up to their knees, fell repeatedly and crawled along in the muddy snow. After seven hours in which they covered less than three miles, they emerged at last on to firm ground. Here they came across some shanties inhabited by wretched folk who had been driven from their homes by war and who, though in dire misery, shared what food they had with the partisans.

It was already night when they came to the first village of unburnt houses, a place named Brodek. Here *Gora* learnt what had happened to the first company, which had been stationed for some days in half-destroyed Derewno. That morning they had been suddenly attacked by a Soviet partisan brigade, who shot ten of their number and led the remainder off into the forest.

A few days later *Gora's* party came upon Warrant Officer *Noc*, the commander of the cavalry squadron, who had been in the countryside with a patrol: he had escaped the Russians and was collecting all the dispersed partisans whom he could find.

Thus *Gora* had to face once more the strenuous task of rebuilding his shattered unit.[36])

VIII

In September 1943, 301 Flight received the long-promised three Liberators, adapted for night sorties by the fitting of silencers to their exhausts. A few other minor alterations had to be made, which held up their use for some weeks. At

---

[36]) This group was the first Polish partisan unit to be broken up as the result of a secret order given on November 30, 1943 by Colonel Gulewicz, commander of the Soviet partisan brigade "Stalin". The order was countersigned by the brigade's commissar, Lt.-Colonel Karpow.

It ran: "...at 7 a.m. on Dec. 1st Polish legionaries ("partisans") are to be disarmed. Their arms and papers are to be confiscated and the men and the arms are to be sent to the Polish camp Milaszewski near the village of Nestorowicze, in the Iwieniecki district. If the "partisans" offer any resistance while being disarmed they are to be shot out of hand..."

This order, found on a dead commissar, was sent to London by the commander of the Home Army on March 4, 1944, in an intelligence report, No. 93, incorporated in coded despatch No. 505.

Major *Waclaw* with his officers was arrested in an ambush a few miles away from the unit. They were taken to the Soviet camp and later sent to Moscow from an airstrip in the forest. They ended up in the Lubianka prison. Many years later some of them returned to Poland.

last they were in service, two being available at any given time[37]) This was a big step forward.

In the second half of October two Liberator flights to Poland were made by route 2, over southern Sweden. The journey was a long one, about 1,100 miles each way, and the flights took 14½ and 16 hours respectively. Once more, the planes only just struggled back on their last drops of fuel.

In these circumstances discussions were pushed on and the British authorities decided to transfer the base to Italy. The first party left, with equipment, at the end of October under Captain Oranowski, the temporary Polish commander of the new base. This was set up at Brindisi in the heel of Italy, 280 miles south-east of Rome, and was known to the Poles as Base No. 11. Their headquarters were close by at Latiano.

The British commander of the base, appointed by SOE, was Lt.-Colonel Threlfall, assisted by Majors Klauber, Morgan and Truszkowski.[38]) The British name for the base was Force 139 with their headquarters at Monopoli. Threlfall also commanded the Czech dropping operations.

The move resulted in a complicated administrative situation. The Polish personnel at the base were under the orders of the Sixth Bureau in London, which as a part of the General Staff was an executive instrument in the hands of the Commander-in-Chief; the latter was answerable to the President and the Polish Government. In course of time the Polish Second Corps in Italy also acquired a measure of authority over the base. At the same time, the Polish command at the base naturally had to act in concert with Lt.-Colonel Threlfall, who was under the direct orders of the Polish section of SOE in London for questions of policy but for administration was also subordinate to General Stowell, the chief SOE representative in Italy. He in turn came under SOE headquarters in London, but was also subject to the orders of General Maitland-Wilson, the Supreme Allied Commander in the Mediterranean. In addition, all flights to Poland came under the authority of Air Marshal Slessor, the RAF Commander-in-Chief for the Mediterranean and Middle East, who was responsible to the Air Staff in London and partly to General Maitland-Wilson.

This intricate set-up demanded great tact and patience, but fortunately harmonious co-operation was achieved.

The organization of the base proceeded during November as more personnel and equipment arrived. In January 1944

---

[37]) Even in normal peace-time conditions, without losses or war time damage, one third of the aircraft are out of service at any given time.

[38]) An Englishman of Polish descent, fluent in Polish. His brother Adam, who has just died, spoke Polish and English without any accent. He spent the war in Poland and took part in the Warsaw Rising.

the Polish command was taken over by Major Jan Jazwinski, whose place in London was taken by Captain Jan Podoski. At this time S section was reorganized and divided into three sub-sections dealing respectively with transport, equipment and the organization of sorties.

The transfer of the base entailed the move of various associated services. The recruiting of parachutists had already been partially taken over by the Middle East command and the Second Corps, and from now on was almost entirely conducted locally. Courses were organized in Italy to avoid moving personnel about unnecessarily, and equipment depots and two holding stations were set up. Wireless liaison with Poland was improved by means of a third station at Mesagne near Brindisi (the other two Polish stations were near London), dealing almost exclusively with parachute drops. This formed part of the base and was commanded by Captain Andrzej Iwanicki; it also comprised a radio-telegraphic transmitter station.

The problem of aircraft was also affected by the transfer. The Polish Flight 301 was withdrawn from 138 Special Duties Squadron and moved southward on November 4th, still under the command of Squadron-Leader S. Krol. As there was not yet room for it at Brindisi airfield it was sent to Tunis. The Air Ministry re-titled it No. 1586 Flight, attached to 334 Special Duties Wing, but in Polish usage it kept its number 301.

The move to Tunis was of course strictly temporary, as the distance from there to Poland is greater than from Britain. On a single night three Liberators left for southern Poland with supplies only and were just able to carry out their mission. Owing to bad weather further flights from Tunis proved out of the question.

Also in December, a British flight which belonged to 138 Squadron and had been temporarily posted to Brindisi attempted several sorties to Poland, but without success: in each case the planes had to turn back. At the beginning of January 1944 this flight returned to Britain and was replaced by the Polish one from Tunis, where the small Polish operational station was disbanded.

At this time the crew establishment for the Flight was brought up to six plus four, though unfortunately these figures, like those for technical staff, were never quite reached in practice.[39]) The number of aircraft varied, but never exceeded ten, including the three Liberators.

[39]) It must also be remembered that as a rule crew trained to fly on Halifaxes could not fly on Liberators without extra training. This caused further complications and made it difficult to change round flying personnel, always in short supply.

Once the transfer to Italy was decided on, flights from Britain ceased and no further use was made of routes 1 and 2 across Denmark and southern Sweden respectively. Instead, three new routes led from Brindisi to southern Poland or a little further.

Route 3 crossed Lake Balaton in Hungary, passed westward of Budapest and over the Tatra mountains. The distance to Cracow was a little over 600 miles, to Warsaw nearly 900. This was the best and most popular route, but had to be abandoned in April 1944 because, as the European front moved westward, the Germans concentrated large anti-aircraft forces and numerous fighters in the Budapest - Balaton area.

Route 4, slightly further east, led via Kotor in Yugoslavia, passed to the east of Budapest and entered Poland east of the Tatras. Its length was similar to that of route 3.

Route 5, still further east, led directly to Lwow, a distance of 684 miles, via Durazzo (Durres) in Albania and Bazias on the Yugoslav - Rumanian border.

On all three routes the aircraft flew high — between 10,000 and 11,500 feet — to avoid flak and, in the case of route 3, to get over the Tatras safely.

As a result of the move to Italy, flights to Poland could not be intensified for some months. In November there were none, in December the three from Tunis, and in January, February and March 1944 only one each. All these carried supplies only. Over five months elapsed between the last flight with parachutists from Britain on October 17/18th and the first from Brindisi on April 3rd.

The falling-off in the number of sorties was not due to the move only, as the weather in the Mediterranean and Balkans was exceptionally bad at the turn of the year. The pilots, eager for action, were frustrated by incessant storms, snow, heavy rain and fog. Many had to turn back, while others did not succeed in taking off. Part of the trouble was due to the Brindisi airfield with its single runway, which was highly dangerous to bombers, especially Halifaxes, when a side-wind was blowing. Two Polish crews crashed when landing in bad weather in the early hours of January 6th.

The experiment was made of flying on moonless nights, first with containers and packages only, but after April with parachutists as well. It turned out that improved navigation methods made it quite possible to fly in the dark and to locate dropping zones accurately.

The severe winter was followed by a fine spring; the nights were still long and the backlog of supplies enormous, so a special effort was made over a very short period. In April the Polish flight effected 100 sorties including 58 to Poland;

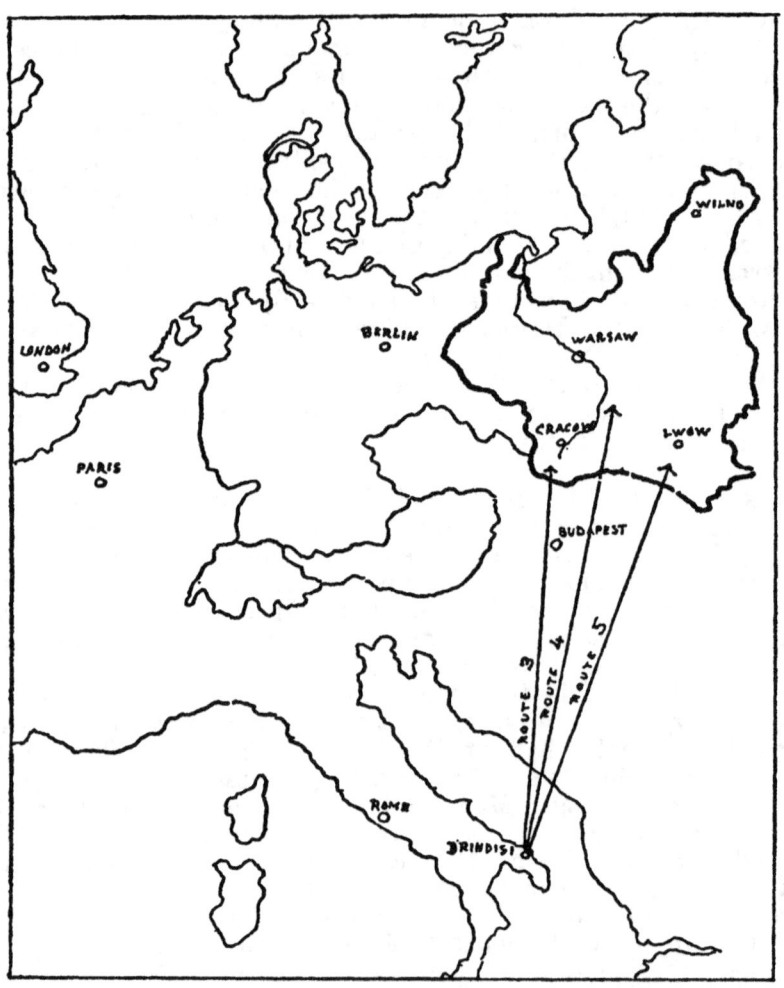

The three routes used on flights from Italy to Poland

in May the numbers were 138 and 72. This was a great advance on the previous record of 24 drops in Poland in March 1943.

The endurance of the Polish crews who achieved these results cannot be measured by any figures. Pilots would fly on five nights in succession, regardless of weather and of the need for sleep. Naturally they became exhausted and the risk of casualties increased, while equipment wore out sooner. The regulations laid down that after a certain number of flying hours the men were to be withdrawn from the unit; this was sometimes disregarded, but it was a dangerous procedure.

It should be borne in mind that the Flight was still making numerous sorties to other occupied countries, in accordance with the rule which had never been rescinded. When the weather prevented flights to Poland, the planes went to Yugoslavia or Greece instead. On the other hand, the commander of 334 Wing sent British-manned planes of 148 Squadron on sorties to Poland.

As a result of these various changes and technical improvements, the reception arrangements of the Polish underground were modified. Up till now, drops had not been very numerous and had mostly taken place in the Warsaw area. Consequently the Home Army command had enforced strict centralization, not only by requiring all parachutists to report to Warsaw and all money and supplies to be brought there in the first instance, but also by controlling wireless liaison with the base, appointing representatives to oversee reception arrangements, and supervising various other details. With the establishment of the base in Italy, things had changed. Drops could take place within a large area of Poland, and the number of reception stations had already grown to over 600; the flight, too, were more frequent, and on a fine night several planes from the base might be over Poland simultaneosly.

In these circumstances centralization was no longer feasible, and Home Army districts were increasingly allowed to maintain, supervise and defend their own reception stations, to keep the supply consignments for their own use in case of an insurrection, and to maintain direct wireless liaison with the base at Brindisi. However, the rule that all parachutists reported to Warsaw and that all money was delivered there remained in force till the end of the operations.

In spite of the shorter routes and increased numbers of aircraft, improved technique and the multiplication of dropping zones, the amount of supplies reaching Poland was still far too small and far short of what was promised and expected. This may be shown by a table:

	Drops promised	Drops carried out
Trial period (Feb. 15, 1941 to April 30, 1942)	30	9
"Intonation" (August 1, 1942 to April 30, 1943)	100	42
"Riposte" (August 1, 1943 to July 31, 1944)	300	205

During this last period, the underground hoped for a total of 500 dropping operations.

There were two main reasons for this shortfall, as a result of which the Home Army was unable to equip itself on an adequate scale.

Firstly, the West's very real technical difficulties. Worldwide strategic planning required attention to the enormous needs of every theatre of war. Priorities were strictly laid down and in general adhered to. For some time now, Poland had ceased to be an important theatre for the Western allies. They were aware of the Home Army's existence and sent it a bare minimum of supplies for diversionary purposes, but they did not turn a friendly ear to representations that more was needed and that supplies should be in sufficient quantity to make an insurrection possible. From the military point of view such plans were of no interest to the West. The Soviet Union, which was beating the Germans, was being sent Lend-Lease supplies on a huge scale, and these must suffice for the eastern front.

The second reason was of a much profounder character. It was not only military and economic but political and moral as well, and concerned the very essence of the world conflict.

On the face of things, the war had become world-wide because certain states had attempted to aggrandize themselves at others' expense, while others again had sprung to the victims' aid. In fact, of course, these states were acting from self-interest; but it was a pity that in so doing they did not show more foresight and plan for the year ahead. Unfortunately the statesmen who held the world's fate in their hands, for all their ability and dynamic leadership, were unable to reach decisions which would have assured the world of a just and lasting peace.

Poland was one of the countries which fell victim to this want of foresight. When the Soviet Union found itself willy-nilly in the allied camp — after having, less than two years earlier, aided Hitler to dismember Poland — the British Government pressed the Poles to conclude a treaty with Russia which contained no guarantee that the annexed territories would be given up. Later, when the Russian giant, fortified by supplies from the West, became Germany's main enemy in the field, the British showed less and less interest in their Polish allies and made it clear as time went on that Poland was an embarrassment to them. Finally the British and Americans decided that Poland would not be covered by the invasion plans or the British theatre of operations and would be regarded as part of the Russian sphere. In other words, Poland was to be left to contend single-handed with victorious Russia, which had no intention of surrendering Poland's eastern territories, but was determined to subdue the whole country and impose on it a Communist regime subservient to Moscow.

Naturally, in such conditions Polish appeals for increased air supplies were unlikely to be heeded. The more it was urged that the Home Army needed assistance not only for the "current struggle" — as the term was — but for an eventual country-wide rising, the more evasive the British and American governments and military staffs became.

Above all, it was a tragedy for the Home Army that Poland was excluded from the allies' operational and invasion plans. Other occupied countries which did not suffer this fate were in a very different position, as the supply figures show.

During the whole war, supplies dropped into Poland from the West amounted to 600 tons. As against this, 5,796 tons were sent into Greece, which was one-third the size of Poland, and 10,000 tons each into France and Yugoslavia. Poland of course was further off, the flights were risky and required specially adapted aircraft, and Greece and Yugoslavia could also be supplied by sea;[40]) nevertheless, the difference in the figures is eloquent.

The decisions having been taken, SOE and the Air Ministry complied with them, the pro-Polish sentiments of individual officers had little effect, since it is the practice of the Anglo-Saxon countries, especially in war-time, that decisions taken at the highest political level are accepted by all and carried out to the best of everyone's ability.

The Polish authorities, whether civilian or military, knew well enough how things were shaping and what the fate of their struggling people was likely to be. But up to the present they had not been officially told of the decisions reached, and they faintly hoped that there might be some chance of altering

---

[40]) After the capitulation of Italy in September 1943 SOE formed its own fleet in the Mediterranean ("Levant Fishery Patrol").

them. But in fact matters were on a slippery slope. Although the Western allies had landed in Italy, their progress was slow; the second front in the west was still at the stage of conferences, plans and preparations, while the Russians were forging ahead and would soon reach the Polish frontier.

In the utmost secrecy and without a word to other interested parties, preparations for the Teheran conference went forward. It was held from November 28 to December 1, 1943. Churchill, Roosevelt and Stalin were the sole participants: no-one else was so much as consulted on the proceedings, although the fate of the world was at stake. From Poland's point of view, the Teheran decisions nullified the whole effort of a people fighting for its freedom.

IX

Lt.-Colonel Iranek-Osmecki fastened up his flying-suit, pulled on his helmet and threw his parachute over his shoulder. Along with others he had just been given his final instructions, reminded of the password and the location of the dropping zone, and issued with a beltful of money. The last farewells had been exchanged and it was time for take-off. In the dark — it was just moonrise — he could descry the blurred forms of powerful aircraft and hear the roar of their revved-up engines.

He paused for a moment in thought, remembering his last trip to Poland over two years ago as a special envoy of the Commander-in-Chief. He had left London on November 7, 1940 and reached Warsaw six weeks later, on December 18th. In those days security had imposed a roundabout route: by flying-boat to Lisbon, thence to Gambia, Freetown in Sierra Leone and Lagos in Nigeria. Three days' rest there, then another series of hops to Lebenge, Stanleyville in the Belgian Congo, Khartoum and Cairo, where he had stopped for ten days and contacted Polish base. Then another flight via Lydda and Nicosia to Adana in southern Turkey, followed by a train journey through Istanbul, Pithion, Salonica, Skoplje and Belgrade to Budapest. There he reported to the Polish authorities once again an was given a companion for the rail journey to Losonc in Slovakia. Then two taxi-rides towards the frontier and a twenty-one hours' tramp across the icy, snowy mountains. Finally Poland — a night's rest at Zubracze, another cross-country hike to Kamionka, a sleigh-ride to Sanok and a train journey to Warsaw.

In those forty-two days he had encountered a series of exotic countries, strange languages, the most varied climates and types of people — and now, all being well he would accomplish the same journey in barely six hours!

With a start, he felt someone touch his arm. He stepped off towards one of the roaring monsters, and a few minutes later they were airborne.

It was a quiet flight, but the drop was a highly uncomfortable one. The navigator mistook the lights of a railway station for those of the reception centre, and the parachutists dropped on to the track. The colonel, who was carried slightly further than his companions, fell into a tree. While struggling to get free he caught his foot in the shrouds of his parachute and fell head-downwards. He extricated himself with difficulty—46 is beyond the age for such acrobatics.

In Warsaw he was appointed to command the Administration Bureau at Home Army headquarters. Staff officers were among the many kinds of specialists who were supplied to underground Poland from the West.

Iranek-Osmecki (promoted to full colonel since his jump) set to work energetically, but was soon transferred to a new assignment. In the late autumn of 1943 he became head of the all-important Intelligence Bureau, which required reorganization and rebuilding after a series of arrests. This was no easy task. Besides enlisting new agents, mending the shattered network, guarding against further threats and re-recruiting those who had been dispersed by the Gestapo, he had to continue the business of gathering information, especially as regards German movements and the state of the eastern front.

Home Army intelligence already had a number of signal achievements to its credit, of which the most notable were the collection of exact data concerning German preparations for the attack on Russia and the discovery of the spot where Germany's "secret weapon", the V1 and V2, was being produced. The first of these enabled Churchill to warn Stalin and, despite the latter's disbelief, had some effect on German chances. As for the "secret weapon" report, it led to a major raid by RAF bombers on the night of August 17/18, 1943, on the installations and launching-pads at Peenemünde, which were so seriously damaged that the Germans had to transfer them elsewhere and lose many precious months.[41])

[41]) General Walter Dornberger, head of the plant, says in his book *V2* that 800 bombers took part in this air-raid, dropped over 1,500 tons of bombs, destroyed a number of buildings and killed more than 700 people. British sources mention 571 bombers and this is the true figure. Michal Wisniewski in his work *Poles in the fight against the German V-weapon* (in Polish) gives the figure of 597 bombers. During the air-raid a number of experts on the "new weapon" were killed. The production of the V1 was delayed by six months and the V2 by nearly a year.

Shortly after the intelligence system was again in working order, its new chief received intriguing reports from the Cracow district that some mysterious activities were going on at Blizna near Mielec in the Sandomierz area, where the SS had a training camp and artillery range. The place was in an extensive forest zone between the Vistula and San rivers, well removed from large centres and major lines of communication.

From these reports, received in November-December 1943, it was clear that the camp had been considerably enlarged in a very short space of time. A branch railway line from Kochanowka had been repaired, the road re-surfaced, new barracks erected, and strange elongated objects, as yet unidentified, were being transported to the camp on tarpaulin-covered trucks. Tighter security regulations had been introduced: some villages had been evacuated, no-one was allowed to enter the forest on foot, and all vehicles were scrutinized.

The district intelligence service was baffled by all this, but it reported to Warsaw every scrap of information that it could get hold of. It also furnished photographs of the rail consignments which confirmed that the objects resembled the fuselage of an aircraft in size and shape.

At the middle of December, district headquarters reported that the activity at Blizna probably consisted of experiments with some kind of aerial torpedo. On two occasions unknown projectiles, similar to aircraft with small wings, had been observed in flight. One had fallen close by, leaving behind it some fragments of metal and a crater of 22 yards' diameetr and $6\frac{1}{2}$ yards deep. At the same time, the Warsaw area reported that a German car had crashed in the Praga suburb, killing two or three passengers. A few days later it was learnt from other sources that the car was from Mielec and the victims were specialists engaged on the new secret weapon.

Colonel Iranek (code-name *Makary* and *Heller*) at once realized what was afoot and how significant the latest reports were. He sent immediate instructions to the district command, emphasizing the importance of the information, and organized a special intelligence unit from headquarters in case the local service should be unsuccessful.

By January 1944 it was already certain that the Blizna artillery range was being used to test aerial torpedoes, which were being fired off regularly. They generally travelled in a northerly direction, sometimes north-west or north-east, and landed in a variety of areas,[42]) making huge craters.

---

[42]) Viz. in the neighbourhood of Czestochowa, Konskie, Sandomierz and Suwin.

Some, as at Rejowiec, fell on dwelling-houses. The Germans had over a dozen motorized patrols stationed about the countryside, and these would rush to the scene of the explosion and meticulously gather up what was left of the missile. A curious form of race developed between these military patrols, which could move about as they wished, and the Home Army intelligence services, which had no technical facilities and had to work in secret, but could penetrate anywhere with the aid of the local population and underground units. In this way it was possible to collect bits of the torpedoes, pieces of metal and wire and tiny fragments of all kinds. The objects fell on the territory of four Home Army districts—those of Cracow, Lublin, Warsaw and Radom —and each of these organized the search in a different manner. On several occasions there were clashes with German patrols.

This was a slow and toilsome method, and plans were made notably by Lieutenant Stachowski, commander of the Debica sub-area, with a view to storming the artillery range and thus getting at the secret of the missiles; but it was so strongly guarded that this was not practicable. Another, more promising line of approach was considered at headquarters, where "Kedyw" received orders to plan an armed assault on one of the rail transports with the object of capturing its cargo. This never took place, as the problem was solved by a lucky accident.

On May 20, 1944 one of the rockets, which had been fired in a northerly direction, fell into a swamp near a village north-west of Sarnaki (on the river Bug, about 80 miles east of Warsaw) and failed to explode. Soldiers of the 22nd infantry regiment of the Home Army, who had been mobilized to collect the pieces, managed to hide the rocket so successfully that the Germans, for all their efforts, could not find it. Some nights later, when the search had died down, it was dragged out of the swamp with the aid of three pairs of horses, loaded on to two carts fastened together and taken to the village of Holowczyce - Kolonia, where it was hidden in a barn. Men of the regiment mounted guard while experts, summoned with all speed from Warsaw, dismantled the object and took measurements, photographs and notes of every single part. It was a V2 rocket, already of an improved type and without wings. The leader of the investigation was Jerzy Chmielewski *(Raphael)*,[43] the director of a

---

[43] Chmielewski, already a very active member of the Second Bureau of the Home Army H.Q., was arrested by the Gestapo in September 1942. The arrest was accidental, nothing was proved against him but he was sent to Auschwitz on May 13, 1943. The present author, who was arrested in April 1943 and against whom nothing was proved either,

Research Commission on new weapons which had been specially set up by Home Army intelligence. He was assisted by Antoni Kocian (*Korona* - Crown),[4]) a young engineer who had devoted himself for years past to problems of aeronautical research and the German secret experiments. The investigators' task was a tremendous one, for the rocket consisted of nearly 25,000 parts.

As soon as the first reports about the work at Blizna came in, urgent messages had been sent to London. The Polish General Staff reacted with equal speed and demanded that every fresh piece of information be sent to them at once. In Britain preparations for the invasion of the continent were in full swing, and the Western Allies were passionately interested in everything to do with German defence methods. They already knew a good deal about the production of new weapons, including the fact that experiments at Peenemünde had partially ceased since the big raid there, and they were therefore much excited by the news from Poland. The Germans had evidently transferred the trials to an area out of range of Western bombers. True, adapted Halifaxes had for some time been flying to Poland and dropping parachutists and supplies, and Liberators with an even longer range had lately come into service; but a raid with several tons of bombs on a distant, blacked-out site would have been a very different matter. The transfer of the base to Italy did not help much, as the Germans could always use sites in central Poland.

Western interest grew even stronger as the reports continued to come in. British and American liaison officers kept in the closest touch with the Sixth Bureau, turned up at its offices daily, put hundreds of questions, clamoured for details and for the utmost streamlining of the reporting process. They were particularly interested in the type of fuel used and the method of steering the rocket by wireless.

---

travelled in the same transport and met Chmielewski in the Penal Company at Auschwitz. He knew a lot about Chmielewski, for before his arrest he was head of the prison intelligence service at H.Q. and information about every arrest in Warsaw passed through his hands. On March 4, 1944, Chmielewski, who had been taken back to prison in Warsaw, was released for a ransom of 150,000 zlote. This was an extremely rare occurrence.

[4]) Not quite two weeks later, on June 1st, the Gestapo in Warsaw got on to Kocian's track and arrested him and his wife Elzbieta. In spite of rigorous interrogation he did not crack and betrayed nobody. On August 13th, during the Warsaw Rising, the Gestapo carried out the last execution of prisoners in "Pawiak" who had not been evacuated. In the ruins of the ghetto, not far from St. Augustine's church, 105 men and women were shot. Among them was Antoni Kocian. Eight days later, on August 21, 1944, the Germans blew up the prison. Kocian's wife survived the war.

Dispatch-riders stood by their motorcycles in front of Polish headquarters and dashed off with each new message as they received it: sometimes the liaison officers would grab half a telegram without waiting for the rest to be deciphered. The reports from Poland covered not only Blizna but towns in Germany where parts of the lethal rocket were manufactured.

The excitement increased still more after D-day (June 6th), when the first allied troops had landed in France and news came from Warsaw that the Home Army had in its possession a complete undamaged specimen of the new weapon. Messages of frantic urgency were sent back demanding further details. The alarm reached its peak when, on June 13th, the first V1's landed in southern England, causing damage to houses, fear on the part of the population and anxiety among its leaders.

Meanwhile in Poland the utmost efforts were being made to exploit the discovery of the new rocket without loss of time. Among its parts the investigators found a wireless transmitter-receiver, also undamaged, bearing the number 0984. This gave *Raphael* the idea that it should be possible to take a hand, as it were, in the German trials and construct a station which would deflect the rockets from their course and render them harmless.

Makary, the head of intelligence, at once followed up this idea, and in the middle of June held a top secret and strictly guarded conference with members of the Research Commission and an Economic Council which was already in being. The essential parts of the rocket were examined by a group of experts, who decided that it would indeed be possible to build in Poland such a station as *Raphael* suggested. A message to this effect went off at once to London.

Raphael's idea was an interesting one and might have had important results, but time was needed to carry it out. Before anything could be done, the eastern front began to shift closer to Poland and the Germans decided that Blizna was no longer safe. On June 24th, they fired off their last rocket and started to evacuate the site.

London continued to press for details concerning the wireless equipment, the chemical composition of the fuel and so forth. Telegrams were sent with the fullest possible answers and descriptions, but it was clear that these would have to be supplemented by some exceptional action. Finally Home Army headquarters decided to send to London all the plans, drawings and analyses, together with the most important parts of the rocket itself. The Research Commission drew up a report of some 4,000 words, to which were attached nearly a score of diagrams, 80 photographs, a sketch of the Blizna camp, a table showing the number of rockets fired and where they had landed, and a list of factories producing the various parts. The document was entitled "Special Report 1/R, No. 242: rocket missiles." It was agreed without demur that the right man to take it to London was *Raphael*.⁴⁵)

X

During the first world war both the Allies and the Central Powers, in despair at the stalemate of trench warfare which swallowed up millions of lives to no apparent effect, made every possible effort to devise a new weapon or strategy which would give them the advantage of surprise. One such weapon was the tank, which made it possible to break the deadlock and played its part in securing the Western victory.

Earlier on, attempts had been made to achieve the same result by the rapid development of aircraft; but these were still so weak and primitive that the air encounters were less like batles than sporting events. Nevertheless, aircraft were useful in reconnaissance and also in secret activities of which we still know relatively little. Agents were dropped in secret behind the enemy lines, and were successfully picked up again. This type of double operation was of course used extensively in the second world war. Since it was evolved earlier than the technique of sending in men and supplies by parachute, it might be supposed that it was simpler. To a certain extent this is true. Passengers who can be landed on a meadow as if on an airfield do not need any special training; they may even be old and infirm. But in all other respects, landing is a trickier operation than the effecting of drops. This applies to such considerations as safety, the size and servicing of the secret landing-ground, the training of the aircrew and the accuracy required of the pilot. All these problems are multiplied if the target is a long way off, when the operation becomes virtually impossible.

During the last war these questions occupied many lively and inventive minds, one of the chief of whom among Poles

---

⁴⁵) Poles played a further part in fighting the German "new weapon". A Lieutenant of the Polish Armed Forces in the West, Wladyslaw Wazny (*Tygrys* - Tiger), who was dropped into France under the auspices of the sub-section (EU/P) of the Polish section of SOE, discovered in Northern France no fewer than 173 V1 rocket sites and informed London by radio telegrams. As a result British bombers destroyed more than 100 of these sites. Lieutentnt Wazny was killed on August 19, 1944, when he was surrounded by German gendarmes near Donai and fought to the death.

was Maciej Kalenkiewicz. After reaching Paris at the beginning of 1940 he busied himself with the problem of rapid liaison with Poland and thought *inter alia* of landings by seaplanes or small aircraft which could be destroyed or buried on the spot. There was not time before the collapse of France for even the most tentative experiment, but his thoughts were to bear fruit in the not very distant future.

As it happened, some members of the underground were thinking on similar lines, as regards both landing operations and the dropping of men and supplies. As early as April 18, 1940 Rowecki, then commander of ZWZ for German-occupied Poland, sent a full report on the subject (No. 18) to military headquarters in Paris, in which he stated that: "I have given orders for the discovery of suitable sites for air liaison in the Kielce, Cracow and Warsaw provinces... with a view to the dropping of mail and especially arms and equipment, either by parachute or possibly by means of aircraft landings."

After the fall of France came the battle of Britain, but in the midst of defending themselves the islanders gave thought to attack, witness the creation of SOE. Within three or four months of the reports by Rowecki and Kalenkiewicz their ideas were taken up, independently or otherwise, by equally ingenious brains.

However, Poland as the most distant allied country presented specially difficult problems, and SOE directed its attention first of all to France, Belgium and Holland. In view of their proximity and the experience of the 1914 war, it was natural to think in terms of landing aircraft. The first experiments were made fairly soon, as the method obviated the long and difficult training of parachutists.

The RAF at this time had Lysander aircraft which were not much good in a fight but were ideal for the present task. They were single-engined planes with a speed of 165 m.p.h. and could fly up to 450 miles if their armament was removed and an extra fuel tank fitted. They carried two passengers besides the pilot, and in emergency four could be squeezed in. The total weight of the aircraft with passengers and fuel was not more than $4\frac{1}{2}$ tons, and it could land and take off over about 500 yards of firm ground. In 1941, after trials had been carried out and pilots trained, the first flights were made to the occupied Western countries, which already possessed men skilled in finding and servicing clandestine landing-grounds.[46])

---

[46]) In 1943, besides the Lysanders, two-engined Hudsons were brought into use. They carried armament and belonged to 161 Squadron at Tempsford base. In 1944 twin-engined American Dacotas came into use: these, like the Lysanders, flew unarmed.

The Poles were the first of the allied nations to train a parachute team which landed in their own country (on February 15/16, 1941), but owing to the distance involved they were still far behind as regards aircraft landings. The heavy, four-engined Halifaxes with its extra fuel tanks, a crew of seven, and six parachutists with their equipment and stores could just manage to fly to Poland and return, but if it had tried to land in a meadow or forest glade it would never have taken off again and the enterprise would have ended in disaster. Parachute drops were multiplied, but the one-way sorties were no use from the point of view of bringing passengers from Poland to Britain. Messengers from the underground had to make the long, dangerous and time-consuming journey by land. It took weeks, sometimes months for them to get to London, by which time the information they brought was of little value. In addition there was the problem of sending older men who could not stand up to the courier journey but who might be needed in London for political or military reasons.

After considering various solutions the authorities reverted to Kalenkiewicz's idea of landing a flying-boat on standing water. Two lakes were chosen (Usciwierz and Biale)[47] not far from Warsaw, as being large and deep enough and relatively safe from enemy observation. Attention was also paid to American experiments in which slow-flying aircraft had picked up passengers from the ground. The collection of mail in this way had been practised in the Polish army before the war. However, neither of these projects was carried out. Flying-boats were not fast enough[48] for the long trip and were beginning to go out of use; while picking up passengers or even mail from a low-flying aircraft was too tricky an operation to be practicable at night, even with a full moon. Only strong, fit men could in any case be picked up in this fashion, and the American experiments, while partially successful, had involved the use of very slow planes which could not have made the trip to Poland.

Thus the question of landing aircraft hung fire, but it was not lost sight of at either the Polish or the British end. Correspondence about it continued, and the Sixth Bureau was in continuous touch with the Polish section of SOE. The Home Army command put forward various ideas such as flying small planes across from Sweden, refuelling with

[47] Both in the Province of Lublin.

[48] The only British seaplane which could have flown to Poland was the Catalina, but it was unable to fly at more than 100 m.p.h. so could not do the double journey in one night, even in winter.

petrol taken from the Germans etc.;[49]) but London turned down these suggestions on the strength of the experience gained in SOE's many landings in the Western countries. These had led to the formulation of rules for two-way operations, which were to apply even more strictly in Poland when such operations became feasible there.

The basic condition of a successful landing was to find a suitable piece of ground over which heavy planes could land and take off. It should be square in shape, measuring about five furlongs each way, so that the aircraft could be sure of landing up-wind. It should be in fairly open country, with no tall buildings, chimneys or trees in the vicinity. The firmness of the ground [50]) must be such that the plane's wheels did not sink in more than an inch or two, and it must of course be flat and smooth, free from stones, tree-stumps and ditches. If it was snowing, the ground must not be covered to a depth of more than three-quarters of an inch.

In the case of flights to the Western countries the Air Ministry had also insisted that every landing-ground should first be photographed from the air. This was a reasonable requirement as regards France or Holland, but was quite impracticable in Poland. The only occasion when a plane managed to fly to Poland and take photographs was when a Mosquito fighter was sent to reconnoitre German warships at Danzig; but it had barely enough fuel for the return journey, and the landing-grounds now in question were a good way further south. After some argument it was agreed to make do with an exact sketch, enlarged and transferred to a map.

Again, it seemed too much to hope that a safe landing-ground five furlongs square could be discovered in Poland, full as it was of German police, gendarmerie, SS and military posts. A further compromise was therefore reached whereby two landing strips could if necessary be prepared, a mile or so distant from each other, running in a north-south and an east-west direction respectively. These might measure five furlongs by a couple of hundred yards, and the pilot could land on one or other according to the wind.[51])

The next important requirement was for a well-trained and experienced crew. This meant using British personnel from 161 Squadron, for no Poles had as yet taken part in night landings. Consideration was however given to making use

[49]) The low-octane fuel used by the Germans and available in Poland was no use to Western aircraft.

[50]) The most suitable turned out to be fields sown with clover.

[51]) This solution was not as simple as it appeared, and was not used in Poland.

of Polish navigators, and some were sent to train at Tempsford. It was expected at that time that twin-engined armed Hudsons would be used for the flight.

The question of ground staff at the Polish end presented less difficulty: the Home Army commander's suggestions, made in the light of local conditions, were adopted. A single "dispatch officer" was in charge of the wireless operators and the men responsible for signal flares, and had also under his orders the commander of the landing-ground patrol. This was divided into two sections, one guarding the field itself and the other the approach roads.[52])

The system of signal lights was somewhat different from that used for parachute drops. The field was bordered with stable-lamps at 80-yard intervals; three green flares were lit on the side from which the pilot made his approach, and three red ones on the opposite side. The direction was further indicated by two oil flares a mile or so up-wind of the green signal.

Wireless communication was a vital factor. The landing-ground must have a transmitter for immediate, direct contact with the base. An operation might have to be called off not only because of a threat from the enemy but in the event of sudden rain or snow. In addition, the "Iodoform" system was still in force.

The crucial date on which actual preparations for the first aircraft landing began was May 21, 1943, when Protasewicz, the head of the Sixth Bureau, telegraphed to General Rowecki in Warsaw that the British had given their consent. From this time on the name "Bridge" was given to these two-way operations, responsibility for which at the Polish end rested with the Air Department of the Home Army, the "Import" organization[53]) and the local military authorities in whose territory the landing-grounds (known to the Poles as "ponds") were situated. In London the operations were directed by the Sixth Bureau, the Polish section of SOE and the Air Ministry.

The next step was a letter of July 2nd, from the Air Ministry indicating dates for the first flight: it was to be known

---

[52]) In Poland all security regulations were necessary and were enforced. In France, where the occupation regime was much milder and landings very frequent, things were different. It happened that casual onlookers turned up at night to see the show. Once one of the onlookers was killed by the aircraft coming in to land.

[53]) At H.Q. of the Home Army there was an Air Department, engaged in planning the use of air forces in Polish territory in the event of a rising towards the end of the war. "Import's" duties were the reception of drops from the West.

as Operation "Wildhorn" and to take place on October 11-18th or 16-18th. Unfortunately it had to be postponed, as the transfer of the base to Italy was decided on meanwhile and was carried out during October. More than six months elapsed before the elaborate arrangements could be set on foot again; they were the same as before except that it was decided to use American twin-engined Dakotas, fitted with two extra fuel tanks. These transport planes, being unarmed, were lighter than the Hudson, and required less space for landing and take-off.

On the evening of April 15, 1944 the first Dakota took off from No. 11 base at Brindisi, with a British crew from 267 Squadron of 334 Wing, a Polish co-pilot and two Polish passengers, Captain Narcyz Lopianowski and Lieutenant Tadeusz Kostuch. As the flight was an experimental one they took only mail. The "Iodoform" signals were duly given — a highland melody on take-off and a tango during transit — and the base wireless station *"Mewa"* (Seagull) was in constant touch with the landing-ground. This was at "Bak" near Belzyce, 22 miles south-east of Lublin.

The wind changed at the last moment, there was no time to alter the signals and the Dakota landed down-wind, but suffered no mishap. The exchange of passengers took ten minutes. Those who made the trip back to base were: General Stanislaw Tatar *(Tabor, Turski)*, director of operations at Home Army headquarters; the commander of "Import", Lt.-Colonel Ryszard Dorotycz-Malewicz; Lieutenant Andrzej Pomian of the information and propaganda bureau; Zygmunt Berezowski, a prominent member of the Nationalist Party; and Stanislaw Oltarzewski of the government *Delegatura*. The take-off was a difficult one, at the ground was too small, too soft and hemmed in by trees; but the Dakota managed it and returned safely to Brindisi.

As a result of this operation, some organizational changes took place in the West. General *Tabor* became a deputy chief of staff and, having just come from Poland and being politically close to Mikolajczyk, took over responsibility for home country affairs in the military set-up. This entailed changes in the Sixth Bureau. Lt.-Colonel Protasewicz, who had been its head for over two years, was transferred to the 2nd Corps on July 6th, and replaced by Lt.-Colonel Marian Utnik *(Warta)*, a young officer in General Tabor's confidence.

No. 11 base was also reorgainzed and given the code-name "Elba". Major Jazwinski followed Lt.-Colonel Protasewicz to the 2nd Corps and the base was taken over on July 1st by Dorotycz-Malewicz *(Hancza)*.

Although the first "Bridge" operation was not faultless,[54]) it showed that the problem of distance could be solved and that further such flights were possible. Preparations for "Wildhorn II" were set in hand. Again a Dakota was used, flying from the same airfield, with a British crew, a Polish co-pilot and two passengers: Lt.-General Tadeusz Kossakowski, a specialist in armoured warfare and war industry, and a sabotage expert, Lt.-Colonel Romuald Bielski. Besides mail, the plane carried 8 or 9 hundredweight of stores. It flew on the night of May 29/30th, again by moonlight and without incident. The landing-ground "Motyl" (Butterfly) was at Zaborow near Tarnow, on a disused German field about 45 miles east of Cracow. After only six minutes the plane took off again with three passengers: Group Captain Roman Rudkowski, chief of air intelligence at Home Army headquarters; Major Zbigniew Leliwa of "Kedyw"; and Jan Domanski of the Peasants' Party, head of a department of the *Delegatura*. The operation was a brilliant success.

Operation "Wildhorn III" did not take place till eight weeks later, towards the end of July. It had been planned for some time, as London was impatient to receive prats and details of the new German weapon; but weather conditions, on which almost everything depended, had not been right, and there were troubles as regards the landing-ground. Strictly speaking, the one used in May ("Butterfly") should have been ruled out as compromised, but it was hard to find another and, as it had proved well-suited, it was decided to use it once again. It was, after all, nearly two months since "Wildhorn II", and "Butterfly" had not only the actual ground to recommend it but also such factors as the reception team, the system of lights and patrols, neighbouring hideouts etc.

Any minor difficulties that might attend the flight were in any case outweighed by the general military situation. In the west the allies were fighting in northern France, in the south they were moving up the Italian peninsula; flying bombs were falling on London, and in Poland the Red Army was approaching the Vistula. It was vital for the Poles in the west to contact their homeland, and the allies were eager to learn the secrets of the Blizna firing-range. The operation was given top priority and it was decided to fly as soon as weather permitted, even on a moonless night.

At 8 in the evening on July 25th, the Dakota took off from

[54]) The Sixth Bureau received a rather unpleasant letter from the Polish section of SOE pointing out errors in the choice, preparation and manning of the landing ground. These rebukes were not without foundation and delayed the next operation.

Brindisi and glided northwards. The crew was again British except for the navigator, Flight Lieutenant Kazimierz Szrajer, who was in command. The plane took 19 suitcases full of special equipment, and four passengers: Captain Kazimierz Bilski, 2nd-Lieutenant Leszek Starzynski, Major Boguslaw Wolniak and Lieutenant Jan Nowak. The first three of these were parachutists on their way to join the underground forces, and the last was a military courier on his way back from a mission for the Home Army commander. He had had long conversations with Mikolajczyk, Sosnkowski and representatives of the different political parties; he had committed to memory their views and requirements in the fullest detail, and was briefed to explain to Warsaw the Commander-in-Chief's estimate of the situation.[55])

The flight was uneventful, and the passengers and crew did not know that up to the last moment it had been doubtful whether it would take place. Some German troops had unexpectedly turned up at the landing-ground, and two Storch reconnaissance aircraft had alighted on it. The reception team were about to send off a telegram cancelling the flight when the German planes took off again. It had been raining and the ground was rather soft, but the westward-bound passengers were determined to start whatever the risk; so the message went out that "Butterfly" was ready, and the flight was confirmed by code-tunes in the appropriate manner.

The landing was naturally intended to take place in secret and with as little noise as possible. But all the neighbouring villages knew what was afoot, as they had helped to man the reception committee and patrols, while the great machine's approach could be heard over the slumbering fields for miles around. It flew over the ground twice with engines roaring and two searchlights blazing. As soon as it landed it was surrounded by a noisy throng of soldiers in the most varied attire, some of them barefooted, who shouted halloos and greetings and dragged off the heavy suitcases to the carts in readiness near by. The cover patrols were of course keeping watch, but the scene would no doubt have been a very different one a year or two earlier, when the German troops were not harried by the pressure of the approaching front.

The incoming passengers alighted and vanished into the dark with their luggage, while the westbound group boarded the plane in strict order of priority. This had been laid down beforehand, and if for any reason the plane could not take the full load, it was known who would have to stay behind.

---

[55]) The information and opinions brought by the courier did not influence the decision to rise in Warsaw, for this decision had been made before he reported to H.Q.

The order was: firstly, a sack containing the V2 parts; secondly Jerzy Chmielewski (*Raphael*), who carried a detailed report on the secret weapon and was ready to supplement it thanks to his unfailing memory; third, Jozef Retinger,[56]) also known as *Brzoza* (Birch) or *Salamander;* fourth, Tomasz Arciszewski, the representative of the Socialist Party, who had been designed by the Council of National Unity in Warsaw as their candidate for the succession to the Presidency of the Republic; and last, Second Lieutenant Tadeusz Chciuk, a political courier, and Czeslaw Micinski, in command of the

---

[56]) Jozef Hieronim Retinger, born at Cracow in 1888, was one of the more colourful and controversial figures of the last war. On finishing school he left Poland and went to Paris. In spite of his youth he made many contacts in France and Britain. He was closely connected with the fighting in North Africa during the Abd-el-Krim rising in the early 20s. Later he played a leading part in Mexico during the anti-Catholic revolution. He was noted for his quick intelligence.

General Sikorski met him in France in 1928 and kept in touch with him. After the collapse of France, when the Polish Government moved to London, Retinger became secretary of the Council of Ministers and from that time on was never far from the Premier's side. When diplomatic relations were established with Russia as a result of the Sikorski - Maisky pact, Retinger went to Kuibyshev as chargé d'affaires before Professor Kot arrieved there as ambassador.

On the night of April 3-4, 1944, after a flight from Italy, two political emissaries were dropped in Poland. One of them was 2nd-Lieutenant Tadeusz Chciuk (*Celt, Sulima*) and the other was Retinger, who had been sent by the Polish Ministry of Interior. (On November 29, 1944, the minister, W. Banaczyk, put forward a request to the Chief of Staff that Retinger should be awarded the Cross of Valour for his jump and for fulfilling "the tasks entrusted to him by the Polish Government"). It has been surmised that the British Government and Churchill were also interested in Retinger's journey, with a view to obtaining exact information about conditions in the Polish underground and, no doubt, a *modus vivendi* with the communists.

Retinger was already 56 and in ill-health when he jumped, but he took the risk although he could have flown with the first "Bridge," which left about a fortnight later. He wanted to try a few practice jumps, but the instructors told him that he was not fit enough for the training and would probably be left crippled after a jump. He therefore decided that his jump by night into occupied Poland would be his very first. He showed great courage in this, and was probably the oldest parachutist of the last war.

Retinger's mission was treated as urgent and top secret. He entered the aircraft wearing a mask.

During the flight he gave evidence of his many-sided temperament: the experienced veteran of so many secret missions, considered to be a cynic, burst into tears when the aircraft flew over the Tatra mountains and approached Cracow.

He hurt his leg badly on landing but made his underground contacts and met a number of people.

He was to have returned on the second "Bridge," but for some unexplained reason he was late. The wagonette which carried him from the secret airfield overturned, throwing him into a ditch. He fell seriously ill and lost the use of his legs.

He died in London in 1960 of lung cancer.

party.⁵⁷) The only infringement of this order was due to the fact that Retinger, being partially paralysed, could not walk and had to be carried by Chciuk, who never left his side.

The doors slammed to, the engines began to roar, but the plane vibrated helplessly without moving forward: its wheels had sunk too deeply into the softened ground. Szrajer made the passengers alight and had the luggage taken off; then he and the pilot examined the landing gear and decided that there was nothing for it but to call off the flight, throw petrol over the plane and burn it. Captain *Wlodek*, the dispatch officer, urged them not to do this, and ordered his men to dig out small trenches in front of the wheels and fill them with straw. Then the cargo was once more taken on board, Retinger was carried into the plane, the others took their places and the engines started up again. Their frenzied roar must have awakened all the Germans for miles around, but the Dakota still refused to budge, and the order to unload was given once more. The aircrew were actually splashing petrol on to the landing-gear when *Wlodek* stopped them a second time: his men rushed to the carts and fetched planks which they laid under the plane's wheels.

It began to look as if the order of priority would after all, play a part in deciding who went on board. Only *Wlodek* and Szrajer knew about it, and they still said nothing. The order to load up was given for the third time. At last, 80 minutes after landing, the roaring, vibrating monster began to move slowly forward. The engines' noise drowned the joyful shouts of the underground soldiers who ran along beside the machine, gesticulating and brandishing their weapons.

At 5.50 a.m. on the 26th, the Dakota touched down at Brindisi. On the following day it flew on to Rabat in Morocco, where Arciszewski, Retinger and Chciuk remained so as to meet Mikolajczyk, who was flying to Moscow for talks with the Soviet government. Chmielewski and Micinski went on with all speed to London. They arrived on the 28th; greedy hands were stretched out for *Raphael's* precious cargo, but he

---

⁵⁷) This order of precedence is given in a despatch of July 20, 1944 (No. 1071/VV/222), sent by Colonel *Hancza*, chief of the operational base in Brindisi, to *Warta* (Lt.-Colonel Utnik, head of the Sixth Bureau).
"Instructions for the landing ground at "Butterfly" and for the pilot are that loading at "Butterfly" shall take place in the following order:
  1) Special material,
  2) Specialist concerned with this material,
  3) Retinger,
  4) The other two couriers."
From this despatch it would appear that at the time it was sent neither the base nor the Sixth Bureau knew that Arciszewski was also to be brought from Poland.

defended it as stoutly as he had done at Brindisi and during the rest of the journey. His report and the vital parts of the V2 were duly delivered to the Polish General Staff, where the document was deciphered and the whole body of information placed in the hands of the British authorities.

The first V2 was not dropped on London till September 18th, by which time such measures of defence as were possible had been organized, and the launching sites pushed back by the advance of the allied armies.[58])

XI

Thus in the west the victorious allies were breaking through the enemy's defences and penetrating into the heart of France; in the south they had taken Rome; bombers in their thousands were pounding German cities into rubble; while in Poland the Home Army, as the eastern front drew closer, made ready for operation "Tempest" and continued to harry the retreating Nazis.

Altogether under "Riposte" 135 soldiers were parachuted into Poland, bringing the total to 285. These men were assigned to sabotage and guerrilla duties, intelligence and communications, the organization of dropping zones and of military training centres and courses for Home Army recruits. They were to be found everywhere occupying posts of the greatest risk; many had already fallen in battle or perished in the course of reaching their native soil. Three were drowned in the North Sea, three were killed aboard a plane which crashed on landing in Poland, and two when their parachutes failed to open; two more were killed immediately after landing, while covering their comrades' escape from the Germans. Of the thirty-two parachutists who served in

---

[58]) A fourth "Bridge" was also planned to take place in September 1944, but after long planning and discussions, it was not till December 15, 1944 that a Dakota left Brindisi for the landing-ground "Swietlik". Unfortunately the weather changed suddenly and the aircraft was recalled to base by radio. This unsuccesful operation went by the code-name "Wildhorn IV".

The number of two-way operations to Poland was very small. The chief obstacle was the distance. It was also difficult to find landing grounds, for the Germans kept the whole country under strict police and military control. The political situation was also unfavourable to frequent flights, which only became technically possible in 1944.

The figure of three "Bridge" landings looks very modest in comparison with the 112 landings on French soil. France was of course close at hand and light aircraft could fly there, but above all she was in an area of key strategic importance to the Western Allies and in a privileged position from the political point of view.

"Fan", five were killed; twelve gave their lives in special actions and nine in guerrilla warfare. Eighteen were captured by the Germans while on special duties and were never heard of again. One suffered a particularly dreadful fate. He was arrested by the Gestapo and broke down under savage interrogation; then he was released in the hope that he would meet and betray others. There was no help for it — he was shot by a Polish bullet.

One of the bravest of them all finally met his fate. On June 15, 1944, *Ponury* fell to a round of German bullets, when commanding the 7th battalion of the 77th infantry regiment of the Home Army under Major Kalenkiewicz. He was killed near Jewlasze in the Nowogrodek region.

His death in the eastern marches of Poland symbolized the end of a chapter in the national struggle during which, despite all losses and sacrifices, no-one had lost hope.

The blackest and most tragic days were still to come.

INTO THE ABYSS

I

Lieutenant-Colonel Leopold Okulicki, who took part in the defence of Warsaw in September 1939, was one of the group of officers who, immediately before the surrender of the city, helped General Tokarzewski to set up the underground military organization known as SZP (in the Service of Poland's Victory). As a member of this organization he went to Lodz towards the end of October to command the local military district. Under the code-name of *Kula* (Bullet) he set about developing the underground network which had been started independently by Colonel Switalski.

After the arrests and deportations, Lodz had become a place of such danger and was so thorougly penetrated by the Gestapo that Okulicki soon found it too hot to hold him. In June 1940 he was recalled by General Rowecki and entrusted with a still more dangerous and difficult task. He was to go to Lwow, in the Soviet zone of occupation, and, while avoiding the attention of the NKVD (the Soviet secret police), attempt to rebuild the military network there, which had been similarly weakened by numerous arrests.

Taught by the experience of Tokarzewski, who had been sent on the same mission but had never reached Lwow, Okulicki organized his journey with the utmost caution. He left Warsaw on October 23rd, and was in Lwow ten days later, on November 2nd. Here he set about his duties with equal zeal under the code-name *Mrowka* (Ant). However, the NKVD proved to be even more efficient than the Gestapo. It was almost omnipresent, thanks to informers who were more loyal to communism than to their own country and people. On the night of January 23/24, 1941 Okulicki was seized in the flat he was using as a hideout and carried off to the Lubianka prison in Moscow.

There he was subjected to the kind of treatment familiar to political prisoners, especially those of Stalin and Hitler. When an ordinary criminal is caught after a career of murder and robbery, the law forbids anyone to lay a finger on him until he has been duly tried and his defence heard; but no such law protects a man fighting for his beliefs and his country. Okulicki was exposed to all the refinements of ill-treatment which the NKVD had devised over the years, but with little result: this stalwart Pole, a native of a small Carpathian village, stood firm.

Suddenly, after more than six months of torture, a warder appeared one day and ordered him to collect his things. Cut off from all news of the world, he imagined that he was being transferred to another prison. In fact he was being set free under the terms of the Polish-Soviet agreement of July 30, 1941, which provided for the establishment of a Polish army in the Soviet Union under General Anders (himself till then also a prisoner of the NKVD).

Okulicki reported to Anders in Uzbekistan and was appointed Chief of Staff of the latter's army. He was now a full colonel, having been promoted on March 31st, while in prison.

In April 1942 he became commander of the 7th Infantry Division, which was transferred from the Soviet Union to the Middle East, there to be rearmed and trained for its part in the allied invasion of Italy. But Okulicki found this too roundabout a way of returning to Poland. Eager to fight on his native soil, he volunteered and was accepted for special duties. On October 13, 1943 he enrolled at the Middle East training base. He was aged almost 45 and his prison experiences had weakened his heart, but he was still fit enough to complete the course. After a few practice jumps he came to London for a briefing from the Polish Commander-in-Chief, General Sosnkowski, and was now ready to be parachuted into Poland.

In view of the military and political situation at the end of 1943, Okulicki well knew that he was almost certain to encounter the Russians and fall once more into the clutches of the NKVD, unless he were first killed or captured by the Germans. Nevertheless he was determined to go back to his own country. On the night of May 21/22, 1944, using the code-name *Kobra 2* he was dropped with five others at a dropping zone near Cracow. He bore a personal letter from General Sosnkowski appointing him one of General *Bor's* deputies and stating that he would be made a general as soon as news was received of his safe arrival in Warsaw.

He reported to General *Bor* (Komorowski), the Home Army commander, on June 3rd and was appointed by him Deputy Chief of Staff and Director of Operations at headquarters. During the next few weeks he had the task of adapting himself to new conditions of life and getting used to the country's altered appearance. It was not like earlier days in Lodz or Lwow, when almost everything lay in ruins and the effects of the September defeat were felt at every turn. Poland had passed through four years of underground activity and fighting; the framework of an underground state had been created; young recruits had grown up to swell the ranks of units that were already engaged against the enemy or would be at any moment. One could feel the nation's inner strength and reborn faith in its own powers. Yet at the same time the world situation had changed in such a way that the achievements of four years' underground activity afforded no guarantee of victory even though the Germans were defeated. Poland's eastern neighbour, which had helped Hitler to despoil it in 1939, had become an ally of the West two years later but had not ceased to be a threat to Poland itself. The tremendous military strength and political influence of the Soviet Union fascinated the world and blotted out the hopes of any weaker states that might stand in its way.

Under Operation "Tempest", which took effect from January 1944, substantial Home Army units were mobilized locally and continued to harry the Germans in their retreat westward. In its original version, this operation did not contemplate fighting in large cities: underground units were to evacuate these and attack the Germans in rural areas, in the hope of avoiding massive reprisals.

Okulicki, having settled into his new command and studied the situation, took a different view. He knew that there was also a plan for a general rising, which had been worked out by the Home Army command in 1942 and involved a battle for Warsaw. The plan as a whole had been discarded, since the Germans were retreating in good order and still possessed formidable strength, but Okulicki believed that the idea of fighting for Warsaw should be maintained.

His chief ground for this view was a military one. In their retreat from Russia, the Germans were making use of every large town, especially if it stood on a river, as a strongpoint in order to prolong their resistance. They could be expected to do the same in Warsaw, which was not only a big city but an important communications centre. If it were destroyed, the German plans would in no way be thwarted; on the contrary, it would suit them admirably. But if a Soviet attack on the city were supported by a rising within it, the battle would be shortened and the destruction of Warsaw averted. Moreover, it would be difficult to use the forces at present in the capital to fight the Germans further west, since this would mean evacuating thousands of Home Army men with the arms which they had concealed on the spot.

The second argument which carried weight with Okulicki was the necessity for the Poles to regain possession of the capital by their own strength in order that the Soviet forces might find Polish civil and military authorities already in being when they entered the city.

It should be recalled that before leaving Britain, Okulicki had had a long conversation with Sosnkowski, whose confidence he enjoyed. This must have covered the question of "Tempest" and of a possible insurrection, since these were the two vital issues of the hour. Sosnkowski, as we shall see, had misgivings about the idea of a general rising; but he cannot have excluded the idea of doing battle in Warsaw, for in a despatch towards the end of July, he spoke of the possibility of gaining possession of the city before the Russians entered it.

On July 21st, Okulicki put his point of view to *Bor*, and the latter's Chief of Staff, General Pelczynski. They both accepted his arguments, as did the rest of Home Army headquarters. However, Colonel Bokszczanin advised against attempting to co-ordinate a rising in Warsaw with the expected attack by the Russians, as he doubted their good faith.

Although military arguments may have played a strong part in the decision to fight in Warsaw, the main justification of that decision seems in fact to have been a political and ideological one.

In 1939 Poland's situation had appeared completely desperate. No-one who knew the facts and the ratio of military strength could have imagined that we would beat the Germans, allied as they were with Russia; yet we had gone to war and fought single-handed, though we possessed allies in the West. Then for five years we had built up an underground state and army in preparation for the day when we could hurl ourselves on the enemy and drive him from Polish soil. That day was now at hand. True, the Germans were being driven back by the forces of a state unfriendly to us, but at all events they were about to evacuate Warsaw. After all the years of preparation and subversion, resistance and hope, was the city now to change hands without any recognition of the fact that it was Polish?

Another strong motive for fighting in Warsaw derived from Poland's unfavourable position on the international scene. If we had had an agreement with Russia placing us on something like the footing which France enjoyed vis à vis Britain and America, there would have been no compelling political need to embark on what was in itself a risky action. We could then have confined ourselves to a modest military demonstration such as took place in Paris, and, a few days later, have welcomed the victorious Red Army in Warsaw, free from any fear of Soviet designs against our territory or political system. Unfortunately the facts were otherwise, and we had to accept the risk of a doubtful struggle against the Germans at a time when the Soviet forces, which seemed about to enter the capital, came as invaders and enemies.

What alternative was there? Were we to allow Stalin's divisions to be greeted in Warsaw by a handful of native communists and Soviet partisans, so that the whole world would be convinced by the Stalinist lie that these were the only forces operating in Poland besides the Red Army?

On July 21st and after, when the Home Army staff was discussing plans for the rising in Warsaw, it had already received the first reports of the arrest by the Russians of *General Wilk*, the commander of the Home Army units which took part in the capture of Wilno, and the disarming of his troops. This was not the first act of hostility committed towards our forces by the Red Army, but so far these had all taken place in territory which the Russians regarded as their own. As General *Bor* has since pointed out, "it did not follow that they would adopt a similar attitude towards the Home Army in territory to which they laid no claim." [1]

On July 25th, after the Home Army command had taken its decision in agreement with the Government Delegate (Jankowski, whom London had raised in May to the rank of Deputy Premier), *Bor* telegraphed to Sosnkowski as follows:

"We are ready to fight for Warsaw at any moment. Participation of the Parachute Brigade would have immense political and tactical effect. Please make arrangements so that Warsaw airfields can be bombed at our request. Will inform you of time fixed for outbreak."

Two facts emerge from this highly important message: that the Home Army command had decided to fight in Warsaw and that they expected substantial help from the West. Unfortunately the signal could not be at once shown to the C-in-C, as he had unexpectedly left London and had been on a visit to the 2nd Corps in Italy since July 11th.

All fronts in the war were important, Poles were fighting for their homeland on nearly all of them,[2] and blood is blood wherever it is shed; but it can scarcely be denied that the most important front for us at that time was the one that ran through the heart of Poland, where the future of our riven country was being decided. Yet the Commander-in-Chief chose the month of July 1944, in which these vital questions

[1] General *Bor's* own words, published in Polish in the monthly of Radio Free Europe *On the Air* (No. 8/9 dated August 16 - September 6, 1964): *How the decision to rise was made.*
Full details of the battle for Wilno can be found in a book by the same author *Between London and Warsaw* in the chapter *For Wilno.*

[2] General Anders expressed this feeling in his order given before the historical battle in Italy: "My brothers and children, the battle for Monte Cassino is the battle for Poland."

were at stake, to leave London and visit Italy for a round of courtesy visits, inspections and the conferring of decorations. This would have been serious even if unanimity had prevailed in our own camp concerning military developments in Poland. In fact it did not, and this made even more fateful the C-in-C's absence from London, the seat of our own and the British authorities, where lines of communication met and decisions were taken.

Sosnkowski knew, of course, that he and the premier, Mikolajczyk, differed in their views regarding the struggle in Poland, and also that the Home Army command did not always agree with his long analyses and directives. A striking example of this had arisen over the Government instruction (part B) to the underground dated October 27, 1943,[3]) which provided in part that if the Russians entered Poland without the prior restoration of diplomatic relations, the local political and military authorities, after fighting the retreating Germans, would not proclaim their existence openly but would remain underground. The Home Army commander, in agreement with the Government Delegate and the chief party leaders, had demurred to this on the ground that the authorities must come into the open in order to assert Polish rights to the territory in question. The Government under Mikolajczyk had accepted the Home Army view and the C-in-C had acquiesced, though he was of a different opinion. From then on his disagreement with Mikolajczyk's policy became more and more marked.

Now that events were moving towards a climax as the Soviet summer offensive progressed, it became essential that all Poles should be united on a single plan, and no less essential that the underground should be fully and frankly informed of what was happening in the West and what help could be expected from that quarter. Finally it was necessary to exert strong and constant pressure on our allies so that, in spite of political decisions which were tragic from our point of view, our suffering country should not be denied help.

Unfortunately the Commander-in-Chief, irrespective of his disagreements with others, had for months been inwardly torn by doubts and irresolution.

As we have seen, he was against allowing the underground authorities to declare themselves, yet he allowed instructions to be issued in a sense contrary to his views, without defending these to the utmost or trying to reach agreement with

---

[3]) Part A of this instruction foresaw a general rising in Poland "after agreement had been reached with the Allies". But in summer of 1943 it was already known that Poland had been excluded from the allied strategic plans. Instructions so formulated suggested to those in Poland that full support for Polish military and political aims by the Allies was still possible.

Mikolajczyk. Similarly, although he expected help from our allies he did not seek to contact them, and when the crisis actually came his intentions were hard to discover.

On July 7th he telegraphed to the Home Army commander: "... If, by a fortunate turn of events, it should prove possible, at the last stage of the German retreat and before the entry of Red Army units, to gain possession even for a brief time of Wilno, Lwow, any other large centre or any clearly defined territory however small, then we should do so and thus appear in the role of undisputed owner..." This fully accorded with the views of the Home Army command.

On July 25th, when still unaware of Warsaw's decision for a rising, he sent the following message from Italy to General Kopanski for transmission to the Home Army: "... This course of action should also be followed in the event of our gaining possession of Warsaw before the entry of Soviet troops..." It seems clear from this that he expected and approved of armed action in Warsaw; but he remained of this opinion for only three days. When he received via London reports of the incident at Wilno, although this was not the first instance of Soviet bad faith that had come to his knowledge, he telegraphed as follows on July 28th: "In view of Soviet policy of violence and *faits accomplis*, armed rising would be devoid of sense politically and might involve needless sacrifice..."[4]

There was thus no more talk of "appearing in the role of undisputed owner." In addition, it would appear that at a time when the Home Army command had given up the idea of a general insurrection, for which the necessary conditions were not present, but had on the other hand decided to fight in Warsaw, Sosnkowski was still thinking in terms of a country-wide rising.[5] Moreover, his message of the 28th was

[4] This despatch was received in London on the evening of July 31st and deciphered in the afternoon of August 1st but, by the President's decision, was not sent to Warsaw in view of the Government's resolutions.

[5] It seems that General Sosnkowski himself did not know exactly what he regarded as a general rising and what the battle for Warsaw only. On September 25, 1944, towards the end of the rising, when there was no doubt as to who was fighting and for what, the C-in-C sent a letter (Ref. No. 1281/GNW/44) to the Commander of the Polish Air Force in which he said: "The development of the operational situation in Poland cannot be foreseen in advance, so that all rigid plans for support are doomed to failure. There is as yet no *uprising* in Poland, and the only current problem is that of supplies for Warsaw, where fighting is now taking place, and for the troops in that part of German-occupied Poland who are able to fight..."

This same General Sosnkowski in 1957, writing the preface to General Sosabowski's book (in Polish) *By the shortest way* states on page XIV: "An uprising in the capital of a country, the seat of the central authorities, both political and military, is nothing else but a general uprising in the full sense of the term."

sent in ignorance of the fact that the Government had decided on July 25th to authorize the Delegate in Warsaw to take on his own authority any decisions made necessary by the speed of the Soviet advance. Similarly, he was unaware that Warsaw had telegraphed to London on the 25th that they were ready to proclaim the rising in the capital.

When one examines the various documents, reports and messages after the lapse of years, one is irresistibly led to the conclusion that if Sosnkowski had really wished to be abreast of events, to make his views clear and secure acceptance of his decisions, the only proper thing for him to do was to fly to Poland and study the position on the spot. There he could have had first-hand information and discussed with the Government Delegate and the Home Army command what to do in the very complex situation that prevailed. If, after such discussions, he had returned to London with solid backing from the home country — if he had shown a firm attitude, and above all if he had been in the right place — then there might have been hopes of a single, resolute Polish policy.

As we have seen, the "Bridge" operations began in the spring of 1944: the first was carried out on April 15/16th, and the second, with complete success, on May 29/30th. This would have been an ideal opportunity to visit the home country, to return and adopt timely decisions.[6]) In actual fact Sosnkowski did think of leaving Britain for Poland, but from a different point of view. On January 11, 1944 he sent a despatch to Warsaw describing the difficulties of his position in London and concluding with the words: "In these circumstances it may soon be my duty to join the ranks of the Home Army." This, however, was more a reaction of bitterness and disgust with the conditions of life in exile.

He returned to the idea once thereafter, but dropped it on receiving a rather coldly-worded message from the Home Army command that they would not be able to guarantee his safety. And so, instead of taking what would appear to have been the obvious decision, he left for Italy at the most crucial and dramatic period of the war as it affected Poland.

II

General *Bor's* historic signal of the 25th had spoken of sending in the Parachute Brigade and also bombing the Warsaw airfields.

---

[6]) General Sosnkowski was then 58 and could have perfectly well borne the hardships of the journey. He was after all the Commander-in-Chief and so a serving officer. Retinger, who was only two years younger, actually made a parachute landing in Poland.

When the first cadres of this unit were created in Britain in 1941, it was certainly with the firm intention that these élite troops would be sent to their native land and join in the battle for final victory. For many months the best and fittest soldiers were selected and given intensive training. Their muscles and courage were steeled and they were taught to be ruthless. They were made expert in the newest weapons and technique of parachute warfare, and naturally they were schooled in actual jumping — all with a view to one day fighting in Poland.

In the early part of the war this prospect could be considered realistic; but the shape of things was transformed at the turn of the year 1942-3, when Russia, aided by huge quantities of Western supplies, beat off the German attack and began gradually to take the offensive herself. The West, which had no desire to see Russia conquer the Germans single-handed, was obliged to accelerate its own planning nad give thought to specific objectives. Churchill, who was a European as well as an islander, perceived the threat looming up from the East and saw the advantages of an attack on Hitler's "Fortress Europe" from the south, striking up towards the centre of the continent. In this way the Western allies might have reached central and eastern Europe before the Red Army and thus won decisive political and strategic gains, as well as shortening the war against Germany.

Unfortunately Roosevelt took a different view. He was only interested in Europe to the extent of wishing to see an order established there which would not threaten the security of the United States. He feared Japan's strength and fanaticism and foresaw hard and bloody contests in the Pacific, in which he was anxious to secure Russia's help. He was apprehensive of a separate peace between Russia and Germany, but did not discern the Russian danger as such. Moreover he disliked the British Empire, and although an ally of Briatin's he wished to see her domination curtailed. He saw in the war a chance of raising his country to the first rank among world powers.

Thus plans to exploit Germany's weakness in the Balkans were rejected, and Churchill as the weaker partner had to give in. The fact that Anglo-American invasion was not supplemented by operations in south-eastern and central Europe[7]) had a profound effect on Poland's political and strategic position, since it was now on the cards that the Red Army would reach the centre of the continent before the Western allies.

The situation began to become clear as far as Poland was concerned in the summer of 1943. On July 2nd Colonel

---

[7]) The decision that the invasion of the continent would be based on Britain was made at the Casablanca Conference on January 14, 1943.

Mitkiewicz, the Polish C-in-C's representative with the Anglo-American Combined Chiefs of Staff in Washington, submitted a long memorandum to that body concerning the use of the Home Army in future allied operations in Europe. This was a subject of the utmost importance to Poland. If the memorandum had been accepted and if the territory of Poland had been covered by allied military plans, it would have meant that the Russians did not have a free hand there and that Poland, like France, Belgium, Holland, Norway and Greece, was still within the sphere of the West's political interests and aims.

The Chiefs of Staff took cognizance of the memorandum, but it was not fully discussed and its recommendations were not acted upon. During the next few weeks Mitkiewicz had several talks with high-ranking American and British officers and learnt, partly through unofficial channels, that it had been decided on the political level [8] that Poland belonged to the Soviet orbit and should seek to come to terms with Moscow. The Western allies were not interested in equipping the Home Army for a general rising, since it was not certain against whom that rising would be directed. They would, however, continue to furnish supplies for purposes of subversion and sabotage. Naturally this was not all spelt out in the official reply which reached Mitkiewicz on September 23rd. This merely said that there were not enough aircraft to meet the full Polish requirements in the way of supply lifts, but that the Americans would send in planes with sabotage equipment.[9]

[8] This probably took place at the conference between Roosevelt and Churchill in Quebec, on August 17, 1943, when it was definitely decided that Poland would be excluded from the area covered by the Allied invasion plans.

[9] Colonel Mitkiewicz gives an account of these affairs in a very interesting article (in Polish) *Prelude to the armed uprising of the Home Army*, printed in *Horyzonty* (No. 131 of April 1967 and No. 132 of May 1967). The author makes a few small mistakes: he gives the full name of SOE incorrectly and assumes that General Gubbins was head of it in July 1943. Also his appraisal of SOE is not in accordance with the facts. All assistance for occupied Europe went through this organization and it was an operational fighting instrument. It had no special ties with the British secret service, and had to assist sabotage and secret armies. SOE carried out its tasks very well in relation to those countries which remained in the sphere of western interests, and was not a "side track" for them but their main support. For instance, all assistance to France went through this channel, yet the privileged strength of France in the political sphere was in no way impaired.

Colonel Mitkiewicz also appears unfair in his judgment of the Americans and the British respectively. His account suggests that the Americans wished to help Poland and that the British were against this and prevented it.

The United States are a great and powerful country, which has twice

The new strategic picture also affected the position of Polish troops in the West. There was little prospect now of their marching into Poland across a defeated Germany and joining forces with the Home Army. Instead, they would have to fight the enemy in distant lands while their home country was reconquered by the Red Army.

This, at any rate, was certain as regards the Polish land and sea forces; but what of the air force and the Parachute Brigade? Was it impossible for them to reach Warsaw and take part in the battle there? Disregarding the political complications, we may consider how the problem looked from the technical point of view.

In the spring of 1944 the Parachute Brigade, stationed in Britain, numbered some 1,500 officers and men. Like all the Polish units in the West it suffered from a chronic lack of manpower, which resulted in the neglect of many of its functions. The men were first-class and were well trained, but they had not practised jumping with full battle equipment, and the unit's supply situation left much to be desired.

At this stage of the war flights from Britain to Poland had a history of over three years behind them, since they had begun in February 1941 and were continued from the base in Italy after the autumn of 1943. Although it was about 1,000 miles from Britain to Warsaw, the problem of distance had been solved by adapting long-range bombers: first Halifaxes, then Liberators towards the end of the period of flights from Britain. But, while this and other practical difficulties had been mastered, it must be recalled that these were flights of a special character, very different from a mass operation by a large military unit. To recapitulate:—

The sorties took place at night, generally at full moon, since they would have been suicidal by day. Weather conditions had to be right, and Reich territory was avoided as far as possible because of flak and night fighters.

The flights were carried out by single, modified aircraft, the supply of which was limited. Each carried from two to

---

saved Europe and is still the main hope of the free world. It would have been impossible to defeat Hitler without their help, but, looking at the last war from the Polish point of view, the facts cannot be ignored. It was not Churchill but Roosevelt who decided that the invasion should take place from the west and not from the south, and thus destroyed all Poland's chances; it was not Churchill but Roosevelt who backed up Stalin at Teheran and Yalta; it was he again who had crypto-communists in his entourage. Many American officers expressed their sympathy to Colonel Mitkiewicz and did not hide their feeling towards Poland. Poles received the same sympathy from many British officers, but in both cases these were only individual reactions and personal views, which had no effect on political decisions.

six parachutists and light stores only, since the distance was too great for heavy ones.

The planes had as their target secret dropping zones, chosen with care and manned by skilled personnel who organized signal flares and the reception of parachutists and stores. Despite these careful arrangements, mistakes were often made, so that parachutists landed far from their destination and supplies were lost.

Sorties took place only in spring, autumn and winter, when the nights were long and the return flight could be made under cover of darkness.

During the thirty-three months in which these difficult, dangerous and expensive sorties were carried out from Britain, between February 1941 and October 1943, a little over 200 parachutists were dropped, including 187 military men and 26 political couriers. But the problem which now presented itself was that of lifting a whole brigade, with its equipment, in a single colossal operation.

Even if Poland had been included in Western strategic plans and the British had agreed to an attempt so foolhardy as scarcely to deserve the name of a military operation, it would have to have been planned for many months ahead. The years of experience had shown that the best aircraft, in fact the only one which could fly to Warsaw by the roundabout route via Sweden, accomplish its mission and return, was the American Liberator. It was armed, which was important since a fighter escort was impracticable over the long distance; but it was basically a daylight bomber, and had to be adapted before it could undertake nocturnal supply lifts. The exhaust silencers were altered and special navigational aids fitted, together with extra fuel tanks and apparatus to facilitate jumping. Thus adapted and with its crew reduced to seven, the Liberator could carry a maximum of six parachutists with their equipment. To lift an entire brigade,[10]) with only the lightest of stores and ammunition for one day's fighting, would have required no fewer than 265 of these giant aircraft, all suitably modified. Where could they have been got from? Suffice it to say that SOE, despite constant efforts, at the peak of its activity covering the whole of occupied Western Europe, never had at its disposal at any one time more than twenty-odd long-range aircraft modified for supply and parachute drops.

Let us, however, exert our imagination further and suppose that the Poles had approached the British authorities in good

[10]) At Arnhem, in September 1944, 1,508 parachutists jumped from Dakotas and 78 landed in gliders with heavy equipment. These figures have been taken into account in calculation.

time and obtained their agreement, and that a swarm of modified Liberators was now in Britain ready to carry out a nocturnal flight to Poland. What would have happened?

Parachute operations on a large scale had already been tried during the war, first and foremost by the Germans, whose main achievement in this line was no doubt the invasion of Crete. This was a success because they had complete air supremacy and barely 120 miles to fly from their bases in Greece. Their paratroopers landed in daylight, after the enemy had been reduced to silence by air bombing on a massive scale.

The Western allies also used airborne troops, their chief operation apart from Arnhem being the landings on the night of June 5/6, 1944 which prepared the way for the invasion of the continent. The distance from the British bases to Normandy was a matter of 90-120 miles, so that various types of aircraft and even gliders could be used. The allies had almost complete air supremacy, they could bomb whatever they liked and provide the paratroopers with a full fighter escort, yet they decided to carry out the landings only at night. They thus had the advantage of surprise, the flights were undisturbed and took only an hour or so; nevertheless, losses were high [11]) and the parachutists so dispersed that some landed twelve miles or more from their destination.

The Germans guarding the French coast, like those occupying Poland, were efficient, disciplined, stubborn frontline troops. Heavy fighting began during the night, and in many places where the parachutists did not receive support from the advancing land forces they were slaughtered by the Germans. The Arnhem operation failed in the same way and for the same reasons.

Let us now imagine a similar attempt in Poland. The vast fleet of Liberators, extended over many miles,[12]) takes off from British airfields and advances eastward. Over the North Sea it is intercepted by German night fighters and suffers its first losses. It flies on in somewhat looser formation as far as Sweden, where it turns south over the Baltic to the Danzig area. In a storm of flak and harried by fighter aircraft with quick-firing guns, the fleet moves southward along the course of the Vistula. By now several planes have been lost in the North Sea and Baltic, some have been shot down in Poland, others have had to turn back with

---

[11]) The American 101st Airborne Division lost 66 per cent of its original strength of 6,000 (*Rendezvous with Destiny*, by Leonard Rapport and Arthur Northwood Jr.).

[12]) The formation plan of a brigade in the air, which extends for twenty-three miles, is given in the book *Polish Parachutists* (in Polish).

engine-trouble and others again have strayed off course in the dark. At last, far below, the flames of the burning city come into view. The planes come down to a low altitude, since otherwise the paratroopers will be dispersed and unable to act as a unit. A fresh barrage of flak shoots up to meet them.

General *Bor* had requested that if the Brigade was sent, the landing should be effected in the Warsaw district of Wola. How many of the paratroopers who reached Warsaw could have landed safely by night in such an area, with its roofs, walls, stone and concrete road-surfaces? How many would have landed in parts of the city occupied by the insurgent forces and not by the Germans? And what would have happened to those few who did land safe and sound and in a condition to do battle? In any case they could not have acted as a coherent force, since they would have been scattered and landed at random destinations. Each man would have had arms and ammunition for one day's fighting, and that would have been the end of it. These, after all, were soldiers trained in the West, used to normal warfare with adequate supplies and equipment. Their brothers in the underground force could have made the ammunition last out longer, but they had five years of experience behind them.

General *Bor's* telegram asking for the Brigade and for the bombing of German airfields reached London on July 26th. Next day the ambassador, Count Raczynski, handed a copy of it to Mr. Eden and informed him that the Polish Government also wished to send to Warsaw the four squadrons from Italy, which, escorted by a fighter squadron, were to land on airfields captured by the Home Army.

The fact that *Bor's* request was passed on as it stood shows that the Poles, both in Warsaw and in London, were unconscious of the practical and technical obstacles. In Warsaw's case this was understandable. Although the underground's liaison with the West was in general efficient, it was never fully informed of the development of the military situation, the allies' intentions and technical possibilities. The exclusion of Poland from the area covered by allied invasion plans was known to it only in a very general fashion. General Sosnkowski furnished the Home Army command with a number of forecasts and shrewd political analyses, but no document can be found to show that London gave Warsaw an exact idea of what was and was not feasible from the technical point of view.

Bor, for his part, was governed partly by psychological motives in making his request. For Poland, the supreme moment of the war was at hand, the contest which was about to determine the nation's fate. The appeal for the Parachute Brigade and the squadrons from Italy was of a symbolic character. Such might well be the reactions and feelings of men who for five years had had no direct contact with the centres of world-wide planning and decision, and had now resolved on a final dramatic stand in defence of the nation's right to live.

The attiutde of the politicians in London is harder to understand. They knew that there could be no question of sending the Brigade to Poland, and for this reason they had agreed to the allies using it for the second wave of the Normandy invasion in June. The Polish Government and C-in-C took this decision jointly and were right to do so, since otherwise the Brigade would not have taken part in the war at all. They knew that no Western bombers had as yet carried out raids on targets as far off as Warsaw was from the nearest Italian bases, and that no such raids would be possible until the Russians consented to the use of their airfields for landing. They must also have realized that to send the four squadrons to Warsaw without ground staff, fuel, spare parts, bombs and ammunition — not to mention the need for the Home Army first to capture suitable airfields — would simply have meant squandering those first-class formations.

The British could do no other than refuse on purely technical grounds, irrespective of politics; and these ill-judged requests only weakened the effect of later Polish efforts which deserved better success, such as those concerning supply drops and the exercise of pressure on Stalin to alter his attitude towards insurgent Warsaw.

III

The second Home Army plan for a general rising in Poland, approved by General Rowecki in the autumn of 1942 and received in London at the beginning of March 1943, envisaged the use of the whole Polish Air Force then in the West. It contained the words: "We assume further that the rising will be supported by the whole of the available air forces, which will by then no doubt have been expanded, or in any case will not be fewer than the present thirteen squadrons." The drafters of the plan recognized that the air force in the West was not then in a position to support a rising in Poland, but they expressed the hope that with time this situation would change. The plan, which was carefully worked out, proceeded from the logical assumption that while all the Polish units controlled by the Government in London were intended to fight the Germans wherever opportunity offered, when the right moment came they should be in Poland to help deliver the final blow against the invader's weaking forces.

This was indeed the intention, but in order for it to be carried out, many circumstances favourable to Poland would have had to coincide. Fate decided otherwise, and it very soon became clear that the plan was over-optimistic. At the very time it was received in London, while the Western allies were planning a cross-Channel invasion in 1944 and were about to enter Italy, Soviet victories in the east were altering the balance of forces in Europe. Instead of our forces returning to their native land in the near future, shoulder to shoulder with the Western allies, the threat of a Red Army occupation already loomed and was given substance by the Western decision to exclude Poland from their sphere of operations.

This made it impossible, for both military and political reasons, for the Polish land units in the West to be used in the home country, even in the event of the direst threat and the most crying necessity. There remained only the question of such help as could be given by the air force. What was its strength, and how far was it capable of independent action?

At the turn of the year 1942-3, the Polish Air Force in the West comprised ten fighter and three bomber squadrons with 176 and 53 aircraft respectively. The special duties flight for sorties to Poland consisted first of six and later of ten aircraft. The size of the force varied with losses and replacements, but plans for expanding it were always frustrated by lack of manpower. This was a problem felt by every Polish commander in the West. The reserves in France were cut off by the events of June 1940; recruiting in the US and Canada was not a success; only a trickle of individuals came from Poland itself; and almost all the evacuees from the Soviet Union were serving in the 2nd Corps. The air force, which had fought uninterruptedly and suffered heavy losses, was in the worst position of all the services. There was no way of bringing bomber crews or ground staff up to strength, particularly as every pilot, navigator and mechanic was a specialist who required thorough training.

Leaving aside the special duties flight, the thirteen squadrons could have been no help to an insurrection if it had broken out in 1943. The allied invasion of mainland Italy, which began on September 3rd of that year, did not alter matters much. The Polish fighter squadrons for the most part used British Spitfire IX's with a maximum range of some 900 miles when fitted with an extra tank, which, however, reduced their speed. One squadron flew American Mustang III's, with a range of only 800 miles. Neither could hope to reach Poland even from the Italian bases. The bomber squadrons of Lancasters, Wellingtons and Mosquitos were also incapable of flying to Poland, carrying out a mission and returning to base. We had no transport planes, for the allies were short of them too, but even if we had been allotted some they would have been no use in view of the distance.[13]) Without long-range transport planes it would have been suicidal to fly the squadrons to Poland during a rising, for they would have had no fuel, ammunition, bombs or ground staff.

Another factor which seriously limited our freedom of action was that the Polish Air Force possessed its own units only up to squadron level, and even these depended partly on British maintenance and communications; nor had we any operational commands of our own. All our difficulties, shortcomings and lack of independence were due to the same ever-present cause, the lack of manpower.

Our air authorities tried to remedy the situation in two ways. They badgered the General Staff for men at every opportunity, and they parachuted into Poland parties of specially trained airmen to inform the Home Army command of the state of affairs in the West and to help with essential preparations for a rising. On the night of January 25/26, 1943 Wing-Commander (pilot) Roman Rudkowski was flown in in this way, and on the following night Flight-Lieutenant (observer) Michal Tajchman, Flying Officer (pilot) Florian Adrian and Flying Officer (aircraftman) Waclaw Pijanowski. The team were instructed by their superiors to discourage undue optimism and make it clear that at that stage help from the West was almost impossible.

Although pressure on the General Staff was kept up, it produced little result. The cry for reserves was heard on every hand — from the Parachute Brigade, the newly formed armoured division and, not least, the Navy. The air force should have had first claim, since it was the only arm that could give direct help to the home country, but this evident fact was sometimes disregarded in favour of local needs.

In 1943 the Inspector of the air force asked the General Staff for 10,000 men to be transferred from the land forces in order to make possible the formation of separate commands, auxiliary services and signal units, and also to bring the bomber squadrons up to strength. Naturally the other commanders resisted this, and the General Staff reduced the

---

[13]) In order to shorten the distance proposals were put forward to operate from neutral countries, such as Sweden and Turkey, but of course these were never put into effect.

number to 3,200 men, of whom 2,456 were actually provided. Some relief was also afforded by the assignment to the air force of the first contingent of the Women's Auxiliary Service; but in general the manpower shortage remained.

Meanwhile events in the east were moving fast; the situation in the home country was altering, and the question of a final struggle was becoming more and more pressing.

On September 10, 1943 the Home Army commander sent to London a long memorandum in which he reverted to the plan for a rising assisted by the air force. Arguing on similar lines to the air force command in the West, he wrote: "Our entire military effort outside Poland should be subordinated to providing air assistance in the event of a rising, since this may prove to be the only way in which the forces in the West can take an active part in the initial and vital phase of such a rising." The memorandum went on to indicate far-reaching operational aims and to emphasize the need for battlefield aircraft, i.e. light bombers which could to some extent take the place of artillery.

These requests reached London on October 1st, and were carefully considered. Three weeks later, Air Vice-Marshal Izycki drafted a reply for the C-in-C containing, *inter alia*, four important points:

(1) In very favourable circumstances and providing the necessary reinforcements are obtained, the Polish Air Force may be in a position to support a rising by the beginning of 1945.

(2) Such support will only be feasible if the relevant plans and timing are fully accepted by our allies.

(3) From the technical and operational point of view, support would entail operating from bases in one or more of the following areas: southern Sweden, the Danish peninsula, or east of the Rhine, or again north of the line Venice - Fiume - Nish (Yugoslavia).

(4) At present, on political grounds, the British do not wish to commit themselves.

General Sosnkowski made some alterations in the draft by hand, deleting the passage about reinforcements and underlining point (4).[14])

In an information report for the Home Army dated February 1944, Izycki once more included the statement that his

---

[14]) It does not appear that this reply was in fact sent to Home Army H.Q. No record of its despatch can be found in the Sixth Bureau archives (register of outgoing correspondence).

squadrons were under strength, but the C-in-C again deleted it. Presumably, his motive was to avoid discouraging the underground leaders by revealing the air force's weakness, but as it was he raised undue hopes. This alarmed the air force command: the Home Army were expecting co-operation that would not be forthcoming, and those whose duty it was to damp their optimism were not doing so. Another team of airmen was sent out and landed near Lublin on April 27/28: Wing-Commander (pilot) Jan Bialy, Squadron Leader (pilot) Jerzy Iszkowski, Squadron Leader Bronislaw Lewkowicz and Flight-Lieutenant Edmund Marynowski. Their orders, drawn up by Izycki himself, were to inform the Home Army command clearly that the squadrons in the West were not strong enough to perform the tasks expected of them in connection with the rising; that shortage of manpower precluded their acting independently; that the British authorities had not consented to the squadrons being sent to Poland, and that even if this were allowed, the allies had no transport planes to spare for supply purposes. Consequently the only practicable form of support would take the form of sorties from bases outside Poland and with the help of the allied air forces.

Such was the position in July 1944, when General *Bor* telegraphed to London that he was "ready to fight for Warsaw at any moment." At the time when this message was sent, the only Polish air unit which was capable of aiding Warsaw was No. 1586 special duties Flight, stationed at Brindisi.

IV

The Polish Fighter Force in the West was, from the very beginning, in a much better situation than the Bombers, for its shortage of personnel was less acute. Only one man was needed to fly a small plane such as the Spitfire or Hurricane, and he made up the whole crew. It was a different matter with the heavy giants, which carried in their hulls, tons of bombs to be dropped on German factories, ports, railway stations and airfields. The four-engined Lancasters, Halifaxes and Liberators required a minimum crew of seven. Practically each one of these carefully trained men was a specialist of a different kind.

When, in 1943, a special duties independent Polish Flight was formed, attached to the British 138 Squadron at Tempsford, Bomber 301 Squadron had to be disbanded to provide a sufficient number of crews. These personnel difficulties never grew less, and after the Flight was transferred to Italy, where it was given the number 1586, they even increased.

Each crew had to undergo special training, different for each type of plane, this took place in Britain and was the cause of extra difficulties and delays. It came to a point when the number of planes was so much greater than the number of crews that the Royal Air Force began to withdraw them and hand them over to other Flights with similar duties.[15])

At the outset the Flight was commanded by Squadron Leader Stanislaw Krol, an experienced navigator, the veteran of many flights to Poland, greatly respected by his own men, the Royal Air Force authorities and SOE. At the beginning of June 1944 he finished a new operational tour, after which he was due to rest. It was, however, decided that, in view of his abilities, he should be used in another, important position. On June 9th he was transferred as liaison officer to the newly-formed British air Group "The Balkans",[16]) while the Flight came under the command of Squadron Leader Eugeniusz Arciuszkiewicz.

After enormous effort during April and May 1944 the sorties to Poland had to be discontinued because of the short nights, but the Polish airmen knew no rest. During June they carried out 169 sorties to Yugoslavia and Northern Italy, luckily without losses. In July they continued these and also resumed sorties to Poland. By the end of this hot, summer month they were exhausted and their worn aircraft required urgent repairs. The Flight had then only six crews, of which two were due to rest. A seventh, newly arrived and inexperienced in night flying, completed this modest number.

[15]) On July 1, 1944, Lt.-Colonel *Hancza*, Polish chief of the "Elba" base at Brindisi, sent Lt.-Colonel Utnik, chief of the Sixth Bureau in London, a telegram No. 999/VV/222, in which he stated that:
"1) The strength of the crews in 1586 Flight will be ten on the third of this month, six on August 1st and four at the end of August...;
2) As a result of the lack of crews and ground staff, the English have taken four of our sixteen planes; there will be further reductions as the crews decrease...
3) The attitude of MAAF [Mediterranean Allied Air Force] is entirely favourable and they will give us as many planes as we have crews and ground staff..."

[16]) This Group was formed on June 7, 1944 and based in Bari. Air Vice-Marshal William Elliot was in command, under Air Marshal Slessor, Air Officer C-in-C of the Mediterranean Area. 334 Wing which included the special squadrons carrying out sorties to the occupied countries, was attached to this Group, as was the Polish 1586 Flight. Altogether the Group contained units of eight nationalities. The Yugoslav partisans under Tito's command had two Flights (one of Spitfires, the other of Hurricanes). There were also two Soviet Squadrons, which the British, after long argument with the Russians, incorporated into 334 Wing. One of them, a transport squadron, which carried out drops, flew Russian-built Dakotas, the other Russian Yak fighters. Both assisted Tito's partisans. They were probably the only Russian units during the war, that served for a time under Western command.

Besides the Polish 1586 Flight, attached to 148 Squadron in 334 Wing, there were also in the Squadron British crews, experienced in night flights to Poland. It has been impossible to find out how many there were, but we know approximately how many specially modified aircraft, Halifaxes and Liberators, the Squadron had at its disposal. Air Marshal Slessor gives the figure as about twenty-four.

At five o'clock in the afternoon of August 1st the Warsaw Rising broke out. The news arrived in London on the following day and immediately the Poles started to urge the Allies, and above all the British, to send the capital the utmost possible help. Our ambassador, Count Raczynski, was the first to make representations on behalf of the Polish Government. Since Eden was engaged in the House of Commons, he was received by the Under-Secretary of State, Cadogan, who reported his request direct to Churchill. The Polish Government required assistance in the form of drops of weapons and ammunition. The following afternoon the Ambassador saw the Prime Minister personally and handed him a letter from President Raczkiewicz.

From this moment the Poles began to press their case more and more urgently. The President, after his letter to Churchill, sent another to King George VI and a telegram to President Roosevelt, while Jan Kwapinski, premier Mikolajczyk's deputy, saw Eden. The Polish Chief of Staff General Kopanski wrote to General Ismay, the Deputy Secretary of the War Cabinet, and later had a personal interview with him; the Minister of National Defence, General Kukiel, tackled other military personages. General Tatar did not remain behind. Individual politicians also tried to use their contacts and influence. On August 6th General Sosnkowski, the Polish C-in-C, at last returned from Italy and immediately began his own intervention, mostly in the form of letters. He wrote to Marshal Alan Brooke, the Chief of the Imperial General Staff, to Air Marshal Portal, to General Wilson, the Allied commander in the Mediterranean area, and to the Secretary of State for Air, Sir A. Sinclair. The demands were three: immediate assistance for Warsaw by air drops, recognition of the Home Army soldiers as combatants, and pressure on Russia to alter her attitude to the rising and give it help.

On August 13th Mikolajczyk returned from Moscow and also began to intercede at the highest levels. It should be recalled that he had gone to Moscow under strong pressure from the British to try to come to a political agreement with Stalin, while opinions among Poles were very divided. Nothing came of his trip, but the Soviet dictator, who at first denied that there was any fighting in Warsaw, towards the end of the talks promised help. This was one more of Stalin's lies, for once again he did not keep his promise.

This great wave of representations, letters, telegrams, interviews and demands bore witness to the fact that the Polish political and military authorities in the West understood the importance of the rising and, in a burst of activity, tried to do everything possible to get help for the city. At the same time, this multiform activity was no better than a vast improvisation.

For years a rising had been planned in Poland. The Home Army command had twice sent detailed plans to the West, the Polish General Staff in London had deliberated on ways of using our armed forces in the West in the event of decisive fighting in Poland; many conferences had been held on this subject, hundreds of telegrams exchanged, urgent couriers sent back and forth; yet when at last the moment for the rising arrived, it turned out that the plans were irrelevant and the real situation very different from what had been foreseen.

All the Polish military plans had been based on the assumption that help by air from the Polish and allied squadrons would only be possible if the Western front was to the east of the Rhine, which would reduce the flying distance considerably. This condition had not been fulfilled and the allied air bases were still in Britain. The transfer of the dropping operations to Italy had afforded access to southern Poland but did not alter the position of Warsaw. The shortest distance to the Polish capital from London is 950 miles, from Brindisi 880 miles. Even the heaviest bombers, used for night flights, could not fly this distance both ways unless they were specially adapted. However the Polish representations took no account of this factor. Some even asked once again for the Parachute Brigade to be dropped and for the Polish Air Force to be sent to Poland, although they must have known that it was quite impossible. A glaring example of this is the telegram sent to Poland on August 8th by General Sosnkowski after a conversation with General Ismay:

"... I am demanding drops, combatant status, parachute help, our airforce..."

It is difficult not to echo General Kopanski's words: "We demanded of our Allies an effort which we had not foreseen earlier ourselves." [17])

The political situation was no surprise either and did not justify improvisation. The fighting in Warsaw broke out

[17]) *War Memoirs 1939-1945* (in Polish), page 334.

eight months after the Teheran Conference, the result of which was known to our authorities. It nullified the British obligations of alliance, handed Poland over to Stalin and was a political reflection of earlier strategic decisions which ruled out an invasion of the Continent from the south to the west and excluded Poland from the military plans of the Western allies. This state of affairs called for a realistic approach to the situation, but of this the Polish Government under Mikolajczyk was incapable. There is no sign that any attempt was made to come to an understanding with the British or to find out their intentions; there are no documents to show that the question was ever put clearly: "What will you do when a rising breaks out in Poland? Will you help and, if so, by what means? What can we count on?" The Polish C-in-C did not put this question either. The argument that it was unnecessary to do so, because in the existing political and military situation a rising in Poland was not to be expected, is untenable and proves only a lack of realism: for in Poland during the war years a spirit of hatred and desire for revenge, together with a remarkable inner strength had accumulated and become a real and visible factor in inspiring action. To ignore or underrate this could only lead to a false appraisal of the situation.

The underground leaders in Poland were also responsible for this improvisation, by reason of their sudden change of plan. It was only decided on July 22nd that Warsaw would be the scene of fighting and that the Poles would attempt to take the city themselves. This was a very serious political decision and had far-reaching military consequences, especially in the matter of help from the West, which was still expected, as General *Bor's* telegram of July 25th proves. Yet the decision to unleash the rising in a big city completely altered the possibilities of the expected air operations.

The demand for the dropping of the Parachute Brigade and bombing of targets near Warsaw was unrealistic and was rejected immediately, as was the landing in Poland of the four bomber squadrons, but even the carrying out of supply sorties became a totally different problem. The aircrews were faced with a quite new and startling task. A solitary night flight to a secret dropping zone in southern Poland, unknown to the Germans, and a drop guided by its light signals was one thing; it was quite another to send regularly up to a score of aircraft a distance of 880 miles over German-occupied territory, and to make drops from a low altitude on the great, fighting city, encircled by fires, hidden in smoke, cut up into small sectors which constantly changed hands and defended by anti-aircraft artillery and night fighters waiting to attack the flight paths.

The very first representation to Churchill brought a result, for in the early morning of August 3rd Slessor received an emergency signal from London that two days earlier a rising had broken out in Warsaw, that the Polish Government had informed the Prime Minister of this and requested immediate help in the form of drops. The British Government considered the matter important and urgent. Drops were to be started at once if it was technically possible.

Slessor's first reactoin, as an airman, was adverse, but Air Marshal Portal explained to him that the problem had a political aspect, that Churchill considered it most important and that sorties must begin immediately.

The night of August 3rd-4th was impossible because of weather conditions, but the following night fourteen aircraft set out. All the seven Polish crews flew, because no-one, of course, took his rest; the other seven were provided by 148 Squadron. Only two Polish aircraft made drops over Warsaw — the insurgents picked them up; ten returned badly shot up; five, all British, failed to return.

After this first experience Slessor forbade further flights, considering that the risk was out of proportion to the results and that in a few nights he would lose all his trained crews and most of his special aircraft. He also considered that, as a commander, he should protect the lives of his airmen when he could not attain his objectives by exposing them. He informed Portal of this, adding that while the moon was full he would not send any more aircraft to Poland at all, let alone to Warsaw.[18])

This refusal aroused an immediate reaction from the Poles. The struggle for Warsaw was for them no ordinary battle; they considered that the capital must receive help, however high the price. The pressure was increased. The airmen of 1586 Flight, although they themselves best knew the danger of flights to Warsaw and how little use they would be, expressed their full readiness to fly.

Under severe pressure Slessor revoked his order and allowed volunteer Polish crews to fly again. On August 8th three aircraft took off and carried out their drops, which fell into the insurgents' hands; the next day four flew but only reached the Kampinos Forest. Luckily there were no losses.

During the next two days the weather did not permit any operations, but the time was used to bring further pressure

---

[18]) During the first phase of the night sorties to Poland, using visual and astronomical navigation, a full moon was necessary in order to accomplish the flight and find the dropping zone; later the flights took place even in complete darkness. During the Warsaw Rising, when the flight-paths were known in advance, the planes fell easy victims to the German night fighters.

to bear on our British allies. Under the influence of this and because the moon was on the wane, Slessor again allowed six British crews to fly, who with five Polish planes set out for Warsaw on August 12th. There were no losses, but only seven aircraft made their drops, five of which were picked up by the insurgents.

These three lucky nights affected further decisions. On August 13th Slessor, with General Wilson's consent, withdrew from flights over the South of France (Operation "Dragoon"), from 205 Group, two squadrons of Liberators, representing half of the Group's heavy aircraft, and detailed them for Poland. These were: RAF 178 Squadron and SAAF (South African) 31 Squadron.

During the four nights, August 13th - 16th, 17 Polish and 62 British and South African giant planes tried to reach Warsaw; 10 of the Polish and 24 of the others succeeded. Of this total only 20 were able to make their drops, 15 of which reached the insurgents. Losses were very heavy. During the operations 3 Polish crews, 7 South African and 5 British were lost, i.e. nearly half as many as reached the capital. Another 2 British planes and 1 South African crashed on landing; almost all that returned were badly damaged, many of the crews brought back wounded.

After these terrible four nights it was clear that supply flights, for which the fighting city was crying out and which it needed so badly, had reached the very limit of what was justifiable as a military operation. The Home Army command, seeing the pitiful equipment of their units, who, as the fighting went on, were threatened by a complete lack of ammunition, demanded so many supplies that between 17 and 20 aircraft would have had to reach Warsaw each night and carry out their drops successfully. This was absolutely impossible. The most experienced crews, accustomed to night flights, had either been killed during the first operations or were on the verge of nervous and physical exhaustion. Their condition might have been adequate for heavy yet unsophisticated fighting, but was quite unsuited for operating a very complicated modern machine, night after night, for long hours without any respite. All the new crews, who had been hastily sent as replacements, trained in instrument flying, without experience and with no conception of visual navigation by night over unknown territory, were often unable even to find their objective, and when they did, they were killed uselessly, not knowing how to get through the clouds of smoke which engulfed the burning city. Signals from Warsaw indicated streets and squares where drops were urgently needed, but to the airmen, dropping from the darkness of the night into the inferno of smoke and fire, they were completely unrecognizable. No wonder that the containers, thrown among bursting anti-aircraft shells, fell anywhere and a large percentage became German booty. And around the blazing city, which lit up the countryside for 90 miles in all directions, hovered the German night fighters, for whom the heavy bombers against the red background of flames made an easy target. To avoid them, the pilots had to fly for miles very low, just above the roofs and treetops. At night that was enough to break up a plane and lose a valuable crew. The Poles, while there were still experienced veterans available, had a slight chance, but the South African boys were doomed to die.

Air Marshal Slessor was in constant opposition to these flights, as he considered that they were more than an airman should be asked to undertake. The fighting man must know that his sacrifice is not in vain, that he is not being sent to his death uselessly.

Such was the opinion of an unemotional Englishman, who had the right to be detached about Poland's fate.[19]) As a professional airman he was entitled to look at the whole problem only from a military point of view and take decisions accordingly.

But what were the opinions of those Poles who knew the problem from their own experience and expressed their views at the same time as the British commander opposed further flights?

General Ludomir Rayski, the pre-war Commander of the Polish Air Force, an experienced pilot, who himself made five flights to Poland during this time, two of them to Warsaw, reported as follows:

"...The crews return in aircraft holed like sieves. Even their parachutes are so shot to pieces that they would be useless if needed...

...In operations over Germany the losses are 3-5%, in operations over Poland more than 30%...

...The crews sent lately are young, newly trained airmen, used to instrument flying. All the flights to Poland require skilled navigation by landmarks. They depend wholly on this and are the very opposite of instrument flying...

...From the Polish point of view this is a suicidal waste of airmen..."

[19]) It should be said, however, that in his memoirs *The Central Blue* Slessor several times stresses the Russians' perfidy and their betrayal of Poles and the Warsaw Rising. He shows a good knowledge of Polish difficulties and problems and comments on them with true concern and friendliness.

The views of Squadron Leader E. Arciuszkiewicz, commander of 1586 Flight during the rising, who himself flew over Warsaw, are quoted in the following message (No. 1338/xxx/222 of August 20, 1944):

"The commander of 1586 Flight informed me to-day that in the present state of the anti-aircraft defence of Warsaw and, as experience has shown, precision drops from a height of 600-800 ft. are impracticable. In his opinion sending aircraft to Warsaw in practice amounts to the loss of aircraft and crews without any guarantee of supplying the troops in the capital..." [20])

From London things looked different. General Sosnkowski, the Polish C-in-C, made his wishes known in this signal to the base at Brindisi:

"Please convey to our airmen my order as follows: the fate of Warsaw and the Home Army now fighting within its walls depends on a sure and precise drop of arms and ammunition to-night in two places, above all Krasinski Square and Napoleon Square.

I realise the great difficulties, but under the present circumstances I demand from our airmen the utmost will-power and self-sacrifice.

These two drops must be carried out unconditionally — if necessary the planes should be sacrificed and the airmen bale out. I am sure that the task will be accomplished, as my faith in the courage and efficiency of our airmen is boundless.

London, 10. 8. 44. Sosnkowski"

During the night of August 13th - 14th this order was carried out and a drop was made on Krasinski Square. A few days later General Sosnkowski sent a telegram to the base, asking for the name of the captain of the aircraft, to whom he wished to award the Virtuti Militari. A meaningless gesture, for the whole crew had been burnt in the wreckage of their plane, which fell on the roofs of the Old Town.

Two experts, who had themselves flown with no thought for their own safety, considered that the flights did not fulfil their purpose. The question was not how many airmen were killed, for war unfortunately devours young lives, but what was the result of their sacrifice.

[20]) This telegram was sent by the Polish commander of the base in Brindisi to the head of the Sixth Bureau in London.

Air Marshal Slessor held to his order and only under pressure, against his own convictions, agreed to Polish volunteer crews continuing to fly. Up to the end of August five British crews flew on a single occasion — on August 18th — but they did not reach Warsaw. Polish crews flew 40 times and only four of them did not return. This was a small percentage of loss, but only because barely three aircraft reached Warsaw and made their drops. None of these fell into the insurgents' hands.

From August 15th to the end of the month the city did not receive a single container, and fourteen aircraft and thirteen vaulable crews were lost. Some of the containers fell on the Kampinos Forest and the Kabacki Woods, but they were practically useless to Warsaw.

On September 1st there was a full moon and Slessor, seeing the fruitlessness of this great effort, which was bringing only losses, forbade further flights. This order included the few Polish crews who were still operational.

V

While one of the bloodiest battles of the war was raging in Warsaw, the Polish eastern provinces were witnessing the last scene of the drama which began on September 17, 1939, when they were first occupied by Stalin, then Hitler's faithful ally. After the years of Germany's victories the front had again moved westward, and the Red Army once more stood on Polish territory.

It had been preceded there by the Soviet partisans, who had been active for two or three years and whose main task was to destroy the Polish character of the area. They were strong enough to threaten townships, villages and Polish partisan units, but did not make much of a stand against regular German troops, nor did they seem very anxious to do so.

However, matters changed when the Soviet armoured divisions once more came rolling from the east. The fate of the provinces was now about to be decided. The question was whether the Poles were to stand aside and make no attempt to assert their rights of ownership, or whether they should carry out local mobilization and attack the retreating Germans in order to seize back the usurped territories, establish Polish administration there and await the Red Army in a state of full preparedness for a further, joint assault on the common enemy.

The Polish political and military authorities decided on

this latter course, and accordingly put operation "Tempest" into effect. The province of Volhynia was the first to rise, and the 27th infantry division was set on foot there at the beginning of 1944.[21]) Then came Wilno and Nowogrodek, and afterwards Lwow, Bialystok and Polesie with the 30th infantry division.[22])

As far as relations with the Red Army were concerned, events always took the same course. First there was military co-operation, then a brief interlude of freedom, followed by treacherous ambushes, arrests and accusations.

As early as July 17-19th this tragic sequence of events occurred at Wilno, where the Russians arrested *General Wilk* (Wolf) and about seventy of his officers [23]) and disarmed over 6,000 men of the Polish partisan brigades who had fought for the city, helped to capture it and remained there for a few glorious days. These brigades, which had assembled at Wilno, belonged to the local Home Army district and were reinforced by five battalions of the 77th infantry regiment from the "Niemen" group which fell within the Nowogrodek district. This district was originally commanded by Lt-Colonel Prawdzic-Slaski, who was succeeded on June 27, 1944 by a parachutist, Lt-Colonel Adam Szydlowski. When the latter was arrested with *Wilk* his place was taken by Major Maciej Kalenkiewicz, who had been dropped into Poland at the end of 1941 and had commanding the 77th infantry regiment. *Ponury*, too had served in this regiment after his transfer from the Holy Cross Mountains.

Kalenkiewicz did not take part in the fighting for Wilno, as he was occupied on other duties and had not fully recovered from an amputation of the hand, carried out in makeshift conditions after being wounded by a German bullet. When the city was captured he was in the Rudnicki forest with some units belonging to his district. He was joined there by such of the Wilno forces as has escaped the clutches of the Red Army. In this way his force numbered in all several hundred fairly well-armed men: some even had horses. The officers included several other parachutists: Captains

---

[21]) Captain Tadeusz Klimowski *(Ostoja)* served in this division, first as an officer in the field and later as chief of staff.

[22]) Commanded by a parachutist Lt-Colonel Henryk Krajewski *(Trzaska)*. A number of parachutists changed their code-names after they got to Poland. Klimowski was previously known as *Klon*, Krajewski as *Wicher*.

[23]) These included three parachutists: *Wilk's* second-in-command, Lt-Colonel Adam Szydłowski *(Poleszuk)*, the chief of staff Major Teodor Cetys *(Slaw)* and the commander of the 6th brigade Major Franciszek Koprowski *(Konar)*.

Jan Skrochowski and Franciszek Cieplik and Lieutenant Adam Boryczko.

The force determined to fight to the last, and Kalenkiewicz's plan — the only one which offered any chance of success — was to escape from the area occupied by Soviet troops and get behind the German front in order to fight the Germans from the forest region around Bialystok. If the Russians should surround and attempt to disarm them, they were to resist.

They set out at once, as Red Army planes were flying more and more frequently over the woods, and scouts informed them that tanks were approaching from the north. Skrochowski led the way with a troop of horsemen and the rest followed in a long column strung out under cover of the woods.

They might have been allowed to escape, but the Russians had finally decided that all Polish units in the area must either lay down their arms or be destroyed forthwith. A motorized column, aided by air reconnaissance, sped after them. As long as it was dark and they could march through the forest there was some hope of evading their pursuers, but for how many days could they do so? Soon they would have to leave the woods for open country, and meanwhile their food was running out.

After a few days Kalenkiewicz divided his force into smaller parties to facilitate cover and the obtaining of food from villages. He himself, with a small detachment of cavalry and a group of his closest comrades, pressed on in a westerly direction in the hope of reaching the Bialystok forest.

On August 21st, a month after they had left the Rudnicki area, the pursuing Russians caught up with them at a forester's cottage at Surkonty. The Poles had no intention of surrendering, and so the bitter, unequal fight took place. The surrounded partisans killed many of the Russians, but only one of their number, Captain Bystromiak, miraculously escaped. Kalenkiewicz was killed, as were Cieplik, Skrochawski and all the other officers and cavalrymen. The Russians conquered the position, along with thirty-two corpses.[24])

[24]) The "Stolpce" group, which also belonged to the Nowogrodek district of the Home Army, was luckier. It was at that time in the Naliboki Forest, commanded by Lieutenant Adolf Pilch (*Gora*). He led a large column to the West, numbering several hundred infantry and cavalry, with a considerable quantity of "transport." Dodging between the two front lines he almost reached Warsaw, then crossed the Vistula and took cover in the Kampinos Forest, which he reached on August 1st, the day the rising broke out. During the fighting in Warsaw Pilch's unit harassed the Germans in the forest and neighbouring area.

VI

From the moment when the Warsaw rising broke out, the key to its success lay with Russia.

While the object of the insurrection was to wrest the city from the Germans and establish Polish rule there, it became clear in the first few days that unless the Russians delivered an attack across the Vistula, the insurgents would not be able to cope with the immensely superior German force.

The Russians' attitude was not only decisive as regards what they might do themselves. The help from the West on which the insurgents counted could not be effectual unless the Russians were willing to make it so. If Stalin, while holding up his own offensive, had at least agreed to Soviet airfields being used to help the insurgents, the problem of supply drops would have taken on a different aspect.

The Polish Government realized this, and in all their appeals to the British stressed the need for pressure on Russia. There was no direct diplomatic or military channel to the Russians, and Mikolajczyk's appeal to Stalin at the Kremlin, which was the only opportunity of its kind, elicited nothing but an insincere promise.

Churchill realized the position too, and apart from the instructions he sent to Italy, he turned his eyes eastward. On August 12th he appealed for the first time to Stalin to aid the fighting city and allow Western planes to land on Soviet airfields. Two days later the British and Americans made a joint appeal. The response from their Russian ally was not long in coming. On August 16th the American ambassador received a curt refusal, and on the same day a similar answer went from Stalin to Churchill. To make their attitude perfectly clear, the Russians added that they would not even permit the use of their fields by damaged allied aircraft with wounded on board.

For the first time since the beginning of the Western-Soviet military alliance, Churchill and Roosevelt lost patience. Doubtless they had no very high opinion of Soviet good faith, but they had not expected such an answer as this. It was, after all, a question of helping a military operation from which Russia could only benefit and in which she need not herself take part; of dealing a blow to the Germans and saving the lives of airmen who were fighting Hitler. Unless the Soviet airfields could be used, there could be no question of substantial aid with heavy aircraft. But this mattered little to Stalin, who had his own political and military aims.

The Western leaders did not give up the struggle, and on August 20th, addressed a further, sharply-worded message to Stalin on the question of landings. Again their faithful ally was prompt in his response: a peremptory "No" came two days later.

Churchill, by this time enraged, was in favour of overriding Stalin's arrogant refusal and informing him that the planes would be sent and would land on Soviet fields with or without permission. But he could not and would not do this without Roosevelt's agreement, and the latter refused to reply jointly in this sense. He too was indignant,[25]) but he did not want to add to the tension, bearing in mind that he still needed Soviet help against Japan.

The Soviet refusal was, in effect, a death-sentence on Warsaw. Only a large immediate airlift with thousands of containers full of arms, ammunition and medical supplies could have redressed the balance of forces and given the insurgents any hope of victory. Such an airlift could only have been achieved by means of a shuttle service of powerful planes flying over Warsaw and escorted by fighters in both directions.

The utmost efforts were made to achieve this. On August 4th, General Kopanski spoke to Colonel Palmer, the representative of the American OSS (Office of Strategic Services) in Britain and urged him to intervene with his superiors. A few days later Sosnkowski raised the matter with General Spaatz, the commander of the American Air Force in Britain. An urgent telegram was also sent to Colonel Mitkiewicz in Washington to take the matter up with the highest military authorities.

The Americans grasped the importance of the matter and before mid-August agreed to the use of their powerful Eighth Air Force of Flying Fortresses, stationed in Britain. Preparations were begun, but the operation was impossible without Soviet help. The colossal machines, flying by daylight only, required a fighter escort and would have had to land behind the Russian lines. The Americans had the use of a base at Poltava, 1,500 miles from Britain, but under the terms of their agreement with the Russians permission had to be sought for every single flight.

Despite Soviet obduracy, pressure was kept up. The Western leaders hoped that in the end they would break down Stalin's resistance, especially as world public opinion was beginning to be aroused. The press was given the facts and made use of them, and millions of people began to alter their opinion of the much-loved and much-admired Soviet Union.

---

[25]) The German historian Hans von Krannhals prefaces his book on the Warsaw rising (*Der Warschauer Aufstand*, published in Germany in 1962) with the dictum: 'Here, and nowhere else, the Cold War between East and West began.'

In the hope that the Russians might after all change their minds, preparations were pushed forward. The Americans were willing to provide the planes and crews and a fighter escort, but the supplies must be furnished by SOE. The Polish section, which had acquitted itself well till then, was faced with an unprecedented problem. Each Fortress, with a crew of ten, could take twelve containers. As it was proposed to send 110 Fortresses, the section had to find 1,320 of the giant metal cigars, weighing a couple of hundredweight each, and fill them with the desired equipment. Colonel Perkins, who had so far been responsible for only a few plane-loads on any given night, had to make a prodigious effort to obtain the necessary stores [26]) and deliver them to four separate airfields: Horham, Thorpe, Abbots and Tramlingham.

At the beginning of September it was still not known whether the flight would take place, but there was some slight ground for hope that the Russians would relent. The Sixth Bureau was in permanent contact with the Polish section of SOE on the question of stores and with the US air force command as regards planning. Many details had to be foreseen and discussed. The Americans, who had plenty of experience of daylight sorties of this kind, expected about forty percent of their planes to be lost and the remainder damaged. The flight, though at a high altitude and protected by fighters, was a long one; the planes would have to cross the North Sea by daylight, passing close to the German shore, and fly over Poland unescorted, as it was beyond the fighters' range and there was no prospect of the Russians providing cover. It was arranged that the Home Army patrols around Warsaw would do their best to rescue any airmen who baled out: they were to use the password

---

[26]) The 1,320 containers were loaded with:

Sten guns	2,976	with ammunition	1,691,400 rounds
Bren guns	211	with ammunition	548,600 rounds
Piats (anti-tank guns)	110	with shells	2,200
Revolvers	545	with ammunition	27,250 rounds
Gammon grenades		2,490	
Hand grenades		4,360	
Plastic explosive		17,523 lbs.	
Instantaneous detonating fuses		59,492 yards	
Safety fuses		9,536 yards	
Detonators		21,990	
Tins of meat		23,520	
Tins of biscuits		2,016	
Tins of margarine		2,016 lbs.	
American rations		5,820	
American milk rations		5,820	
Medical equipment		12 containers.	

"America", to which the countersign was "Polska" (Poland). Signal tunes were duly chosen under the "Iodoform" system.

Warsaw was in flames, the extent of the city controlled by the insurgents grew less and less, yet Stalin still delayed. At long last, on September 12th, the Russians agreed to the landing. It is not clear whether they did so in response to the allies' unremitting pressure, or in order to prolong the insurgents' agony and increase their losses. The latter is more probable, for on the night of September 13/14th the Russians themselves began to carry out supply drops.[27])

The four US airfields were immediately put into a state of readiness, and three combined wings of Flying Fortresses made final preparations for take-off. The weather was good and it was hoped that they would fly next day, but the number of containers was still not fully made up.[28]) The 13th passed, and fog then caused further delay. On the 15th the planes took off and some got as far as Denmark, but the weather became so bad that they had to turn back.

At last, at 5.50 a.m. on the 18th, the great armada took off once more. A hundred and ten giant B-17's forged eastward, in three large groups, spread out over many miles and flying at between 13,000 and 16,500 feet. They started despite local fog and were joined on leaving the British coast by seventy fighters, after which they made for southern Denmark. The BBC duly broadcast the signal. In Warsaw the weather was fine, but the burning city was engulfed in heavy clouds of smoke. The insurgents were fighting with their last remnants of strength and ammunition. It was thirty-four days since they had received a single drop from the West, and they had ceased to expect any.[29])

The first part of the flight was uneventful, but three planes had to turn back with engine trouble. The fleet crossed the Danish peninsula and continued south of Bornholm. German planes came up to meet them, but the fighters drove

---

[27]) According to insurgent sources about 55 tons of supplies were received, including 15 tons of food. Although the Russians made their drops from a low altitude they did not use parachutes, so that part of the supplies were destroyed. The flights were carried out by small aircraft known in Russian as *Kukuruzniki*.

[28]) This is the version given in the Sixth Bureau report. The Polish section of SOE maintained that the delay was not due to lack of containers but that the Russians gave their consent too late.

[29]) According to the table in Vol. III, p. 798 of *Polskie Siły Zbrojne w Drugiej Wojnie Swiatowej* (History of the Polish Armed Forces in the Second World War), seven drops were carried out over Warsaw on September 10th, of which the insurgents received five. A careful search of the archives of the Sixth Bureau and the Polish Air Force has not brought to light any confirmation of this statement.

them off without trouble.[30]) Unfortunately, after this the escort had to turn back, while the great fleet continued on its way via Torun, Plock and Plonsk to Warsaw. German fighters appeared again, and this time they were able to be more aggressive. Near Warsaw, eight ME-109's and two FW-190's attacked the third group of Fortresses and set fire to one. The crew managed to drop the containers, and one airman baled out.[31])

In Warsaw, only those members of the Home Army command who knew the secret of the signal tune were aware that a great American fleet was approaching; the civilian population and the soldiers on the barricades had no idea what was afoot. Suddenly their straining ears caught a sound different from that of the artillery bombardment, the roar of mortars and the rattle of machine-guns. A dull, monotonous throbbing, ever more powerful, could be heard from the northwest. Every single person who was not at that moment covered by enemy fire ran out into the street or climbed on to a roof-top and stared at the sky. Nothing could yet be seen, but the heavy throbbing grew louder every moment. There could be no doubt that it came from hundreds of powerful engines.

A few minutes later, tiny patches of different colours could be seen high in the sky. As they drifted down and grew larger the crowd began to shout: 'It's the paratroopers!' It was a natural mistake: from that distance they could not see the containers, and the exhausted defenders of the city were clinging to the hope of some impossible change of fate, of a miracle. But of course it was not parachutists that were gently floating downwards. If it had been, the soldiers and inhabitants of the still free capital would have had to witness a fearful massacre. The heavy flak[32]) was unable to reach the flying giants, but the chattering machine-guns were now

[30]) One source states that four German aircraft were shot down at this stage.

[31]) The aircraft was shot down over Dabrowa, six miles north-west of Warsaw, between the Vistula and the Kampinos Forest. The airman broke his leg, either on landing or as a result of jumping too violently, and unfortunately fell into German hands. He was a tall, fair young man of about 20. The Germans immediately took him in for interrogation. He suffered great pain, for he was interrogated without his leg being dressed, but he showed great courage, treating the interrogating officers with contempt. After some hours he was shot in the forest. These details are to be found in a report from a local unit of the Home Army, which was sent to the Sixth Bureau in London via H.Q.

[32]) Photographs taken from aircraft showed that Warsaw was defended by about 45 heavy (88 mm) anti-aircraft guns and a large number of light ones.

directing their fire at the swaying parachutes [33]) as they came closer to the ground. Many of the coloured canopies caught fire; bullets struck the containers and pierced them from side to side. How many defenceless parachutists could have survived such an attack?

No, it was neither a miracle nor a landing of airborne troops; but Warsaw, fighting to its last breath, was filled with joy. True, the containers fell far and wide, mostly into German hands, and the defenders felt a pang of loss as the great planes flew on and away from the city. But the mere fact that a huge American fleet had suddenly appeared, that someone in the West had at last remembered and sent help, was perhaps even more precious than the supplies. These, of course, were sorely needed, and there was a rush to pick up the containers that had fallen in Polish-held districts. A good many were retrieved, but only in the central district and the Mokotow area. All the supplies that fell further north, in Zoliborz, were picked up by Germans. Elsewhere, some fell in no man's land and were fought for, or retrieved at night if German machine-guns made it impossible by day.

As a result of the drop, the Home Army commander reported the safe receipt of 228 containers, adding that 32 more would have to be fought for and 28 had reached the ground in a damaged state, as their parachutes had been destroyed in the air. Some, containing food, had been retrieved and kept by the civilian population.[34]) The American assessment was that the operation was correctly carried out and the result highly satisfactory: only three planes had had to turn back and 1,284 containers had been dropped. This assessment was of course based on air observation, and took no account of what had happened on the ground or whose hands the containers had fallen into. As a rule, operations of this kind were carried out over areas which, for a considerable distance around, were in friendly hands.

The German fighters did not pursue the Fortresses east of the Vistula, but they succeeded in damaging one so severely

---

[33]) A container dropped by parachute from a height of 13,000-16,500 ft. took about 7 minutes to reach the ground. SOE at that time did not have in Britain parachutes with an automatic delayed opening device. When these were used, the containers reached the ground much faster and were not so widely scattered. According to American estimates, from one to three per cent of the parachutes did not open and the stores were destroyed.

[34]) These figures are taken from the archives of the Sixth Bureau. They differ from those given in Vol. III of *Polskie Siły Zbrojne*. Some of those who took part in the rising state that more supplies were received. Naturally they only know about their respective sectors. It will probably never be possible to ascertain the exact figures.

that it came down in Soviet-held Polish territory. The crew survived, but the plane was a write-off. Ten more badly damaged planes managed to reach Poltava. In addition to ten airmen who lost their lives in or over Poland, including one captured and shot by the enemy, another died on board a plane which had been shot up by the Germans.

Six days later the great fleet left Poltava and returned to Britain by the safe roundabout route via Italy.

A second expedition of the same kind was planned, but was forestalled by the surrender of the city.

VII

At the same time as the great American operation was being mounted, in London further efforts were being made to get help for Warsaw. At midnight on August 29th - 30th the British Cabinet decided that from that moment it would recognise the Home Army as an integral part of the Polish Armed Forces. This recognition of combatant rights applied to all members of the Home Army and was a warning to the Germans that they would run the risk of reprisals if they did not treat the underground soldiers according to international conventions. The following day the Times published this important decision.

It came very late, for which the Poles themselves were partly to blame; it could not affect the outcome of the fighting in Warsaw and it conspicuously referred only to the behaviour of the German forces; as if the Russians had not imprisoned and deported thousands of Home Army soldiers in violation of international law. Nevertheless it constituted a great step forward and was a symbol that the Polish-Western brotherhood of arms still existed.

At the same time as the British Government adopted and published its decision, the Government of the United States did likewise.

The moon was still full, so for eight nights there were no flights to Warsaw. It was September 10th when five Polish, four British and eleven South African planes took off. Seven reached the capital and carried out their drops, none of which fell into the insurgents' hands. Two Polish planes flew on the following night, but their effort was in vain. That was the last attempt that the men of 1586 Flight made to carry help to their brothers fighting in the capital. The losses were so heavy and the exhaustion of the remaining airmen so great that they were unable to make any more sorties. On two more occasions British aircraft took off, but they did not reach Warsaw. The last flight took place on September 21st.

On October 2nd, after exceptionally bloody fighting that had lasted longer that anyone had anticipated, Warsaw had to capitulate.

Defeat always leaves a taste of bitterness, someone has to take the blame and thus the Warsaw Rising, which brought no victory and led to heavy losses and the destruction of the city, has left behind it a trail of sorrow and reproach, claims and accusations.

Some of these reproaches were addressed to those who carried air supplies to the city. After all, the Polish Air Force alone possessed thirteen squadrons, and the Allies had to their disposal "some tens of thousands of planes of all sorts and types".[35])

In earlier pages I have given a number of facts which serve to outline the political and military background to the problem and the great technical difficulties attending flights to Warsaw. In the situation that had arisen, with Russia's attitude hostile and the allied bases so far away, these difficulties were so serious that they influenced decisively the effect of the aid supplied.

The rate of loss was enormous, probably the highest of any during the war, and the results of the effort small, giving little chance of success from the outset.

Of the 18 Polish crews that flew over Warsaw during the rising, only 2 survived this period, so that 160% of the establishment of the special duties flight, together with the reserve, was lost. The British and South African percentage of loss was almost the same, in actual figures even greater, for altogether 22 crews were lost. Only the Americans, in their big flight, completed their difficult task almost unharmed, mainly because that single operation was carried out according to the normal American practice of those times. They flew by day at a high altitude, they had a fighter escort most of the way and they landed on the Soviet side. Therefore, when counting the losses, one has to make a separate summing up for the night flights from Brindisi and for the American operation respectively.

From the Italian base 196 Polish, British and South African aircraft took off, of which 42 managed to get to Warsaw and drop supplies. To achieve this small result 39 planes were lost, more than 90%! Of these 42 drops the insurgents picked

---

[35]) This phrase comes from Order No. 19 issued by General Sosnkowski on September 1, 1944, in which he reproached the Allies for inadequate assistance to Warsaw.

up only 25. Another 43 drops were made also on the Kampinos Forest and the Kabacki Woods, but they had no serious significance for Warsaw and the percentage of losses was very small.

The Americans in their great operation lost only 2 planes and 11 airmen, but they flew under privileged conditions and the effect of their drop, made from a great height over the small area of the city still in Polish hands, was minimal. Out of 107 drops involving 1,284 containers, only 19 (228 containers) were picked up by the Poles, and even this figure is not certain.[36])

Altogether, out of 149 drops made over Warsaw the insurgents picked up only 44. Even if it is presumed that a certain number of parachutes failed to open and the containers shattered, and also that a small proportion, consisting of food, fell into the hands of the civilian population and was kept by them, we still get figures which prove that the great sacrifice of airmen was of more help to the Germans than to the insurgents, who picked up barely a third of the supplies dropped. Here again it must be stressed that the American operation distorts the statistics. The night sorties from Italy show a much better result. Out of 42 drops the insurgents picked up 25, i.e. 59.5%. This, however, relates only to the first period, up to August 14th, while the Germans had still not mustered sufficient anti-aircraft defence.

Many reproaches have been directed against the British military and air authorities, particularly Air Marshal Slessor. He has been accused of opposing the flights, forbidding them and thereby reducing the aid to Warsaw. In the earlier chapters his attitude and motives have been explained: let us now examine the facts and figures.

Out of the 60 nights of the rising, from August 3rd [37]) to October 2nd, 25 were lost because of bad weather and on 12 more there was a full moon, so that flights were banned. During the remaining 23 nights sorties were carried out to the maximum possible limit of the number of crews and aircraft. A look at the table of sorties shows that from August 15th onwards the drops on Warsaw did not reach the insurgents. Even if sorties had been undertaken during the forbidden periods, they would probably have been of no use to the fighting city and would only have increased the losses, which, as it was, were colossal. It must be added that the

---

[36]) The description "drop" always refers to the whole load of a plane and not to an individual container. Generally the planes — Halifaxes, Liberators and Flying Fortresses — carried 12 containers each. Sometimes it was less and the load was made up by parcels.

[37]) It was only on this day, in the early morning, that Air Marshal Slessor heard of the rising and received orders to commence the sorties.

cessation of the sorties after September 21st was due not to their lack of success and the shrinking of the area held by the insurgents, but to very bad weather.

Looking back on the whole question through the perspective of the years, remembering the historical significance of the Warsaw rising and the heroism of the young soldiers who died on the barricades in the hope that they would win freedom, remembering too the suffering of the population, the destruction of the large city and the military defeat once again inflicted on the Poles by German hands — it is important to realise that everything that happened was the result of earlier political decisions. Strategy and military plans were adapted to these decisions, and the concurrence of all these factors caused Warsaw to find herself in a situation in which victory was impossible.

One can and must blame the Western leaders who abandoned Poland to Stalin, oblivious of the fact that in sacrificing our country and the whole of central and eastern Europe, they were allowing the Soviet peril to come closer to their own frontiers. Part of the blame rests on the Polish political and military leaders who refused to face facts and deluded themselves with hopes of a sudden change, which led them to resort to dangerous improvisation.

There is no reason to impute blame to any of those who carried out military orders. On the contrary, the great sacrifice of the young airmen, Polish and Allied, who died with the full knowledge that their death could not alter the course of events, is an example of the utmost heroism.

Under forced conditions of improvisation, against all the logic of normal military operations, a tremendous effort was made, which unhappily was doomed to failure.

AIRMEN WHO FLEW TO AID WARSAW, THE NUMBER SHOT DOWN AND THEIR SUBSEQUENT FATE

	Poles	British and South Africans	Americans	Total
Number that flew	637	735	1,100	2,472
Number shot down	112	133	11	256
Number that survived being shot down	34	7	—	41

Of the 112 Polish airmen whose planes were shot down, 78 were killed, 28 were taken prisoner after baling out and 6, after baling out, reached Home Army units. Similarly 7 British and South African airmen were saved because, after baling out, they fell in with Home Army units.

There is a document in the archives to prove that 4 of them, at their own request, were helped to reach the Soviet lines. Probably the others made the same decision, because it appears that allied airmen were under instructions to make their way to the nearest Soviet unit if they were shot down and managed to bale out. An Anglo-Russian agreement was in force which gave ground for hoping that such airmen would be evacuated to the rear and sent back to the West.

The figures in the above table are taken from the archives of the Sixth Bureau, which compiled them on the basis of reports from the base at Brindisi, supplemented by reports from Poland. Since the Polish, British and South African airmen each flew several times, the figures in the first horizontal line are higher than the number of individuals who actually flew. This does not apply to the Americans, who flew only once.

TABLE OF FLIGHTS AND DROPS

Drops on Warsaw, Kampinos Forest and Kabacki

No.	Date	Took off					Mission carried out				
		Polish	British	S. African	American	Total	Polish	British	S. African	American	Total
1	4. 8.	7	7	—	—	14	3	—	—	—	3
2	8. 8.	3	—	—	—	3	3	—	—	—	3
3	9. 8.	4	—	—	—	4	4	—	—	—	4
4	12. 8.	5	6	—	—	11	4	3	—	—	7
5	13. 8.	4	4	20	—	28	3	2	4	—	9
6	14. 8.	5	6	15	—	26	2	3	8	—	13
7	15. 8.	3	4	—	—	7	3	2	—	—	5
8	16. 8.	5	4	9	—	18	2	2	3	—	7
9	17. 8.	4	—	—	—	4	1	—	—	—	1
10	18. 8.	2	5	—	—	7	—	—	—	—	—
11	20. 8.	4	—	—	—	4	3	—	—	—	3
12	21. 8.	4	—	—	—	4	2	—	—	—	2
13	22. 8.	2	—	—	—	2	—	—	—	—	—
14	23. 8.	3	—	—	—	3	2	—	—	—	2
15	24. 8.	6	—	—	—	6	6	—	—	—	6
16	25. 8.	7	—	—	—	7	4	—	—	—	4
17	26. 8.	5	—	—	—	5	—	—	—	—	—
18	27. 8.	4	—	—	—	4	1	—	—	—	1
19	1. 9.	7	—	—	—	7	2	—	—	—	2
20	10. 9.	5	4	11	—	20	1	2	6	—	9
21	13. 9.	2	—	—	—	2	1	—	—	—	1
22	18. 9.	—	—	—	110	110	—	—	—	107	107
23	18. 9.	—	5	—	—	5	—	—	—	—	—
24	21. 9.	—	5	—	—	5	—	3	—	—	3
Total:		91	50	55	110	306	47	17	21	107	192

DURING THE WARSAW RISING

Woods from Aug. 1st do Oct. 2nd, 1944

	Lost					Warsaw		Kampinos and Kabacki Woods		Notes
Polish	British	S. African	American	Total	Dropped	Picked up	Dropped	Picked up		All aircraft that crashed while landing are included in the table
—	5	—	—	5	2	2	1	1	1 aircraft crashed while landing. 3 drops outside Warsaw
—	—	—	—	—	3	3	—	—	
—	—	—	—	—	—	—	4	4	
—	—	—	—	—	7	5	—	—	
—	2	—	—	2	9	5	—	—	Also 2 "blind" drops outside Warsaw
1	3	4	—	8	11	10	2	2	1 aircraft crashed while landing
—	—	—	—	—	—	—	5	5	
2	2	4	—	8	—	—	7	7	2 aircraft crashed while landing
—	—	—	—	—	—	—	1	1	Only 7 packages were picked up
—	—	—	—	—	—	—	—	—	1 "blind" drop outside Warsaw
1	—	—	—	1	1	—	2	1	1 aircraft crashed while landing, crew saved
—	—	—	—	—	—	—	2	—	From 1 drop on Kampinos 12 packages were picked up
—	—	—	—	—	—	—	2	—	
—	—	—	—	—	—	—	6	4	
—	—	—	—	—	—	—	4	—	
3	—	—	—	3	—	—	—	—	1 aircraft crashed while landing
2	—	—	—	2	1	—	—	—	
4	—	—	—	4	—	—	2	1	1 drop outside Warsaw
3	1	1	—	5	7	—	2	—	There is no confirmation that Warsaw picked up 5 drops
1	—	—	—	1	1	—	—	—	
—	—	—	2	2	107	19	—	—	1 aircraft landed completely shot up
—	—	—	—	—	—	—	—	—	The aircraft turned back on the way
—	—	—	—	—	—	—	3	1	
17	13	9	2	41	149	44	43	27	

VIII

After being parachuted into Poland in May 1944, General Okulicki made for Warsaw. Through an address which he had been given immediately before leaving the base in Italy, he was directed to a secret apartment in the Old City where his "aunt", Janina Pronaszko, was expecting him. She was a young woman, full of energy, courage and initiative. Okulicki was able to devote himself heart and soul to underground work while she dealt tactfully, quietly and efficiently with all the day-to-day problems of housekeeping, liaison, security and the organization of premises for clandestine activities.

Just before the Warsaw Rising it was decided to form a duplicate headquarters in case the rising should end in defeat and further underground work be necessary. Okulicki volunteered for the heavy responsibility of taking over the Home Army command in such circumstances. *Bor* considered that he would be a good choice, as he was little known inside the country and therefore ran less risk of detection.

As a result of his appointment as "shadow" commander, Okulicki was for a time unable to take part in the rising itself. He remained in hiding in a small room under *Janina's* firm though solicitous care — cut off from the fighting city, pacing about like a caged tiger and cursing the decision that had led him to put his name forward. However, before long he was made Chief of Staff in succession to General Pelczynski, who was hit by a fragment of shell during the bombardment of the Savings Bank on September 4th. For a week or two this post afforded an outlet for his impatient, pent-up energy.

Then came the surrender. In a parting conversation *Bor* handed to him a small card on which he had written a few words to the effect that Okulicki was his successor. On October 3rd, in a final order to district commanders, *Bor* confirmed this appointment with the words: "I designate *Niedzwiadek* [Bear-cub — Okulicki's new code-name] as my successor for purposes of underground work." This order was broadcast in a final radio signal, and in the early morning of the 3rd, Okulicki and the faithful *Janina* left Warsaw under cover of a vast exodus of refugees. Laden with a large bundle tied together with string, he looked like one among the thousands of homeless people who made their way to the Western station. Here, under German supervision, he climbed aboard a goods wagon and was carried to the transit camp in the suburban locality of Pruszkow.

A few days later the Germans, on a day of torrential rain, packed some thousands of people into open tenders which moved off to an unknown destination. Okulicki, *Janina* and two other women members of the resistance who were in the same truck decided to escape. They jumped out at Kielce, hid from their pursuers amongst the station buildings and managed to reach the town, where the General knew an address which fortunately proved to be still safe. Here he found *Jelita* (Guts), the chief of staff of the local Home Army district whose headquarters were at Radom. The district recognized Okulicki without demur as its new commander-in-chief, and he set about the arduous task of reconstituting the Home Army command.

The first problem was to find the officers who, like himself, had been appointed members of the "shadow" command, and who had not gone into captivity at the time of the surrender. This could only be done by the invaluable *Janina*, and Okulicki sent her back to the Warsaw area to pick up the traces of the dispersed officers as best she could. It might have been better if the whole team had been able to stay together and leave the capital with Okulicki himself, but in the chaotic atmosphere at the end of the rising this proved impossible. Not all the officers in question even knew that Okulicki was their new commander.

Janina set off in a crowded train, with her arm in plaster as though she were an invalid, which conferred some practical advantages. After various adventures she reached Milanowek, where she found that an address dating from before the rising was still in working order. She managed to contact Lt.-Colonel Jan Szczurek-Cergowski and, not long afterwards, General Emil Fieldorf *(Nil)*, the head of "Kedyw", and a number of other officers. They did not know the circumstances of Okulicki's appointment, but they took *Janina's* information on trust and made ready to assemble at the monastery town of Czestochowa (about 65 miles north-west of Cracow), which was to be the new command headquarters. *Janina* returned to Kielce to report progress, and then herself went on to Czestochowa to make the necessary arrangements.

Meanwhile in London General Kopanski, the Chief of the General Staff, was taking stock of the situation in Poland and endeavouring to guess what precisely General *Bor* had in mind when he appointed Okulicki his successor "for purposes of underground work." Did this refer to the Home Army command or to the organization known as "Nie" (the Polish word for "No", also short for "independence"), which it was planned to establish after the whole country came under Russian occupation? The whole situation was extremely confused and difficult: the more so as the President had dismissed Sosnkowski from the position of C-in-C and appointed *Bor* in his place on September 30th, immediately before the surrender of Warsaw. Since *Bor* was now a prisoner in German hands, he could neither perform his military functions nor explain his intentions as regards the succession in Poland.

The first word that reached London after the surrender was a message from Okulicki dated October 6th, stating that he was at Radom and would "start to sort matters out as far as possible" on the following day. This did not clear up the doubt about his exact position. A few days later a message dated October 7th was received in which Okulicki stated that he had left Warsaw on *Bor's* orders "to take command of the entire underground activity in Poland, whether under German or Soviet occupation"; but it was still not clear what the possibilities were of his exercising command and carrying out operations. Kopanski therefore decided to send to Poland someone he could trust to assess the situation and report to London. The need was urgent, for the headquarters of the underground State had been wiped out at the same time as the city of Warsaw, while the collapse of the rising and the attendant devastation were a severe blow to the country's morale. Chaos and anarchy prevailed, and in some cases people's mood was changing. There were those who felt that underground activity was useless since the catastrophe, and began to wash their hands of it; while others suddenly became extremely active, hoping that with the disappearance of the former leaders they themselves would come to the top and inscribe their names on the pages of history. Naturally such people adopted a critical attitude towards everything that had been done so far; they endeavoured to make contact with the authorities in London, but not through normal military channels.

The officer chosen by Kopanski was Group Captain Roman Rudkowski (*Rudy* — Red-head), who had been parachuted into Poland in January 1943 and had returned to the West by the second "Bridge" at the end of May 1944.[38]) He now proceeded to Brindisi and was one of a party dropped near Piotrkow on the night of October 17/18th. He reported to Okulicki at Czestochowa and was given every opportunity to study the situation, which he summed up in a message received by Kopanski on October 29th:

"... The districts are in a state of chaos and authority is disintegrating ... *Poldek* [diminutive of Okulicki's Christian name] is the only one capable of coping ... I am sure he can

---

[38]) There were only two Poles who jumped twice into Poland during the war. One of them was Group Captain Rudkowski (*Rudy*), the other a political courier, 2nd Lieutenant Tadeusz Chciuk (*Celt, Sulima*).

remedy the prevailing anarchy if you recognize him as *Bor's* successor and inform districts accordingly... Ruthlessness is the order of the day here and a firm hand is essential."

Unfortunately this prompt and accurate appreciation did not lead to immediate action, as the President, who could have confirmed Okulicki's authority by a stroke of the pen, wished first to obtain the concurrence of the new Premier and to consult the Government Delegate in Poland (Jan Jankowski, who possessed the rank of Deputy Premier). This led to delay and complications, but Okulicki showed iron determination in overcoming all difficulties and re-creating a nucleus of command. The new Chief of Staff was Colonel Bokszczanin, while personnel, intelligence and operations were in the hands respectively of Major Gorazdowski, Lt.-Colonel Zielinski and Lt.-Colonel Kamienski. Press and propaganda were looked after by K. Moczarski and diversionary activities by Lt.-Colonel Jan Mazurkiewicz, who had distinguished himself in the Warsaw fighting. A woman named *Henryka* was in charge of liaison. The new command operated in makeshift conditions, in a town filled to overflowing with refugees, with no proper premises or money and without adequate personal documents. Okulicki's own "identity card" was a scrap of paper which might just have passed muster in a run-of-the-mill police raid. The officers usually held their meetings at the houses of two priests, and used various churches as letter-boxes.

The surrender of Warsaw, which had such a shattering effect on the Polish underground and destroyed all hopes of a victorious conclusion to the war, naturally also came as a shock to Poles in the West, but had much less effect on the daily course of life there. The base at Brindisi, which for two months was entirely concerned with aid to fighting Warsaw, succeeded shortly before the surrender in landing six parachutists near Cracow: this was on the night of September 21/22nd, at the same time as the last attempt was made to get supplies through to the burning city. After that there was an interval to allow the few surviving airmen to recuperate, to make up fresh crews and replace aircraft; but on the night of October 17/18th another sortie was made by two Liberators with Polish crews, carrying twelve parachutists of whom Rudkowski was one.

During this last period after the Warsaw rising, the principle of centralization at the receiving end ceased to be observed. The districts communicated directly with the base in Italy, acknowledged drops promptly by telegram and kept the supplies for themselves. Even the rule that parachutists must first report to headquarters no longer held good, since headquarters had ceased to exist. An attempt was made to revive the principle with a centre at Radomsko near Czestochowa, but this worked only partially and for a very short time.

It was clear from the course of military events in Europe that the years of lunacy might come to an end in another few months. Desperate as Poland's political and military situation was, our people in the homeland and in the West fought to the uttermost and strove once again to raise themselves from the depths. The new Home Army command was functioning at Czestochowa, although Okulicki was still waiting for his official appointment and could not overcome the resistance of some districts which refused to recognize him. He took this calmly, went on inspections, visited forest units and established contact with the Government Delegate, who supported him unreservedly. This was the time of the Government crisis in London which led to Mikolajczyk's resignation over the question of relations with the Soviet Union and Poland's future frontiers, and his replacement on November 29th by the socialist leader Arciszewski, who had come to the West on the third "Bridge", and who took a stiff political line. At the Italian base, the tremendous effort imposed by aid to the Warsaw rising had not exhausted everyone's energies but seemed rather to have stimulated them. Much was of course done for morale by the proximity of the victorious 2nd Corps.

The last period of flights to Poland, known as "Retaliation", had begun on August 1, 1944, the same day as the rising, but there was no question of discontinuing sorties because the capital had surrendered. Further important operations were planned, as may be shown by figures. The period was due to end in May 1945, and by then it was proposed to carry out 140 flights and drop 400 tons of supplies as well as further parachutists.[39]) Lt.-Colonel Threlfall, the British commander at Monopoli, who did his utmost to help throughout the rising and constantly pressed the Polish point of view with the Air Force authorities, now used every endeavour to get hold of the most suitable aircraft. The Polish commander, Lt.-Colonel Dorotycz-Malewicz *(Hancza)*, went even further and considered the possibility of a daylight sortie by twenty

---

[39]) Immediately after the cessation of the fighting in Warsaw, on October 3rd, a conference took place between the Polish Chief of Staff, the commander of the Polish Air Force and Air Marshal Slessor. It was on this occasion that 140 flights were mentioned. Slessor also accepted plans for further "Bridges" and promised that when Warsaw was finally occupied by the Russians he would agree to flights with food and medicines, provided the politicians had reached agreement on the matter by then. This of course did not happen, and there were therefore no flights with food and medicines.

or thirty American bombers, presumably Liberators, escorted by Mustang fighters, in the direction of Nowy Targ and Wloszczowa, about 35 miles south and north of Cracow respectively. Drops were to be made just before sunset so that the supplies could be picked up and removed under cover of darkness. This scheme did not work, as the day bombers required an escort of long range fighters, which were not evailable. *Hancza* accordingly considered afternoon drops, but these presented great practical difficulties and were not carried out.

An unexpected change took place in the attitude of the Air Ministry. Hitherto it had always refused to agree to the expansion of the special duties Flight, but now, when the period of direst need was over, it suddenly gave permission, on November 7th, for the Flight to be expanded into a Squadron with the old number 301.[40]) When studying the archives it is difficult to resist the impression that some decisions were marked, unintentionally no doubt, by savage irony.

All the plans, schemes and decisions adopted by military men at this time had little practical result, for the politicians, who had the last word, had long since adopted arrangements which sealed Poland's fate. What was the point of intensifying parachute drops now that Warsaw had fallen, the rest of German-occupied Poland was stifled by the retreating Nazi divisions and the Red Army was preparing for a new offensive which might well be the last?

After the three drops of parachutists mentioned earlier, two more were carried out in the second half of November, as well as some with supplies;[41]) then suddenly everything came to a halt. On November 26th, General Tatar, the Polish Deputy Chief of Staff, received a secret letter from Colonel Perkins stating that he had had to send urgent instructions to Lt-Colonel Threlfall at Brindisi cancelling the sortie which had been planned for that night. Perkins added orally that this did not affect the fourth "Bridge" operation. Next day Major Truszkowski, a British subject who was on Lt-Colonel Threlfall's SOE staff at Monopoli, handed to the Polish com-

---

[40]) Even Polish officials called the special duties Flight a "squadron". The error arose from a mis-translation of the British terms. A flight is the equivalent of a Polish *eskadra* and a squadron is a *dywizjon*. The misunderstanding was compounded by the fact that 301 Squadron was disbanded to form the special duties Flight, and this flight, in memory of the squadron, was known by the number 301 in Polish unofficial usage.

[41]) These drops were carried out very badly, without warning and "blind", at a distance of about 22 miles from the target areas. This was a consequence of the great losses suffered during the Warsaw rising. The new crews were quite raw and inexperienced.

mander a written order from London suspending all further flights for an indefinite period: no reasons were given. Twenty-four hours later Air Vice-Marshal Elliot informed General Rayski, the Polish senior officer in the RAF Mediterranean command, that the ban also covered "Bridge" operations. The shut-down was thus complete.

This was a political decision, due no doubt to Soviet pressure, and the military had to carry it out whatever their own feelings. The Poles made emergency appeals in many quarters, which led to only small concessions. Permission was given to prepare for a fourth "Bridge" on December 15th, but the Dakota which took off on that day had to turn back owing to a sudden change in the weather.[42])

Another exception was made for the British military mission to the Home Army, which had been ready for months and was waiting at Brindisi for the political green light and for suitable weather. The story of this small mission is worth further study, for the circumstances connected with it were highly curious and give a striking picture of our country's situation in the last phase of the war.

From the middle of 1942 onwards Soviet propaganda, at first with caution and then more boldly, put about the view that nothing special was happening in occupied Poland: the underground movement, especially on the military side, was a myth created by the Government in exile to serve political ends, and the only real opposition to the Germans came from Polish communists and Soviet partisans. This picture of the facts, absurd as it was, gained acceptance the more easily because Russia was a valued ally and her good opinion was courted. The Western press used Soviet propaganda material which it reproduced in its own articles; Polish periodicals in London were censored and could not obtain a sufficient allocation of paper. Efforts were made through personal contacts to convince politicians and other leading figures in the West that matters were otherwise, that the underground movement existed and was growing day by day, and that it had been fighting the Germans from the very outset. But these efforts failed, because it became harder and harder to reach the right people, who preferred not to listen to the Poles and to ignore their presence.

In these circumstances, the only answer seemed to be for Western observers to be sent to Poland and see for themselves what was going on there. In February 1944 the Polish Government sent notes to Churchill and Roosevelt suggesting the dispatch to Poland of military missions which, in close

[42]) There is no record of the names of the persons who travelled in this Dakota or who were to have been picked up in Poland.

contact with the Home Army command, could send full information to their governments. Unfortunately the governments showed no desire for such information: in April the Polish suggestion was rejected.

This was discouraging, but the Polish leaders did not give in and made several further attempts. At last, at the beginning of July, when events in Poland were approaching a crisis and the Russians were nearly on the Vistula, Churchill changed his mind and decided that it was right to send a reliable emissary to the scene of such heavy fighting and political complications. The officer chosen was Colonel D. T. Hudson, who had carried out a similar mission in Yugoslavia. Churchill held two conversations with him which were not recorded but which were presumably concerned wholly with Polish-Soviet relations. Churchill at this time was devoting much attention to the Polish question and to the search for a compromise. He was exerting constant pressure on Mikolajczyk, whom he persuaded to go to Moscow and seek agreement with Stalin. No doubt the plan to send a military mission was closely connected with this.

The arrangements for the mission were entrusted to the Polish section of SOE, which was to provide the rest of Hudson's team as well as the aircraft and crew. The party was to set out from Brindisi. It might have done so at once, but was delayed because Mikolajczyk had just left for Moscow and his talks there might result in one of two ways. If they were successful, it was planned to send part of the mission via Moscow and the rest direct to Soviet-held Polish territory; but if not, the mission would be sent into German-occupied Poland and make contact there with Home Army partisans.[43])

Mikolajczyk's talks were a failure and to that extent the situation was clarified; but the mission did not take off, because the British Government unexpectedly took the strange view that the consent of their Soviet ally must be sought beforehand. Stalin, of course, refused: how could he agree to the presence of observers whose task was to report what he was up to?

A deadlock ensued for over two months. Then in October, after pressure from the Polish Government, long discussions and a report by General Gubbins, the British agreed that the mission might be sent without consulting the Russians. Those at Brindisi comprised three British officers, a Polish interpreter using an English name, and an NCO wireless operator.[44])

[43]) These details are to be found in a dispatch No. 6113 of August 2, 1944 sent by the Sixth Bureau to General *Bor*, at that time in fighting Warsaw.

[44]) The mission consisted of: Colonel D. T. Hudson, Major Peter Solly-Flood, Major Peter Kemp, Captain Tony Currie (Antoni Pospieszalski) and Sergeant D. Galbraith.

After waiting for suitable weather they were about to take off in November, when an urgent message was received from Churchill. The Polish Government crisis had resulted in the replacement of Mikolajczyk by the unyielding Arciszewski. The whole plan for a mission was closely connected with British attempts to get the Poles to make concessions and come to terms with the Soviet Union. Churchill required time to consider the new circumstances, and the flight was postponed for some days. Finally the officers, by now impatient, again got the green light at the beginning of December.

Okulicki, who was still waiting for confirmation of his appointment from London, was informed of the dispatch of the mission. If it had been decided on some months earlier and could have reached Poland before the rising, all Poles who had anything to do with the West would have greeted it with approval and even enthusiasm. But what was Okulicki to think of it now, at the beginning of December 1944, confined as he was to a hiding-place in Czestochowa and to a tiny fraction of what had been the extensive area controlled by the Home Army? What was the mission coming for and what did it expect to achieve? It had not been sent when large Home Army units were mobilized in the east for operation "Tempest" and co-operated tactically with the Red Army against the Germans, only to be disarmed by the same Russian troops when the fighting was over. Nor had the mission been sent during the battle for Warsaw, when the Home Army put forward its supreme effort against the Germans while the Russians displayed unmistakable hostility. What was the point of its coming now? The Polish underground State, which had embraced so many aspects of the nation's life, had virtually ceased to exist. The Home Army command had been restored but was in a desperate situation; large units had had to be demobilized because they would not have been able to maintain themselves in the field. It was not even possible to guarantee the safety of the gallant officers who were to be parachuted in. But orders were orders, and Okulicki accepted the plan without demur.

A rare moment of consolation came when, at Christmastime, he was informed that on December 21st the President had at last signed his appointment as commander of the Home Army. But on the very next day his cheerfulness was shattered by the news that his only son had been killed fighting with the 2nd Corps in Italy. The General said nothing, but appeared to collapse inwardly. Only those closest to him knew that the heart disease which he had neglected had suddenly struck violently.

Immediately after the holiday, on the night of December 26/27th, the British mission landed at a secret dropping zone north-east of Czestochowa. They had flown in a Liberator with a Polish crew commanded by Fl.-Lieutenant Ladro.

On the same night, another Liberator under Fl.-Lieutenant Krzywicki dropped six parachutists in the region of Nowy Targ near the Slovak frontier. Two nights later, a supply drop was carried out in southern Poland — the last flight from the West to Poland which took place during the war.⁴⁵)

IX

When Hitler, in December 1944, ordered von Rundstedt to launch a final offensive in the Ardennes, the West was taken by surprise. The offensive, however, was bound to collapse, since it was a desperate effort undertaken without reserves and with inadequate equipment.

A few weeks later another offensive was launched, this time in the east, which equally surprised the Western powers. In the heart of winter, on January 12, 1945, Stalin struck on a broad front and drove the Germans back some distance in disarray.

Stalin's offensive was far from being a desperate manoeuvre. He had broken with the rule of delaying the advance till spring because he well knew that the purpose of military actions is to attain political ends. The object of his calculations, which were as cold and precise as usual, was the three-power conference which it had for some time been planned to hold at Yalta in February.

⁴⁵) The special duties squadron (301) still went on flying to Czechoslovakia, Austria, Bulgaria and Yugoslavia. On February 28, 1945, as a result of the new military situation, night flights were discontinued and the squadron became a transport unit.

The losses of the special flight (towards the end a squadron), from October 25, 1941, when the first three Polish crews started to fly, up to the end of January 1945, amounted to 24 and 1/3 crews on flights to Poland and 9 and 3/8 crews on flights to other countries. On flights to Poland 28 crews were lost, but 4 of them survived as prisoners of war. 65 officers were shot down, of whom 48 were killed, and 119 other ranks. These were the highest losses in comparison with other units of the Polish Air Force in the West. They amount to 10,37% of all the losses of the Polish Air Force.

Members of the crews of the special flight received altogether 3 awards of "Virtuti Militari" Class IV, 42 of "Virtuti Militari" Class V and 339 Crosses of Valour. The technical personnel received 2 Silver Crosses of Merit with Sword, 14 Bronze Crosses of Merit with Swords, and 12 Bronze Crosses of Merit. In addition, on September 15, 1944, the whole flight was awarded the title Defenders of Warsaw.

The Polish command did not overlook the great efforts of the Allied Air Forces during the Warsaw Rising. British and South African airmen were awarded 1 "Polonia Restituta", 1 "Virtuti Militari" Class V, 8 Crosses for Valour and 1 Cross of Merit with Swords. American airmen received 1 "Virtuti Militari" Class V and 10 Crosses for Valour.

The Western leaders too had prepared for the conference, which was to discuss the political ordering of postwar Europe, but they had done so only in routine fashion. They had already reached agreement with the Russians on spheres of influence in Europe, and were resolved to adhere strictly to existing decisions.

Stalin's attitude was different. He had been promised a great deal; he knew that he was winning the war and stood to gain more that he had expected in his most optimistic moments, but he still did not trust the Western powers. Being himself capable of any treachery, he feared that the others might suddenly go back on their engagements. This was why he launched his January offensive in Poland. He had been promised the country anyway, but he preferred to have the whole of it in his hands before the conference opened.

Okulicki too was surprised by the Soviet offensive, which he had expected later and on a smaller scale. When it began, he was in Cracow conferring with the Government Delegate. They hurried back to Czestochowa, which they reached three days later than the Red Army.

During the week or two since the confirmation of his appointment, Okulicki had been extremely active. He had visited several districts and inspected the skeleton partisan units which remained in being despite the winter and the congestion of German troops throughout the countryside; he had also received the British military mission and had a long talk with Colonel Hudson.[46]) The revived Home Army headquarters was by now working quite efficiently.

Suddenly, in a few days, everything was changed: the Germans were driven back, and almost the whole country was under the control of the Red Army and Soviet administration. The historic period of fighting against the German invader was over. The Home Army, which had been so active in the past years, was coming to the end of its existence. Poland was about to undergo a new occupation, for the Soviet forces which had expelled the Germans had clear political aims of their own. These must be resisted, but whatever happened, the methods used up to now would no longer be serviceable.

---

[46]) After the start of the Soviet offensive the mission received radio instructions from London to make their way to the nearest Soviet command. This they did on January 18th. All the members of the mission were arrested, no doubt on Stalin's orders, and thrown into prison at Czestochowa. They were not released till February 12th, the day that the Yalta Conference ended. They returned to Britain via Moscow, Odessa and the Near East.

Okulicki faced a grave decision, the saddest perhaps that he was called upon to take in all his life. After the disaster of September 1939 he had gone underground, been arrested by the Russians, suffered prison and interrogation and been unexpectedly freed; then, a few weeks before the Warsaw rising, he had returned home to fight once more with the underground army. He might have remained in the West and commanded a well-equipped, regular division while enjoying all the glory and privileges of a front-line soldier. Instead, he volunteered for service in Poland and, after the bitter, dramatic weeks of the Warsaw rising, was offered the supreme dignity of taking over the Home Army command. Since then he had rebuilt its organization with great difficulty, mending the broken threads of the vast underground network; he had fought to restore morale after the catastrophe, inspiring the troops by his own example.

Now the moment had come in which he must tell them that the battle they had waged was at an end, that the Home Army was ceasing to exist. With a heavy heart he drafted the order which was issued on January 19, 1945:

"Officers and men of the Home Army!

This is the last order I shall issue to you. From now on, your activity and energies are to be devoted to the restoration of the full independence of the Polish State and the protection of its population from destruction.

You must strive to be leaders of the nation and to bring about the independence of the Polish State. In this endeavour, each and every one of you must be his own commander.

In the conviction that you will carry out this order and remain eternally loyal to Poland, to facilitate your work in the future I hereby, with the authority of the President of the Republic, release you from your oath and disband the Home Army.

I thank you in the name of the Service for the devotion you have shown up to this moment. I profoundly believe that our sacred cause will triumph and that we shall meet once more in a truly free, unoccupied Poland.

May our country live long in freedom, independence and happiness!

The Commander of the Armed Forces in Poland."

The dissolution of the Home Army was confirmed by the President in a broadcast from London, on February 8th;[47])

---

[47] The speech began: "From the moment that the German invader was driven out of Poland by the Red Army, armed operations in our country ceased and the Home Army units disbanded..."

but this did not mean that the demobilization of the many thousand troops took place automatically and easily. The war and the occupation had left an imprint on the soul of the fighting nation which was too deep to be erased by a single order. This would have been so even had the outcome been victorious; how much more when Poland was only changing masters; The country was in a state of mental and physical confusion, dazed by the headlong rush of military events and torn by conflicting views of the new situation. Some of the disbanded units came out of hiding, laid down their arms and were imprisoned by the Russians: these, about 50,000 in number, were deported into the depths of the Soviet Union. Others hid or buried their arms and reverted quietly to their peace-time occupations, concealing the fact that they had belonged to the Home Army. All such were pursued relentlessly by the NKVD. Finally there were those who did not lay down their arms but formed a new patriotic organization to do battle with the Soviet occupying forces.

All the problems of this situation converged upon Okulicki, who had to offer advice and explanations, tell his subordinates what they should do and relieve their doubts, hesitations and fears, at the same time as he himself was pursued by the Soviet police and was at his wits' end to decide on the best course of action.

After issuing his final order to the troops, the main task was to wind up Home Army headquarters. Part of the organization was transferred to Lodz, where it had to remain in being for a time, as demobilization proceeded slowly. After two weeks things got so hot there that a fresh move was necessary. The choice fell on Milanowek near Warsaw, where there were still some premises and contacts that could be used. The utmost caution was required, as the NKVD was especially interested in capturing those responsible for disbanding the underground army. At one time they had transformed into "lobster-pots" sixteen of the Home Army's former premises and meeting-places in Milanowek alone.

Despite danger and ill-health, Okulicki remained active and in contact with the Government Delegate, the representatives of political parties and the officers engaged on demobilization. It was a slow job, as arrests became more and more frequent: every day someone else disappeared and another link in the underground network was broken. Letters for headquarters were still being sent to Lodz, whence *Janina* fetched them from time to time. Wireless communication with the West still functioned, but with increasing difficulty.

The tragic conference at Yalta, fraught with disaster for eastern Europe, was held from February 6th to 12th. Stalin's victory was complete: he was now the undisputed master of Poland, which in any case he held in a tight grip, as his armies had advanced as far as the Oder.

During the first half of March, Okulicki received a curious letter through the underground postal service. It had evidently travelled by a slow, roundabout route, for it bore the signatures of many who had handled it on its way. It was crumpled and dirty but had not been opened, for the large wax seals were intact.

The General tore open the envelope and found inside a letter in Russian from Colonel Pimenov, a guards officer of the Red Army, politely inviting him to attend a meeting with General Ivanov, the representative of the commander of the 1st Byelorussian front,[48] to discuss co-operation and various important problems.

The first fact that struck Okulicki was that the Russians had established access to him. He had already received a similar invitation at the end of February, but it had been a vague, word-of-mouth affair and had gone through several intermediaries.

He at once contacted Jankowski, the Government Delegate, and found that he had received a similar invitation, showing that the NKVD had access to that quarter also. They debated what their answer should be.

Okulicki, who had experienced arrest by the Russians, imprisonment and interrogation in the Lubianka, was convinced that the invitation was a trap. The Russians could do anything they pleased — what need had they of "co-operation"? They might, of course, have decided that it was worth while seeking a *modus vivendi* with the Polish underground, but why then had they recognized the Lublin Committee of Polish communists as the legitimate government of the country? In any case, the question of coming out of hiding was one on which Okulicki's superiors in the West had views. When he received the previous invitation in February he had telegraphed to Kopanski, the Chief of Staff in London, asking for guidance but saying that for his part he preferred to remain underground. Kopanski had replied at once that this was the correct course, and General Anders, the Acting C-in-C, had followed this up with a telegram forbidding him to declare himself to the Soviet authorities.

The second invitation caused great excitement in underground circles. It could not be hidden from them, as Pimenov had also contacted the Party leaders through the Government

---

[48]) The commander of this front was Marshal Zhukow.

Delegate. The great majority, wearied by years of clandestine activity, were for accepting the invitation and coming out of hiding. The Delegate sought instructions from London and was told the Government were also in favour of acceptance, especially as the Russians had promised that the underground delegation would be transported to London in the first instance to consult the Polish authorities and obtain the necessary powers and instructions.

Okulicki was thus subject to strong pressure. He was still convinced that the invitation was a trick: he knew and distrusted the Russians and did not want to accept, but his colleagues were of a different opinion. The Government Delegate attended a preliminary meeting with the Russians and returned unscathed, nor was he apparently shadowed thereafter. The same happened with the party leaders, who came back from the talks with Pimenov still more enthusiastic for negotiation. However, they all agreed in reporting that the Russians demanded the presence of the Home Army commander, without whom nothing could be done.

What was Okulicki to do? He knew that by maintaining his refusal he would probably be saving his own life, as well as obeying superior orders. He would thus be fully justified in acting as his own convictions dictated; but was it right to be guided by these arguments alone? Voices were beginning to be heard to the effect that he did not understand the situation and that through excess of suspicion he was throwing away a chance of coming to terms with the Russians. Some even began to accuse him of cowardice. This he might have ignored, but could he entirely rule out the possibility that the Russians were in good faith? There was no real hope of this and no good ground for believing it — but what hopes were there, what grounds for any other course of action? When he had decided to fly into Poland in May 1943, he had known what to expect: a final battle with the Germans and then, whether it were won or lost, a fresh invasion by the Red Army. Now that things had turned out in this way, it behoved him to play his part to the last. The nation had offered him one of its most exalted posts and had placed in his hands the last weapon that it possessed on Polish soil. That weapon no longer sufficed, and he had had lay it down. Unable to fight on or to meet force with force, what could he do except sacrifice himself in a hopeless attempt to save his country and people?

The decision was taken. A delegation was formed, and the names of its members were announced to the Soviet authorities. Documents were to be issued to them for the journey to London — which did not prevent the NKVD from shadowing them till the last moment, although they were to come forth of their own accord in the near future. Okulicki was felt to be in such danger that preparations were made for him to go into hiding in the Carpathian foothills near Cracow. But as a result of further pressure the date for the meeting was advanced, and his projected journey came to nothing.

On March 25th *Janina* brought Okulicki to a small room in the Mokotow district of Warsaw, which she had used before the rising and which, by a miracle, was still intact. Next day, as the morning sun gleamed on the battered walls, they made their way towards the centre of the city by narrow paths leading through heaps of rubble and shattered pavements. The General walked along in silence. He was to meet Jankowski and Puzak, the Government Delegate and the Chairman of the Council of National Unity, a body representing the political parties, for a last exchange of views before deciding on their plans. The Russians had once again promised that the whole delegation would be flown to London, but they wanted them first to meet a representative of the Red Army, who was expected to be Marshal Zhukov himself.

In front of a small café which had sprung into existence in a burnt-out house in Koszykowa street, Okulicki took *Janina's* hand and said with a smile: 'Don't worry, I'll see you again in a few hours.' Then he turned away and walked slowly into the dark interior.

The headquarters of the First Byelorussian Front were in a farmhouse at Pruszkow, just outside the capital. Okulicki, Jankowski and Puzak arrived there on the evening of March 27th and were received by General Ivanov, who was to discuss with them arrangements for the meeting with Marshal Zhukov on the following day.

It is not clear whether the three delegates were arrested at Pruszkow or later at Wlochy, the NKVD headquarters on the outskirts of Warsaw. Probably it was the latter, for in the course of the 28th the other underground leaders were held there under armed guard.[49]) By this time Okulicki and his two colleagues had already been flown to Moscow, where

---

[49]) They were: Adam Bien, Peasants' Party, Stanislaw Jasiukowicz, National Party, and Antoni Pajdak, Socialist Party, all members of the Council of Ministers in Poland; also Kazimierz Baginski, acting chairman of the Peasants' Party, Jozef Chacinski, chairman of the Labour Party, Eugeniusz Czarnowski, chairman of the Democratic Party, Kazimierz Kobylanski, National Party, Stanislaw Michalowski, Democratic Party, Stanislaw Mierzwa, Peasants' Party, Zbigniew Stypulkowski, National Party, Franciszek Urbanski, Labour Party, Aleksander Zwierzynski, acting chairman of the National Party, and Jozef Stemmler, interpreter.

the thirteen others were brought two days later. All were imprisoned in the Lubianka.[50])

X

On April 25, 1945 an international conference opened at San Francisco for the purpose of founding the United Nations Organization on the basis of the Dumbarton Oaks and Yalta proposals. The war was still going on, but Hitler's Germany was at its last gasp and the cease-fire in Europe was expected any day. Roosevelt had died on April 12th and was succeeded by Vice-President Truman. At the last moment before the conference, the Soviet Government announced that it would be represented by Molotov, the Foreign Minister.

The League of Nations, which ceased to exist in 1940, had its faults, but it was vastly superior to the institution which came to birth towards the end of the last war in a cloud of opportunism and defeatism. The war had supposedly been fought in defence of the weak and oppressed, of human rights and the Four Freedoms; but little was left of these exalted principles when the delegates of four dozen countries assembled in California, surrounded by hundreds of advisers and secretaries and over two thousand journalists and radio commentators. The Organization came into being under the shadow of the Great Powers, who possessed the right of veto and decided everything in their own interest. In practice the most important matters were decided by the Russians, who fascinated the world by their strength and ruthlessly pursued their own political ends.

Unfortunately Poland was not in a position to defend herself at the conference which sealed the tragic Yalta decisions, for her representatives were not accorded a place among the delegations of 46 and later 49 countries. On the pretext that it was necessary to await the formation of a "Govern-

---

[50]) At this distance of time it may appear strange that men experienced in the underground, who had lived through more than five years of occupation, who knew of the treacherous arrests of Polish commanders and officials after the Bolsheviks entered Poland, should have fallen so easily into a trap. The reason, however, lay in the situation that obtained at that time. These men were not naive, but deprived of all help, worn out by years of underground activity, powerless against the might of Russia, they grasped at the offer of talks as their one remaining hope. Only a sudden change in Russia's attitude to Poland could have saved the country at that time, and the proposal for talks suggested that there might be a possibility of such a change. It should be remembered that in 1956 the commander of the Hungarian rising, General Maleter, agreed to talks in exactly the same way, although he knew Soviet methods and all that had happened in Poland earlier. He accepted the *rendezvous* because it was the only chance left to him.

ment of national unity," which in practice meant merely adding one or two London politicians to the Lublin Committee, the Polish Government which was then recognized by almost every country in the world was not invited to the conference. Yet this was the government which had, throughout the war, directed the nation's struggle against the Nazi hordes, and had had under its orders both the Home Army and the Polish armed forces in the West.

At the outset of the conference the question of Poland—her government, her frontiers and her future—predominated over the discussion of other problems, important as these were. Russia's predatory attitude and the weak compliance of the Western powers were too blatant to escape attention. Unfortunately, though Poland's wrongs were recognized and a few of the bolder statesmen made speeches on the subject, nothing was done to remedy them.

Before the conference opened, those delegates who took an interest in European affairs knew that towards the end of March a dozen or so of the chief Polish underground leaders had been invited to talks with the Soviet authorities, and had not returned. There was speculation as to the reason, but it was generally thought that secret negotiations must be in progress, perhaps with an element of compulsion, but with the general object of achieving a compromise and agreeing on a new Polish government. The matter was of especial concern to the British Government, for on January 27th they had asked the Poles in London to give them the names of the underground leaders for communication to the Russians, in order to "facilitate the protection of valuable individuals." At San Francisco the Soviet delegation were repeatedly asked what had happened to the missing men, but always replied that they had no definite information.

On the evening of May 3rd—the Polish national day, anniversary of the 1791 Constitution—the US Secretary of State, Stettinius, entertained Eden and Molotov to dinner. While they were still at table he asked Molotov once again if he had any news of the Polish leaders. In reply the Soviet minister growled: 'They have been arrested by the Red Army.'

The Western ministers were dumbfounded, Eden recalled vividly the moment when he had handed over the leaders' names to the Russians, hoping to ensure their protection but in fact making certain that they would land in an NKVD gaol. Not only had his government abandoned Poland to the Russians, but it had become an accessory in the arrest of allied leaders who had kept faith till the end.

The Lubianka prisoners knew nothing of all this, since they were totally cut off from the outside world. They received no newspapers and of course no letters; no-one gave them the slightest information about the war, and they had no idea that far away, on the other side of the Western hemisphere, a conference had assembled that was to seal their country's fate.

Every night they were called up for interrogation and kept for hours under the glare of powerful lights, while they were grilled about the minutest details and ordered to confess to crimes they had not committed. Then they would be taken back to their cells and routed out again when they had scarcely had time to close their eyes. They were starved and deprived of exercise, and every attempt was made to stifle their human feelings and deprive them of resilience, dignity and the will to live.[51])

Some of the sixteen arrested men were no strangers to Russian prisons. Puzak, a dyed-in-the-wool socialist, had known the dark Schlüsselburg dungeons in Tsarist time. Baginski had been in gaol in the same era, and Zwierzynski had been transferred straight to the Lubianka from another Soviet prison; but Okulicki was the only one who was now confined in the Lubianka for the second time.

On the first occasion, during Stalin's honeymoon with Hitler, he had endured over six months' interrogation by the NKVD without breaking down, though they had at their disposal every implement of force and coercion. By the time he was set free his health was undermined, and he felt now that he was less strong than before; yet the task confronting him was a much graver one.

None of the prisoners knew precisely why they had been arrested and what the torture of incessant interrogations was designed to achieve; but there were many signs that they might be intended to appear in a show trial, staged in order to further the aggressor's policies. Okulicki knew how relentlessly the NKWD had tracked him down and how insistent the Russians had been on his taking part in the supposed talks. It was more than likely that he might be the main figure at the trial, and he must conserve enough strength to defend himself. It was not a question of saving his own skin—he knew well enough that he would not escape from the lion's den twice. His strength was needed to defend the cause entrusted to him as the Home Army's last commander.

After eleven weeks of interrogation the Russians showed their hand. The indictment presented to the prisoners conformed to the line followed by Soviet propaganda for the past two or three years. The main charge was that the Polish

---

[51].) Stypulkowski writes in his memoirs *Invitation to Moscow* that he was interrogated 140 times.

underground had been "planning armed action together with Germany against the USSR." Various "crimes" were enumerated which the underground was alleged to have committed in the way of sabotage against the Red Army etc., and a false picture was given of the situation in Poland. According to this, the Home Army and the Council of National Unity were illegal bodies, and their leaders were accused of controlling armed bands and possessing stores of weapons, wireless transmitters, secret printing-presses and meeting-places.

The charge of collaboration with the Germans was farcical in the mouths of those who had invaded Poland and shared out its territory with Hitler in 1939. Equally it was worthy of Goebbels to describe the Polish underground, active on Polish soil, as "illegal." But only those who were at a safe distance from the Russians could afford to dismiss the charges in this way. They had a very different sound to the defenceless captives in the Lubianka, who were at the end of their physical and mental endurance after ceaseless interrogation and ill-treatment. Some of them indeed gave way to the merciless pressure and owned to crimes they had not committed. What could now prevent the accusers from proclaiming to the whole world that the "Polish criminals" had admitted to collaborating with the Nazis?

On June 21st, the prisoners were taken to Trade Union House on Pushkin street, a former Noblemen's Club with a stately Hall of Columns which was used as the venue for show trials. It was here that Rykov, Bukharin and Kamenev had been tried and sentenced—all communist leaders of the past whom Stalin had swept out of his way with unexampled brutality. Here, too, Marshal Tukhachevsky had been tried *in camera* on the charge of treasonable relations with Germany.[52])

The Collegium of the Supreme Military Court of the USSR consisted of General V. Ulrich, the President, and two colonels. The prosecutors were General N. Afanasiev and State Counsellor R. Rudenko. The latter was soon to achieve the dignity

---

[52]) This was the result of a trick planned by Heydrich and agreed to by Hitler. Documents were forged to show that Tukhachevsky was in league with the German general staff to bring about a coup in Moscow. This information was planted on the Czechoslovak President Benes, who provided it in good faith to Stalin. A special messenger from the latter went to Germany, collected the documents and paid 3,000,000 gold roubles for them. (Later it turned out that the roubles were marked and German intelligence agents, who used them in Russia, were arrested). Tukhachevsky was arrested on June 4, 1937 and brought to trial seven days later. He was sentenced to death and shot the same evening. The prosecutor was Vyshinsky. This trial brought in its train a purge in the Red Army and weakened it considerably.

of Soviet prosecutor at the Nuremberg trial which convicted Goering, Hess, Ribbentrop and other Nazi leaders of war crimes.

The Hall of Columns was crammed full. Most of the spectators were in uniform, but there were a large number of foreign correspondents. The organizers, who had much practice in the smooth running of this type of show, had also invited the British, French and American embassies to send representatives.

Although the accused were seated together, each of them was still absolutely alone, as the slightest contact between neighbours was forbidden. During the past few days they had been forcibly fed and restored to some decency of appearance, but they were still human shadows, holding on to life with their last scrap of will-power. The supreme test had now come: a public arraignment to which they had no valid means of resistance.

Thanks to his two terms in the Lubianka, Okulicki spoke Russian with fair fluency, and decided to conduct his own defence.[53]) He concentrated his thoughts on a single line of argument. He was the commander of an underground army which was itself being placed in the dock but whose only aim had been to fight for its people's freedom. His duty was to forget all other aspects of the case and especially his own interests,[54]) and to vindicate the obvious truth which his persecutors were seeking to obscure and besmirch.

Naturally he enjoyed none of the right which are customarily accorded to an advocate or to a prisoner defending himself. Apart from his physical and nervous exhaustion, his freedom of speech was limited by the presiding judge and he was prevented from calling witnesses. He had asked to be allowed to question six senior Home Army officers [55]) who were in Soviet hands and whose statements, undoubtedly made under duress, supported the indictment. Okulicki well knew that if local fights had taken place with Red Army units or Soviet partisans, it because Home Army troops had been attacked and ambushed for the purpose of disarming or destroying

---

[53]) Jankowski and Stypulkowski also elected to conduct their own defence.

[54]) The indictment stressed that his guilt was aggravated by the fact that he had been dropped into Poland "by a Liberator aircraft of the Royal Air Force from the British air base near Brindisi (Italy)." It added that "... The object of sending Okulicki to Poland in May 1944 was to intensify the struggle against the Red Army."

[55]) These were all commanders of the Eastern Districts of the Home Army: General Ludwik Bittner, Colonel Wladyslaw Filipkowski, Colonel Jan Kotowicz, Colonel Kulczycki, Colonel Adam Switalski and Colonel Kazimierz Tumidajski.

them. But his request for a confrontation was refused by the court on flimsy technical grounds.[56])

The prosecutors suffered from no such disablement, and their witnesses, one by one, were duly led into court. All had come direct from prison, all were scarcely able to stand on their legs, and all were well coached in their parts. At the prosecutors' request, or even without waiting to be asked, they recited a long string of allegations concerning attacks by the Home Army on Soviet troops and representatives of the civil administration.

Deprived of witnesses and documents, harassed by the judges, prosecutors and warders, emaciated by hunger and with a weak heart, Okulicki summoned up his last reserves of strength and measured his answers with iron self-control. The opposing counsel never once succeeded in causing him to deviate from the path he had set himself.

On the fourth day of the trial, when the defence was permitted to reply, he was at last able to state his case at length and with relatively little interruption.[57])

He was addressing a Soviet court which might at any moment deprive him even of that opportunity, in the presence of spectators who, as a body, were at best indifferent to his cause. Here and there, no doubt, there were some who were hanging on his words and sympathized with him heart and soul. But the great majority had been educated by the Soviet regime in one simple truth: if a prisoner of the NKVD is allowed to speak, it is in order that he may do penance, fall on his knees before his persecutors and acknowledge the truth of their charges, lick their boots and beg for mercy. This was the iron rule of Soviet show trials, the purpose for which they were organized. It is no wonder then that a hush fell on the assembly as the chief defendant, who was to all appearances at the end of his tether, continued to speak quietly and slowly, with pauses to recover his strength, but without departing from the line he had taken since the very outset of the merciless interrogation.

'... This is a political trial... its object is to blacken the Polish underground movement...

[56]) One pretext for not producing these witnesses was that of bad weather. Apart from the absurdity of such a reason in the context of a major political trial, it must be remembered that it was held in June.

[57]) The only source from which extracts from Okulicki's speech can be quoted is the court report of the trial published in 1945 by the Peoples Commissariat of Justice of the USSR. Another source of information is an article by the Daily Express correspondent Alaric Jacob, published on June 21, 1945, entitled "Okulicki says: I fought for Freedom."

'The truth is that the Polish underground is endowed with moral credit as a result of its fight against the Germans. No-one can deny this, or bring any evidence to show that the Polish underground did not fight the Germans for five long years...

'In accusing us of collaborating with the Germans, you are impugning our honour. To accuse the three hundred thousand soldiers of the Home Army is to accuse the whole Polish nation...

'The Warsaw rising... was a heroic struggle and in no way justifies political reprisals...'

Rejecting the charge that the Home Army had attacked advancing Red Army units, Okulicki recalled that he had not been allowed to summon witnesses.

'During this trial the prosecution has presented in a lurid fashion certain shocking accusations of terror. In so doing it has cast a slur on the Home Army, which it has portrayed in a despicable light. I requested that certain witnesses might be summoned—the commanders of the Home Army areas, districts and divisions concerned—so that I might question them before the court and discover the true cause of such useless and harmful activities. These men were in command at the time and they must know what happened. Unfortunately I was not enabled to question them...

'What is my opinion of Polish-Soviet relations? I will give it, not for the purpose of justifying myself to the court... I must declare that I feel no hostility whatever towards the Soviet Union. My actions were not hostile, nor were they inspired by hostility. I acknowledge that they were inspired by distrust of the Soviet Union... That distrust was not born during this war; it has existed for centuries. We lived as an independent State for only twenty years. We have not forgotten the hundred and twenty-three years of slavery imposed on us from the east, from Tsarist Russia...

'My actions were not aggressive but defensive. I know that the Polish people sincerely desires friendship with the Soviet people. And I should regard myself as a criminal of the first order if I did not desire it too, on the inviolable condition that Poland's independence is preserved.

'This is—*conditio sine qua non*.'

The hush that had lasted throughout Okulicki's speech was still unbroken. He was too exhausted to say more, but he had said what was necessary. His voice, weak though it was, vibrated over the heads of the judges, prosecutors, warders, uniformed spectators, journalists and diplomats.

At last one of the prosecutors rose to his feet and, glaring at the accused with a fury he could no longer control, exclaimed contemptuously:

'So, General, you feel no gratitude whatever to the Red Army for liberating your country?

Okulicki replied:

'I honour the Red Army for liberating Poland. But I honour still more those Polish soldiers who were done to death by soldiers of the Red Army.[58])

---

[58]) Okulicki's last words spoken at his trial were cited by Puzak after he returned from Soviet imprisonment and was, for a short time, at liberty in Poland.
Okulicki, who was sentenced to ten years, died after a few years in a Soviet prison. The Government Delegate, Jan Stanislaw Jankowski, sentenced to eight years, met the same fate.

APPENDICES

STATISTICS OF DROPS DURING THE FOUR OPERATIONAL SEASONS

I. *TRIAL PERIOD* (FEBRUARY 15, 1941 - APRIL 30, 1942)

Flights: 12 (10 Polish crews, 2 British)

Drops
carried out: 9 (8 Polish crews, 1 British)

Dropped: 48 parachutists (41 military, 7 political couriers)
19 containers } (arms, explosives, communications and
13 parcels } photographic equipment). Total 2 tons
1,660,850 dollars in bills and gold
    1,775 gold sovereigns
    885,000 German marks

Lost: 1 Polish aircraft and crew
2 parachutists (killed in fighting immediately after landing)
5 containers } about 1,100 lbs. (25%)
2 packages }
8,200 dollars
an unknown quantity of German marks

II. "*INTONATION*" (AUGUST 1, 1942 - APRIL 30, 1943)

Flights: 65 (49 Polish crews, 16 British)

Drops
carried out: 42 (29 Polish crews, 13 British) [1]

Dropped: 119 parachutists (109 military, 9 political couriers,
    1 Hungarian)
241 containers } ("OW" loads, "MD" loads, radio parts,
86 packages } field dressings, materials for forging
58 kit-bags [2]) } documents, maps). Total 49,5 tons
13,022,000 dollars in bills and gold
5,158,000 German marks

[1] The proportion of Polish and British crews is an estimate: no exact data are available.

[2] Kit-bags were dropped together with the parachutists on the same parachutes.

Lost: 6 aircraft (3 crews were saved, 3 were lost — 2 Polish, 1 British)
4 parachutists
42 containers
14 packages } 8,1 tons (16,4%)
7 kit-bags
606,000 dollars
70,000 German marks

III. "RIPOSTE" (AUGUST 1, 1943 - JULY 31, 1944)

Flights: 381 (213 Polish crews, 168 British)

Drops carried out: 205 (131 Polish crews, 74 British)

Dropped (or sent by "Bridge"): 146 parachutists (135 military, 10 political couriers, 1 woman)
1,996 containers } (arms, explosives, communications equipment, field dressings, uniforms, blankets). Total 263,4 tons
2,073 packages
16,109,325 dollars in bills and gold
6,586,500 German marks
40,569,800 Polish "occupation" zlote

Lost: 16 aircraft and crews (5 Polish, 11 British)
4 parachutists
87 containers } 13,4 tons (5,1%)
201 packages
1,149,000 dollars
150,000 German marks

IV. "RETALIATION" (AUGUST 1, 1944 - DECEMBER 31, 1944)

Flights: 410 (167 Polish crews, 133 British and South African, 110 American)

Drops carried out: 229 (72 Polish crews, 50 British and South African, 107 American)

Dropped: 33 parachutists (31 military, 2 political couriers)
2,546 containers } (arms, explosives, communications equipment, field dressings, uniforms, blankets). Total 286 tons
799 packages
4,030,988 dollars in bills and gold
6,460,000 German marks

Lost: 47 aircraft (21 Polish, 24 British and South African, 2 American. Crews saved: 1 Polish, 3 British and South African, 1 American)
1 parachutist
1,465 containers } 158 tons (55,2%)
216 packages
380 German marks

THE WARSAW RISING IN THE FRAMEWORK OF "RETALIATION"
(August 1, 1944 - October 2, 1944) [3]

Flights: 306 (91 Polish crews, 50 British, 55 South African, 110 American)

Drops carried out: 192 (149 over Warsaw, 43 over Kampinos and Kabacki woods). *Polish crews:* 47 drops (16 over Warsaw, 31 over Kampinos and Kabacki woods — 2 drops consisted of only 19 packages altogether). *British and South African crews:* 38 drops (26 over Warsaw, 12 over Kampinos and Kabacki woods). *American crews:* 107 drops over Warsaw.

Dropped: 2,154 containers (1,711 over Warsaw, 443 over Kampinos and Kabacki woods). *Polish crews:* 461 containers (177 over Warsaw, 284 over Kampinos and Kabacki woods). *British and South African crews:* 409 (250 over Warsaw, 159 over Kampinos and Kabacki woods). *American crews:* 1,284 over Warsaw only.
557 packages. **Total 239 tons.**

Picked up by the insurgents: 742 containers (Warsaw 463, Kampinos and Kabacki woods 279).
381 packages (Warsaw 182, Kampinos and Kabacki woods 199. **Total 88 tons (36,8%).**

[3] The statistics of the drops into Poland, with special regard to Warsaw during the rising, are based on the archives of the Sixth Bureau and of the Polish Air Force in the West. The figures for the first three periods are practically identical with those given in the official publication "The Polish Armed Forces during the Second World War (Vol. III, The Home Army)," but for the fourth period, inclusive of the Warsaw Rising, there is a wide difference. The chapter on help from the West in the above-mentioned volume is based almost entirely on the archives of the Sixth Bureau and so certain inaccuracies have crept in. They were difficult to avoid, for the material on assistance to the insurgents is incomplete, frequently contradictory and difficult to analyse. The author has spent a great deal of time and effort on checking the available sources, he has used both Polish and British material and has drawn up a table of the flights and drops which is probably fairly accurate and has served as basis for further researches.

The figures regarding the rising appear to be exact, though it is impossible to be completely certain. The conditions in which the insurgents fought, the division of the city into small sectors cut off from each other, the difficulties of night drops and reception, the impossibility of exact recognition of the aircraft (Polish or British) which made a particular drop, the wide dispersal of the containers — all these factors combine to make conclusive data impossible. It was easier to establish the number of drops made, using the archives of the Sixth Bureau and the Polish Air Force as well as British sources, but it was far harder to establish the figures for the amount picked up. Here there is only one source: despatches and reports from Warsaw. They are very inexact, often contradictory. It had to be judged which figures were the most probable, taking into account the state of the city, what percentage of its area was in the insurgents' hands and the conditions under which the operations were carried out (e.g. the great American drop of September 18, 1944).

Lost: 41 aircraft and 36 crews (Poles 17 aircraft and 16 crews, British and South African 22 aircraft and 19 crews, Americans 2 aircraft and 1 crew).

1,412 containers
176 packages } 151 tons (63,2%)

TOTAL FOR ALL THE OPERATIONAL SEASONS

Flights: 868 (Polish crews 439, British and South African 319, American 110)

Drops carried out: 485 (Polish crews 240, British and South African 138, American 107)

Dropped (or sent by "Bridge"):
346 [4]) parachutists (316 military, 1 woman soldier, 28 political couriers, 1 Hungarian)
4,802 containers
2,971 packages } Total 600,9 tons
58 kit-bags
34,823,163 dollars in bills and gold
    1,775 gold sovereigns
19,089,500 German marks
40,569,800 Polish "occupation" zlote
   10,000 Spanish pesetas (in which season is unknown)

Lost: 70 aircraft (30 Polish, 38 British and South African, 2 American)
62 crews (28 Polish,[5]) 33 British and South African, 1 American)
11 parachutists
1,599 containers
433 packages
7 kit-bags
1,763,200 dollars
The exact quantity of German marks has not been established.

---

[4] This is the number of parachutist drops, but actually only 344 persons were conveyed, as two men jumped twice.

[5] Of these 28 crews 4 baled out and were taken prisoner by the Germans. Therefore only 24 crews are given as lost in the tables drawn up immediately after the war by the Polish Air Force. Another 6 airmen were saved by Home Army units. This only came to light later. Of the 33 British and South African crews posted missing after being shot down, at least one crew was saved also by joining a Home Army unit.

SOURCES

A) BOOKS AND PUBLICATIONS IN ENGLISH

Julian Amery	Special Operations (Routledge and Kegan Paul)
Władysław Bartoszewski	Warsaw Death Ring 1939-1944 (Interpress Publishers, Poland, 1968)
Tadeusz Bór-Komorowski	The Secret Army (Victor Gollancz, London, 1950)
Winston S. Churchill	The Second World War (Cassell and Co., London, 1948-54)
Hugh Dalton	The Fateful Years (Memoirs 1931-1945), (Frederick Muller, London, 1957)
Walter Dornberger	V. 2. (Hurst and Blackett, London, 1954)
Guy Eden	Portrait of Churchill (Hutchinson and Co., London)
John Ehrman	Grand Strategy (History of the Second World War), (H. M. Stationery Office, London, 1956)
M. R. D. Foot	SOE in France (H. M. Stationery Office, London, 1966)
Brian Gardner	The Wasted Hour (Cassell and Co., London, 1963)
Colin Gubbins	Resistance Movements in the War (lecture given at the Royal United Service Institution (RUSI), (1948)
David Irving	Accident. The Death of General Sikorski (William Kimber, London, 1967)
Alaric Jacob	Okulicki says: I fought for Freedom (Daily Express, June 21, 1945)
Peter Kemp	No Colours or Crest (Cassell and Co., London, 1958)
Stefan Korboński	Fighting Warsaw (George Allen and Unwin, London, 1956)
Stanisław Mikołajczyk	The Pattern of Soviet Domination (Sampson Low, Marston and Co., London, 1948), (US title: The Rape of Poland)
Edward Raczyński	In Allied London (Weidenfeld and Nicolson, London, 1962)
Leonard Rapport and Arthur Northwood, Jr.	Rendenzvous with Destiny (A History of the 101st Airborne Division), (101st Airborne Association, Greenville, Texas, 1948)

Lord Russell of Liverpool	The Scourge of the Swastika (Cassell, London, 1954)
Cornelius Ryan	The Longest Day (Victor Gollancz, London, 1960)
Walter Schellenberg	The Schellenberg Memoirs (A record of the Nazi secret service), (André Deutsch, London, 1956)
John Slessor	The Central Blue (Cassell, London, 1956)
Edward R. Stettinius, Jr.	Lend-Lease: Weapon for Victory (Macmillan, London, 1944)
Zbigniew Stypułkowski	Invitation to Moscow (Thames and Hudson, London, 1951)
Jerrard Tickell	Moon Squadron (Allan Wingate, London, 1956)
Alexander Werth	Russia at War (1941-1945), (Barrie and Rockliff, London, 1964)
Charles Wighton	Heydrich, Hitler's most Evil Henchman (Oldham's Press, London, 1962)

* * *

Collective works

Documents on Polish-Soviet Relations 1939-1945, Volume I and II (Heinemann, London, 1961 and 1968.).
Destiny Can Wait (The Polish Air Force in the Second World War), (William Heinemann, London, 1949).
Proceedings of a Conference on Britain and European Resistance, 1939-1945 (St. Antony's College, Oxford, 1962).
Reports of Congress of the United States of America.
The Unseen and Silent (Sheed and Ward, London, 1954).

B) BOOKS AND PUBLICATIONS IN POLISH, FRENCH, GERMAN AND RUSSIAN

Witold Babiński	*Odpowiedzialność Naczelnego Wodza* (Responsibility of the Commander-in-Chief), Letter to the London Polish weekly *Wiadomości*, No. 9, March 2, 1952.
Witold Babiński	*Powstanie warszawskie, rząd i wódz* (Warsaw Rising, Government and Commander-in-Chief). *Wiadomości*, No. 42. Oct. 21, 1951.
Adam Borkiewicz	*Powstanie Warszawskie* (Warsaw Rising), *Instytut Wydawniczy Pax*, Warsaw, 1964.
Aleksander Bregman	*Dzieje pustego fotela* (The story of an empty chair), Światpol, London, 1948.
Aleksander Bregman	*Najlepszy sojusznik Hitlera* (Hitler's best ally). Orbis, London, 1958.
Marek Celt	*Pojedynek z latającą śmiercią* (Duel with flying death). *Na Antenie*, No. 50, May 28, 1967.
Marek Celt	*Trzeci Most* (The third "Bridge"). *Na Antenie*, No. 47, February 26, 1967.

Cezary Chlebowski	*Ponury. Wrocławski Tygodnik Katolicki*, No. 12 (705), March 19, 1967.
Cezary Chlebowski	*Rozbicie więzienia w Pińsku* (Armed raid on the prison at Pinsk), *Wojskowy Przegląd Historyczny*, No. 3 (39), Warsaw, 1966.
Rudolf Hoess	*Wspomnienia komendanta obozu oświęcimskiego* (Memoirs of the Auschwitz commandant). *Główna Komisja Badania Zbrodni Hitlerowskich w Polsce*, Warsaw, 1956.
Czesław Hołub	*Jeszcze o rozbiciu więzienia w Pińsku w 1943 r.* (More about the armed raid on the prison at Pinsk in 1943). Letter to the Polish quarterly *Wojskowy Przegląd Historyczny*, No. 2 (42), Warsaw, 1967.
Kazimierz Iranek-Osmecki	*Ostatnia podróż Rafała* (Raphael's last journey). *Wiadomości*, No. 1086, January 22, 1967.
Stanisław Jankowski	*Cichociemny skok* (Secret parachute jump). *Życie Warszawy*, January-February 1967.
Stanisław Kopański	*Wspomnienia wojenne 1939-1945* (War memoirs 1939-1945). Veritas, London, 1961.
Hans von Krannhals	*Der Warschauer Aufstand 1944* (The Warsaw Rising, 1944). Frankfurt am Main, 1962.
Władysław Pobóg-Malinowski	*Najnowsza Historia Polityczna Polski. Okres 1939-1945* (The recent political history of Poland, 1939-1945). Gryf, London, 1960.
Leon Mitkiewicz	*Mikołajczyk, Eden, Powstanie* (Mikolajczyk, Eden and the Rising). Polish monthly *Horyzonty*, No. 128, January 1967.
Leon Mitkiewicz	*Preliminaria powstania zbrojnego AK* (Prelude to armed uprising of the Home Army). *Horyzonty*, No. 131, April 1967.
Jacques Mordal	*25 siècles de guerre sur mer*. Marabout Université, France, 1959.
Zygmunt Nagórski, Snr.	*Wojna w Londynie* (The war in London), Księgarnia Polska, Paris, 1966.
Jan Nowak	*Operacja Wildhorn* (Operation "Wildhorn"), *Kultura*, No. 4/5, Paris, June-July 1949.
Adam Pragier	*Czas przeszły dokonany* (The past definite). B. Świderski, London, 1966.
Zbigniew Siemiaszko	*Retinger w Polsce w 1944 roku* (Retinger in Poland in 1944). *Zeszyty Historyczne*, No. 12, Paris, 1967.
Kazimierz Sosnkowski	*Materiały Historyczne* (Historical materials), Gryf, London, 1966.
Tadeusz Stypniewski	*Powstanie i działalność bojowa "Wachlarza"* (Organization and activity of "Fan"). *Wojskowy Przegląd Historyczny*, No. 2 (42), Warsaw, 1967.
Stanisław Stroński	*Powstanie i Naczelny Wódz* (The Rising and the Commander-in-Chief). Letter to *Wiadomości*. No. 45 (293), November 11, 1951.

Stanisław Stroński	*Spór czy Upór* (Argument or obstinacy). Letter to *Wiadomości*, No. 11 (311), March 16, 1952.
Tadeusz Sztumberk-Rychter	*Artylerzysta piechurem* (A gunner footslogging). Pax, Warsaw, 1966.
Tadeusz Szumowski	*Polska Organizacja Wojskowa we francuskim ruchu oporu w latach 1943-1944* (Polish Military Organization in the French Resistance in 1943-1944). *Wojskowy Przegląd Historyczny*, No. 3 (12), Warsaw, 1959.
Michał Tokarzewski-Karaszewicz	*Jak powstała Armia Krajowa* (How the Home Army was created). *Zeszyty Historyczne*, No. 6, Paris, 1964.
Olgierd Tuskiewicz	*Działania na korzyść Armii Krajowej* (Assistance to the Home Army). Polish monthly *Skrzydła*, No. 20 and 21, November 1 and 11, 1946.
Stanisław Urbanek	*Przyjęcie Cichociemnych* (Reception of parachutists). Letter to *Wojskowy Przegląd Historyczny*, No. 2 (42), Warsaw, 1967.
Leon Wanat	*Za murami Pawiaka* (Behind the walls of the "Pawiak"). Książka i Wiedza, Warsaw, 1967 (4th edition).
Michał Wiśniewski	*Polacy w walce z niemiecką bronią V* (Poles against the German V weapon). *Wojskowy Przegląd Historyczny*, No. 2 (38), Warsaw, 1966.
Michał Wojewódzki	*Na tropie Wunderwaffe* (On the trail of the Wunderwaffe). Ministry of National Defence, Warsaw, 1961.
Melchior Wańkowicz	*Hubalczycy* (The Hubals), Instytut Wydawniczy Pax, Warsaw, 1959.
Józef Żbik	*Pierwszy skok* (The first jump). London, 1946.

* * *

Collective works

Istoria Velikoy Otechestvennoy Voiny Sovietskogo Soyuza (The History of the Great Patriotic War of the Soviet Union), Moscow.

Na Antenie, No. 8/9, August 16 - September 6, 1964 (Issue devoted to the Warsaw Rising).

Polskie Siły Zbrojne w drugiej wojnie światowej, Tom III, Armia Krajowa (Polish Armed Forces during the Second World War, Volume III, the Home Army). General Sikorski Historical Institute, London, 1950.

Polscy Spadochroniarze (Polish Parachutists), Fundusz Wydawniczy Plutonu Opieki 1 Samodzielnej Bryg. Spadochronowej, London, 1949.

Sprawozdanie sądowe w sprawie organizatorów, kierowników i uczestników polskiego podziemia na zapleczu Czerwonej Armii na terytorium Polski, Litwy oraz obwodów zachodnich Białorusi i Ukrainy. Rozpatrzonej przez Kolegium Wojskowe Sądu Najwyższego ZSRR 18-21 czerwca 1945 roku (Polish translation from Russian of the record of Okulicki's trial). People's Commissariat of Justice of the USSR, Moscow, 1945.

C) UNPUBLISHED SOURCES IN POLISH, ENGLISH AND FRENCH

Colin Gubbins	SOE and Poland (additions and corrections to the present author's text).
Albert Guérisse	SOE and Belgium (written answers to the author's questions).
Czesław Halski	Polish Radio in London (oral answers).
Józef Hartman	Training courses for parachutists sent into Poland.
D. T. Hudson	Report of a British observer to German-occupied Poland, 26th December 1944 (Polish Underground Movement (1940-45) Study Trust).
Kazimierz Iranek-Osmecki	A Courier's route to Poland in 1940.
Tadeusz Klimowski	The Home Army in Volhynia: I. "Fan", II. 27th Volhynian infantry division.
Stanisław Kopański	The independence of the Polish Armed Forces in the West; co-operation with General Sosnkowski and the Allied military authorities (oral answers).
Marian Kukiel	Polish Armed Forces in the West (oral answers).
Franciszek Kwieciński	The Sixth Bureau (oral answers).
Zygmunt Milewicz	Personnel of "Import".
Tadeusz Pełczyński	Home Army Headquarters (oral answers).
Adolf Pilch	The fate of the "Stołpce" group.
Jan Podoski	Report on the activities of Section "S" of the Sixth Bureau, 1941-1945 (Polish Underground Movement (1939-45) Study Trust).
Antoni Pośpieszalski	Report on British Military Mission in Poland (Polish Underground Movement (1939-45) Study Trust).
Janina Pronaszko-Konopacka	About General Okulicki (Polish Underground Movement (1939-45) Study Trust).
Antoni Rawicz-Szczerbo	The Independent Parachute Brigade (oral account).
Ludomir Rayski	Flights over Warsaw (oral answers).
Franciszek Rybka	Preparations for a parachute jump and service in the Home Army (oral account).
Józef Smoleński	The Sixth Bureau (oral account).
Henry McLeod Threlfall	The SOE base at Brindisi (additions and corrections to the author's text).
Olgierd Tuskiewicz	Polish Air Force abroad, London, 1947.
P. A. Wilkinson	The Polish Section of SOE (written answers).

D) ARCHIVES

The Sixth Bureau (Polish Underground Movement (1939-45) Study Trust).
The Polish Air Force Abroad (General Sikorski Historical Institute).

INDEX

(All ranks are omitted, code names in *italics*)

A

Abd-el-Krim, 162
Abington, Lord, 62
Adrian, Florian, 183
Afanasiev, N., 230
Aldenham, Lord, 60
Aldenham, Lady, 60
Anders, Wladyslaw, 119, 168, 171, 223
Arciszewski, Tomasz, 162, 163
Arciuszkiewicz, Eugeniusz, 186, 193
Azor, 111, 114

B

Badoglio, Pietro, 120
Baginski, Kazimierz, 225, 228
Banaczyk, Wladyslaw, 162
Banasikowski, Edmund, 109
Benes, Eduard, 229
Berezowski, Zygmunt, 159
Bialy, Jan, 185
Bielski, Romuald, 160
Bien, Adam, 225
Bilski, Kazimierz, 161
Bittner, Ludwik, 230
Bocian (Stork), see Eckhardt
Bokszczanin, Janusz, 170, 213
Boryczko, Adam, 196
Bor (Komorowski), 120, 134, 168, 170, 171, 174, 180, 185, 189, 210, 211, 212, 213, 217
Braybrooke, Lady Dorothy, 61
Brekiewicz, Antoni, 39
Brooke, Alan Francis (Lord Alanbrooke), 187
Brzoza (Birch), see Retinger

Bukharin, Nikolay, 229
Bystromiak, 196

C

Cadogan, Sir Alexander George Montague, 187
Canaris, Wilhelm, 46
Celt, see Chciuk
Cetys, Teodor, 195
Chacinski, Jozef, 225
Chciuk, Tadeusz, 162, 163, 212
Chmielewski, Jerzy, 151, 152, 162, 163
Churchill, (Sir) Winston, 19, 20, 21, 22, 23, 26, 29, 32, 42, 53, 93, 148, 149, 162, 175, 176, 177, 187, 190, 197, 198, 216, 217, 218
Cieplik, Franciszek, 196
Currie, Tony, see Pospieszalski
Curzon, Lord, 121
Czarka (Bowl), 111, 112, 113, 128, 130, 133, 134
Czarnowski, Eugeniusz, 225

D

Dab, 138
Dalton, Hugh (Lord), 19, 20, 22, 26
Daniel, 126, 128, 130, 131
Dobrzanski, Henryk, 35
Domanski, Jan, 160
Donovan, William J., 96
Dornberger, Walter, 149
Dorotycz-Malewicz, Ryszard, 159, 160, 214
Dubow, see Sidoruk, 138
Dzwig, 136

E

Eckhardt, Mieczyslaw, 111
Edek-Monter (Eddie the fitter), 111, 112, 114
Eden, (Sir) Anthony (Lord Avon) 19, 20, 180, 187, 227
Elliot, William, 186, 216
Evans, 60

F

Farley, 67
Fehér, Istvan, 28
Fielden, Edward, 63, 67
Fieldorf, Emil, 211
Filipkowski, Wladyslaw, 230
Foot, Michael, 99

G

Gabcik, Josef, 45
Galinat, Edmund, 30
Galbraith, D., 217
Gaulle, Charles de, 28, 29
General Wilk (Wolf), 171, 195
George VI, H.M. King, 187
Goering, Herman, 62, 230
Goebbels, Joseph, 229
Goliath, see Grocholski, 101, 102, 106, 108, 111
Gora (Mountain), see Pilch, 136, 137, 138, 139, 140, 196
Gorazdowski, Jan 213
Gorski, Jan, 36, 37, 43, 50
Grabica, see Rowecki
Grazyna, 115, 116
Grocholski, Rémi, 101, 105
Grom, 136, 139
Grot, see Rowecki, 114
Grot, 126, 128
Gubbins, Sir Colin, 24, 25, 26, 27, 73, 176, 217
Gulewicz, 140

H

Habdank, 126, 127, 128
Halski, Czeslaw, 80 81
Hambro, Charles, 26
Hancza, see Dorotycz-Malewicz, 159, 163, 186, 215
Hartman, Jozef, 55, 57, 61
Hazell, Ronald, 28

Heller, see Iranek-Osmecki
Hellinger, 113
Henryka, 213
Hess, Rudolf, 230
Heydrich, Reinhard, 45, 229
Himmler, Heinrich, 44, 45, 46
Hinsley, Arthur, 81
Hitler, Adolf, 19, 21, 23, 25, 29, 32, 40, 44, 45, 50, 51, 68, 85, 93, 95, 101, 110, 111, 117, 147, 167, 175, 177, 194, 197, 219, 226, 228, 229
Holland, J. C. F., 24
Hubal, see Dobrzanski, 35, 128
Hudson, D. T., 217, 220

I

Idzikowski, Zbigniew, 64
Ikwa, 136
Iranek-Osmecki, Kazimierz, 148, 149, 150
Ismay, Sir Hastings Lionel (Lord Ismay), 187, 188
Iszkowski, Jerzy, 185
Iwanicki, Andrzej, 142
Ivanov, 223, 225
Izycki, Mateusz, 184, 185

J

Jabotinski (Zabotynski), Vladimir, 26
Jacek, 126
Jacob, Alaric, 231
Janina, see Pronaszko, 210, 211, 222, 225
Jankowski, Jan Stanislaw, 171, 213, 223, 225, 230, 233
Jasinski, Wladyslaw, 127
Jasiukowicz, Stanislaw, 225
Jazwinski, Jan, 40, 73, 75, 76, 77, 142, 159, 160
Jedrus, see Jasinski
Jelita (Guts), 211
Jurek, 126, 128, 130

K

Kalenkiewicz, Maciej, 35, 36, 37, 38, 43, 50, 73, 74, 155, 156, 165, 195, 196
Kalina, see Rowecki

245

Kamenev, Lev, 229
Karaszewicz-Tokarzewski Michal, 30, 33, 34, 50, 167
Karpow, 140
Katya, 116, 117
Kawa (Coffee), 111, 112, 113, 114
Kemp, Peter, 217
Kennedy, Angus, 61
Kisielewski, 115
Klauber, George, 141
Klimecki, Tadeusz, 68, 120
Klimowski, Tadeusz, 70, 72, 73, 74, 76, 103, 104, 105, 106, 107, 108, 122, 195
Klon, see Klimowski
Knowles, 47, 64
Kobra (Kobra 2), see Okulicki, 168
Kobylanski, Kazimierz, 225
Kocian, Antoni, 152
Kocian, Elzbieta, 152
Komorowski, Tadeusz, see *Bor*
Konar, see Koprowski
Kopanski, Stanislaw, 94, 120, 125, 173, 187, 188, 198, 211, 212, 223
Koprowski, Franciszek, 61, 195
Korona (Crown), see Kocian
Kossakowski, Tadeusz, 160
Kostka, see Krzymowski
Kosturch, Tadeusz, 159
Kot, Stanislaw, 162
Kotowicz, Jan, 230
Kra (Ice-floe), 111, 112
Krajewski, Henryk, 195
Krannhals, Hans von, 198
Krizar, Leopold, 84
Krol, Stanislaw, 69, 70, 118, 142, 186
Krzymowski, Stanislaw, 49
Krzywicki, Antoni, 219
Kubis, Jan, 45
Kukiel, Marian, 187
Kula (Bullet), see Okulicki, 167
Kulczycki, 230
Kwapinski, Jan, 187

L

Ladro, Edmund, 219
Lawrence, T. E., 24
Lewald, 139
Lindbergh, Charles, 40, 65

Leliwa, Zbigniew, 160
Lewkowicz, Bronislaw, 185
Lopianowski, Narcyz, 159
Lukasiewicz, Juliusz, 33

M

Mackus, Adam, 61
Maisky, Ivan, 119, 162
Mak (Poppy), see Piatkowski, 84, 109, 115, 117
Makary, see Iranek-Osmecki, 150, 153
Maly, 139
Maleter, 226
Marianski, 128
Marynowski, Edmund, 185
Mazurkiewicz, Jan, 213
Meinertzhagen, R., 26
Michalowski, Stanislaw, 225
Micinski, Czesław, 162, 163, 164
Mierzwa, Stanislaw, 225
Mikolajczyk, Stanislaw, 120, 124, 159, 161, 163, 172, 173, 187, 188, 189, 197, 214, 217, 218
Milewicz, Zygmunt, 82, 83, 84, 90
Mira, 109, 115, 116, 117
Mitkiewicz, Leon, 96, 176, 177, 198
Moczarski, Kazimierz, 203
Molotov, Vyacheslav, 226, 227
Morawicz, Jerzy, 61
Morgan, Alun, 141
Moscicki, Ignacy, 33, 55
Motor, see Wojnowski, 113, 125, 130, 133
Mouse, see Fielden
Mrowka (Ant), see Okulicki, 167
MSZ, 111, 112, 113, 114
Mussolini, Benito, 120

N

Naturalista, Tadeusz 109
Nelson, Sir Frank, 26
Niedzwiadek (Bear-cub), see Okulicki, 210
Nil, see Fieldorf, 133, 211
Nimitz, Chester, 93
Noc (Night), 138, 140
Northwood, Arthur, Jr., 179
Nowak, Jan, 161
Nowodworski, Leon, 33

Nurt (Current), 125, 126, 127, 128, 130, 133, 134

O

Okulicki, Leopold, 31, 167, 168, 169, 170, 210, 212, 213, 214, 218, 220, 221, 222, 223, 224, 225, 228, 230, 231, 232, 233
Oranowski, Zygmunt, 40, 141
Oltarzewski, Stanislaw, 159
Oset (Thistle), 126
Ostoja, see Klimowski

P

Paczkowski, Alfred, 110
Pajdak, Antoni, 225
Palmer, 198
Pelczynski, Tadeusz, 170, 210
Perkins, H. B., 27, 40, 75, 76, 120, 199, 215
Piatkowski, Bohdan, 109
Pijanowski, Waclaw, 183
Pilch, Adolf, 134, 135, 136, 196
Pilsudski, Jozef, 34, 55, 121
Pimenov, 223, 224
Podoski, Jan, 40, 142
Poldek, see Okulicki
Poleszuk, see Szydlowski
Pomian, Andrzej, 159
Ponomarenko, 137
Ponury (Grim), 106, 111, 112, 113, 114, 115, 125, 126, 127, 128, 129, 130, 131, 132, 133, 134, 165, 195
Popov, 137
Portal, Sir Charles (Lord Portal), 187, 190
Pospieszalski, Antoni (Currie Tony), 217
Prawdzic-Slaski, Janusz, 195
Promaszko, Janina, 210
Protasewicz, Michal, 119, 120, 121, 124, 125, 158, 159, 160
Puzak, Kazimierz, 33, 225, 228, 233

R

Raczkiewicz, Wladyslaw, 33, 187
Raczkowski, Czeslaw, 49
Raczynski, Edward, 180, 187
Rafal, 128

Rakon, see Rowecki
Raphael, see Chmielewski, 151, 153, 154, 162, 163
Rapport, Leonard, 179
Rataj, Maciej, 33
Rawa, see Protasewicz
Rayski, Ludomir, 192, 216
Rekiszko, Zygmunt, 108, 115
Retinger, Jozef, 162, 163, 174
Ribbentrop, Joachim von, 230
Rommel, Juliusz, 30
Robot, 126, 127, 128, 130, 133
Roosevelt, Franklin D., 68, 96, 148, 175, 176, 177, 187, 197, 198, 216, 226
Roper-Caldbeck, Terry, 61
Rowecki, Stefan, 34, 35, 39, 49, 50, 51, 53, 102, 105, 111, 115, 119, 120, 125, 155, 158, 167, 181
Rudenko, R., 230
Rudnicki, Tadeusz, 76
Rudkowski, Roman, 160, 183, 212, 213
Rudy (Red-head), see Rudkowski
Rundstedt, Gerd von, 219
Ryba (Fish), 115
Rybka, Franciszek, 136
Rykov, Aleksiej, 229
Rys, 111, 114

S

Salamander, see Retinger
Selborne, Lord, 26
Sidoruk, 138
Sienkiewicz, Henryk, 107
Sikorski, Wladyslaw, 31, 33, 34, 35, 39, 48, 52, 53, 63, 68, 69, 78, 96, 119, 120, 122, 124, 162
Sinclair, Sir Archibald (Lord Thurso), 69, 187
Skrochowski, Jan, 196
Slaw, see Cetys
Slessor, Sir John, 141, 186, 187, 190, 191, 192, 194, 205, 214
Smigly-Rydz, Edward, 30, 33
Smolenski, Jozef, 39, 76, 78
Sokolowski, Tadeusz, 115
Solly-Flood, Peter, 217
Sosabowski, Stanislaw, 60, 173
Sosnkowski, Kazimierz, 34, 35, 37,

38, 39, **48**, 94, **120**, 122, 125, 161, 168, 170, 171, 172, 173, 174, 180, **184**, **187**, **188**, 193, 198, 204, **211**, 217
Spaatz, Carl, 198
SS, 111, 113
Stacey, 60
Stachowski, Mieczyslaw, 151
Stalin, Joseph, 110, 117, 119, 148, 149, 167, 171, 177, 181, 187, 188, 189, 194, 197, 198, 200, 206, 219, 220, **222**, 228, 229
Starzynski, **Leszek**, **161**
Starzynski, Stefan, 30
Stettinius, Edward, Jr., 227
Stowell, 141
Strawinski, 60
Stypulkowski, Zbigniew, 225, 228, 230
Sulima, see Chciuk
Sweet-Escott, B., 27
Swir, 138
Switalski, Adam, 167, 230
Szabó, Iván, 28
Szczurek-Cergowski, Jan, 211
Szort, 127, **128**, 130
Szrajer, **Kazimierz**, **161**, 163
Sztumberk-Rychter, **Tadeusz**, 122
Szydlowski, Adam, 195
Szymanski, Jerzy, 61

T

Tabor, see Tatar, 159
Tajchman, Michal, 183
Tarzan, 128
Tatar, Stanislaw, 159, 187, 215
Thompson, Miss J., 79
Threlfall, Henry McLeod, 141, 214, 215
Tickell, Jerrard, 119
Tito, Josip, 186
Tokarzewski, see Karaszewicz-Tokarzewski
Torwid, see Karaszewicz-Tokarzewski
Trop (Trail), see Sokolowski, 115
Truman, Harry, 226
Truszkowski, Richard, 141, 215
Truszkowski, Adam, 141
Trzaska, see Krajewski
Tukhachevsky, **Mikhail**, 121
Tumidajski, Kazimierz, 230

Tumry, 115, 116, 117
Turski, see Tatar
Tygrys (Tiger), see **Wazny**

U

Ulrich, W., 229
Urbanski, Franciszek, 225
Utnik, Marian, 159, 163, 186

V

Vansittart, Sir Robert, 22
Vlasov, Andrey, 127, 130
Voelnagel, Antoni, 64
Vasilevich, 137, 139
Vyshinsky, Andrey, 229

W

Waclaw, 138, 139, 140
Wania, see Paczkowski, 111, 112, 114
Warta, see Utnik
Wazny, Wladyslaw, 154
Wdowinski, David, 25
Wejtko, A., 61
Wicher, see Krajewski
Wieronski, 61
Wilk, see General Wilk
Wilkinson, P. A., 27
Willetts, H. T., 29, 92
Wilson, Maitland Henry, 141
Wisniewski, Michal, 149
Witek, 130
Wlodarkiewicz, Jan, 101
Wlodek, 163
Wlodek, see Raczkowski
Wojnowski, Jerzy, 133
Wolniak, Boguslaw, 161
Wroblewski, S., 107

Z

Zabielski, Jozef, 49
Zagiew (Fire-brand), 108
Zabotynski, see Jabotinsky, 26
Zbik, see Zabielski
Zelner, 113
Zielinski, 213
Zhukov, Georgi, 223, 225
Zwierzynski, Aleksander, 225, 228

For Product Safety Concerns and Information please contact our EU representative GPSR@taylorandfrancis.com
Taylor & Francis Verlag GmbH, Kaufingerstraße 24, 80331 München, Germany

www.ingramcontent.com/pod-product-compliance
Lightning Source LLC
Chambersburg PA
CBHW070600300426
44113CB00010B/1335